THE TEMPORAL DIMENSION IN COUNSELLING AND PSYCHOTHERAPY

A Journey in Time

Sue Wright

Routledge
Taylor & Francis Group

LONDON AND NEW YORK

First published 2020
by Routledge
2 Park Square, Milton Park, Abingdon, Oxon OX14 4RN

and by Routledge
52 Vanderbilt Avenue, New York, NY 10017

Routledge is an imprint of the Taylor & Francis Group, an informa business

British Library Cataloguing-in-Publication Data
A catalogue record for this book is available from the British Library

Library of Congress Cataloging-in-Publication Data
A catalog record for this title has been requested

ISBN: 978-0-367-82070-1 (hbk)
ISBN: 978-0-367-81965-1 (pbk)
ISBN: 978-1-003-01177-4 (ebk)

Typeset in Bembo
by Taylor & Francis Books

Printed and bound in Great Britain by
TJ International Ltd, Padstow, Cornwall

To "Gee" who always supported my "future self".
Even though his "falling away" was hard, after a life span-
ning nine decades, he still showed interest in this book in
his final days.

CONTENTS

PART III
Ruptured time   **161**

PREFACE

To be present in the moment is not hard. But it takes all of you.
You have to listen well and look long.
You have to engage your heart,
 bringing your fear and your hope to the same place …

(Inge, 2014, p. 193)

I am going to invite you to join in an adventure, a journey in time – and see where it takes you. When I embarked on the project I had certain ideas and questions in mind. A plan emerged for what the book would cover. Four years on it has changed shape dramatically. My encounter with new ideas, events in the world, my life and my client's lives, along with a deepening exploration of my place in time took me along unexpected paths. As in any adventure, there have been false paths, places where I got stuck, mountains climbed which opened up startlingly new views. The subject has called me to bring the whole of myself, to listen well and look long in order to find something new. And undoubtedly there will be more to discover about time because, like all living beings, my existence is bound up in time.

"Our present swarms with traces of our past", said Carlo Rovelli (2018, p. 154). Traces of the past are everywhere. "The craters of the moon testify to impacts in the past. Fossils show the forms of living creatures long ago. Telescopes show how far off galaxies were in the past. Books contain our history; our brains swarm with memories" (p. 144).

ACKNOWLEDGEMENTS

Writing this book will leave many memories and indelible traces on my future. And in turn I hope it will leave traces for you and invite you to be curious about your personal relationship to time, and that of the people you work with. I have been inspired by a wealth of writers, one book revealing others to explore, and by rich discussions with friends. Amongst them I would like to thank in particular Jim Pye and Pippa Smethurst who have accompanied and encouraged me throughout this journey in time. Thanks are also due to colleagues who have read chapters en route and offered valuable feedback – Helen Hastings-Spital, Miriam Taylor, Raje Airey and Sarah Tate. I also want to honour the people who have allowed me to accompany them for a while on their life journey and all that they have courageously shared. I have done all I can to disguise the identity of individuals by changing details and sometimes using composite examples. I have appreciated the wise, efficient and encouraging support of Russell George, my editor, Elliott Morsia, Singhania Solani, Pamela Stewart and Nick Craggs. They have always been there to answer the many questions an author has and to accommodate my ideas about how the book should look and take shape. Last, but not least a huge thank you to Paul who has been my companion on so many journeys and who has supported this particular adventure in numerous ways. And so, with no more ado, let us begin the journey …

References

Inge, D. 2014. *A Tour of Bones*. London: Bromsberg.
Rovelli, C. 2018. *The Order of Time*. London: Allen Lane.
Watts, A. 1992. *The Wisdom of Insecurity: A Message for an Age of Anxiety*. London: Rider. (1st edition, 1951, Pantheon Books).

PART I

Our individual and cultural relationship to time

1

THE LURE OF TIME

What is time? I know, but when you ask me I don't.

(St Augustine, Watts, 1992, p. 51)

Time is a subject that is central to our existence as well as being a common theme in psychotherapy and counselling. In this book I want to explore our complex, multi-faceted relationship with time and what time means to us. Like much research, the theme crept up on me – a coming-together of many strands, different life events, issues emerging in my work, interesting books read, or things heard on the radio. Finding a remarkable Anglo-Saxon sundial inspired research on how people in the past marked time. Little did I know how much would emerge! There was also turning 60 which unexpectedly drew me to look back on what has formed me thus far and to reconnect with earlier versions of myself, including my historian self, and former activities and pursuits. Because elderly relatives began to occupy more and more of my time and because during the year this project began I learned of so many deaths, some very difficult and tragic, I was also compelled to contemplate my own senior years and to ask some searching questions about my personal relationship to time. Rich discussions with friends and colleagues fuelled my interest. Everyone seemed to have interesting stories to tell and thoughts about time.

As a psychotherapist the following questions began to preoccupy me:

- In what ways is our sense of self and our identity shaped by our existence in time?
- How often do people seek therapy because they are struggling with their place in and relationship to time and its passage?
- How is time experienced and dealt with in therapy and how do the inter-locking histories of client and therapist colour the work?

- Why is our lived experience of passing time sometimes at odds with "real" time so that we can be both selves-in-time and selves-out-of-time? And how does this dissonance influence how we live our lives?
- Why is it that some people frequently seem to lose all sense of linear time, whereas others are obsessively preoccupied with the ever-ticking clock?
- Lastly, how do we work with the impact on our sense of time of experiences such as traumatic events and overwhelming losses when the known becomes utterly dislocated?

As a former social historian I also became interested in how people have marked and measured time and defined the stages of life across the ages; in the different ways that the notion of time has shaped how we live our lives, and in changing philosophical ideas about time as reflected in the arts. At various points I will bring a historical perspective to my current audience because I believe that to really understand and be able to help those who seek our help we need to understand, not just the influence of "the presenting past", a concept central to psychodynamic approaches, but to appreciate how our relationship to time has altered over the centuries and to understand our work in the context of a world which is changing in ever more rapid, dramatic ways. This is part of what I see as the "contextual turn" that psychotherapy has embraced over the last 30 years – an understanding that the social, cultural, historical, political and ecological milieu in which we and our clients live informs the narratives we develop about ourselves and how we interact with others.

The words of an erudite professor whom Oliver Sacks met during his travels, capture what I mean about the need to know our context. The two men were standing looking at a large glacial basin in the Rockies. First the professor pointed out the magnitude of time:

> This prodigious bowl was filled with ice to a depth of three hundred feet. And when we and our children are dead, seeds will have sprouted in the silt and a young forest will nod over these stones. Here before you in one scene of a geological drama, past and future implicit in the present you perceive, and all within the span of a single human generation, and a human memory.

Reading this I thought, we could say something similar about the human body, for the past is etched on its landscape. Then the man said wisely,

> Travel the right way, the way I travel. I am always reading and thinking of the history and geography of a place. I see its people in terms of these, placed in the social framework of time and space. Take the prairies for example; you're wasting your time visiting these unless you know the saga of the homesteaders, the influence of law and religion at different times, the economic problems, the difficulties of communication, and the effects of successive mineral finds.
>
> *(Sacks, 2015b, pp. 49, 50)*

In the same way, as a psychotherapist, an explorer of the human psyche, I need to be aware of my own place in a social framework of time and space. We exist in many different contexts, the geological drama being one of them, and how our individual dramas relate to these bigger ones will be one of the leitmotifs of the book. There are other reasons too why I believe it is important to have some understanding of our individual and collective relationship to time.

The first is that it underpins many of the problems that bring people into therapy. We encounter people who are incredibly time-poor. They are hyperconscious about clock time – anxious not to be late or to waste time; unable to take time off to rest; stressed about how much they have to do and often troubled with a range of somatic complaints. Other people find that time drags and getting through a day can seem a daunting task when each moment feels like an eternity and everything seems meaningless. We see men and women troubled by life-stage challenges, perhaps because reaching a particular age has forced them to face their place in time or to deal with the loss of former dreams, expectations or capacities. We also see people who lose time and cannot live fully in the present because they are haunted by memories of the past. Many of these problems are malaises of the modern world. We have become preoccupied with doing and time-management, enslaved by the notion that time is money and anxiously driven to meet targets and deadlines. As I shall argue in Chapter 4, it is also a world obsessed with keeping up to date and trying to deny the passage of time. Our inventive minds have discovered numerous strategies to save time, go faster and extend the duration of our lives, and writers and scientists play with the notion of travelling in time. Yet however hard we try to defy Chronos, our lives are conditioned and corralled by the relentless march of time. Is it any wonder that some people experience crises when life situations force them to face the reality that life is finite?

Another reason for studying time is that psychotherapy offers a unique, temporal experience. For example, and I discuss this in detail in Chapter 5, it provides a boundaried temporal space in which the dance between Kairos, our subjective experience of time, and Chronos, clock time, is heightened. Although structured within a time-frame, what goes on during a session often takes us out of time – in the leaps backwards and forwards in time of the client's narrative; during enactments when we are caught in positions belonging to earlier time-frames, and in our felt-experience of how time passes – dragging, rushing by or losing touch with what time it is. Such experiences often have things to tell us. The dialectic between Kairos and Chronos is another leitmotif in the book. It is a dialectic that T. S. Eliot confronted us with in the paradoxical words: "To be conscious is not to be in time". But "only in time can moments", good and bad (my words), be remembered and become "involved with past and future. Only through time time is conquered" (1969, p. 173). *Only through time time is conquered.* And by this I would read: Only when we engage in a dialogue with time, can past experiences become woven into our self-defining narratives.

Another aspect of the unique temporal experience provided by psychotherapy, is the particular way that it engages with the past and the unfolding present moment. Although not Eliot's meaning, those words from "Burnt Norton" are a wonderful way of describing the change process and the potential for something new to emerge as a result of remembering and reliving aspects of the past with someone prepared to go there with you. It is a process of interaction between past, present and future, of "memorial activity" which I shall discuss in detail in Chapter 12. And in more everyday ways we all need an anchoring in the past, to believe in a future and feel motivated to work towards future events – *and* we need to inhabit the present moment. We have to understand and work on our relationship to time in order to come to terms with the ways it stresses and challenges us. The contrast, excessive "mental time travelling", often leads to obsessional thinking, endless comparing, a susceptibility to reliving traumatic moments, and to anxiety, shame and hopelessness – difficulties that we often encounter during our work and are not immune from ourselves.

The final reason for reflecting on our relationship to time is that in our interior life, and psychotherapy is concerned with our inner world, temporality provides a backdrop that colours many of our thoughts, feelings and responses. One of my aims is to give words to a domain of our lives, the temporal one, which we experience through the body and which often preoccupies our thoughts. As part of my heuristic research I have endeavoured to track my own moment-to-moment subjective experience of time, my temporal phenomenology, as I live my life and as I work. And as you read this book, I invite you, now and then to notice your own experience of time – the moments when you are time-conscious; when you lose track of it; how present you feel, or when something mentioned catapults you into remembering something past or ideas or feelings about the future. To begin that process of enquiry, how you have been impacted by time so far today?

Did you wake with a start because the alarm went off or to your own timing? Did you have a leisurely start or rush to fit in a lot before leaving home, perhaps to take children to school or go somewhere for work? If your day has been spent at home, how many "events" have been conditioned by time? How aware of the clock have you been? If you travelled today how conscious were you of time during the journey? How often did you check your watch or the car clock? Did you get to your destination with lots of time to spare or at the last minute? And which is the more familiar of the two?

I also invite you to become curious about your clients' temporal phenomenology. How do they manage their time? What is their attitude to time passing and where they are in the life-stage? What do you notice about the pace and rhythms of their movements and how these change in response to what is being said? We can also learn a lot by paying careful attention to the temporal dynamics of each person's conversation – his or familiar rhythms and the timing and nature of pauses in speech – and to the pace of his thinking. Do his thoughts race? Are they sluggish? Halting? And do these patterns offer clues about our client's earliest experiences of time?

Two women come to mind. Bree always arrived and left in a rush, announcing her presence with a loud knock on the door which seemed to call for an urgent response. Her words poured out even before she had fully given her weight to the chair, and I would often invite her to pause, take a breath and allow herself to notice me and her surroundings or check what she felt in her body. Our earliest sessions proceeded at a breakneck pace leaving me trying hard to keep up, having to think fast and when Bree left, needing to go out and walk briskly in order to dissipate the racing energy I felt in my body. Bree's experience was of never being held or heard and she would often cry out, "why didn't anybody listen to me?" She had learned to hold herself together through action, rapid movement and addictive behaviours. She grabbed hold of anything that might provide a semblance of nurture, yet paradoxically never felt satisfied. The "drive" state that Paul Gilbert described in his neurobiologically, evolution informed Three Circles Model comes to mind (2005). Bree managed the experience of perceived threat by shifting into drive, a dopamine fuelled state that kept her in the fast lane. What she found hard, but gradually began to explore in therapy, was to slow down and nurture herself in more compassionate ways.

By contrast, as Lucianne climbed the stairs to my room her pace was slow, and when she spoke it was halting and hesitant. It could take a while before she let me know what was on her mind or how she was feeling. Sometimes, after a long pause, a statement would burst out – part of a sentence which did not immediately make sense as I lacked the background narrative. On other occasions when she felt calmer and safer, Lucianne conversed a little more freely. Then as if realising what she was doing, engaging in a contactful turn-taking, her words dried up. She felt uncomfortable and embarrassed. She did not know how to do it. And no wonder. As a child Lucianne learned to sit quietly and say nothing in order to stay safe. Time was not shared in this household, either in doing things together or conversing, and that meant endless, unendurable hours spent alone with her thoughts. She never had that needed experience of people willingly giving her their time, being available, protecting her and putting her first. The emotional, embodied and intersubjective experiences of shared time were very different for these two women and the imprints of early patterns emerged in their relationship to time during our meetings. This is true for other people, indeed for us all because we carry imprints of our earliest experiences and sometimes that of our parents too, and I believe that these imprints colour how we inhabit time. I will say more about this later in the book.

Before going further, I should explain what I mean by our relationship to time. As "selves-in-time" the passage of time evokes a range of thoughts and emotions which change according to circumstances and our stage of life. We have emotional responses to the changes in ourselves and the world around us, some subtle, some dramatic, which occur because of time passing. We objectify time in the language we use about it. In the modern world it has become a commodity we have too much or too little of and we make judgements about how we use time. In ancient civilisations time was often depicted as a god. It has also been personified as a judge or a destroyer, like the popular image of Old Father Time with his sickle (Whitrow, 1988, pp. 38–9). These myths and archetypes speak of time's power over us, of its inescapability, and of fate. We also have a relationship to past, present and future, and again this changes according to our age and context. For instance, we might speak of the past with nostalgia – "the good old days", or with fear or anger – the days of "the Troubles", the Depression, the Cold War. Our personal history and current context informs our relationship to time, but we are also influenced by how our family and community perceive and relate to time.

There is of course a debate about whether there is such a thing as absolute time, and scientists and philosophers have grappled with the question "what exactly is time?" for centuries, Aristotle being one of the first. He argued that time is the measurement of change. From this perspective, explained Rovelli, "time is our way of situating ourselves in relation to the changing of things". It is the measure of flow and movement, internal and external. If nothing moves or changes, there is no time (2018, pp. 57–8). In the seventeenth century Newton challenged the Aristotelian position. He believed that even if everything were completely motionless time would still pass. It exists independently of things. As Newton stated in his *Principia:* "Absolute, true and mathematical time, of itself, and from its own nature, flows equably without relation to anything external", and he regarded moments of absolute time as forming a continuous sequence like the points on a geometrical line (Whitrow, 1988, p. 129). The rate at which these moments succeed each other is independent of particular events and processes. Newtonian time held sway for several centuries until Einstein challenged this seemingly commonsense belief that time is a given independent of the universe. Einstein's Theory of Relativity states that, to the contrary, the length of time between events depends on the observer and is not completely separate from and independent of space (p. 173). The Aristotelian perspective raises interesting thoughts about our subjectivity and our core sense of existence. Newtonian time gives us a far more "I-it" relationship to time.

Core propositions

As well as holding certain overarching questions in mind, eight fundamental propositions have underpinned my heuristic research. I will describe each in turn.

- We exist in time.
- Although we exist in time, we experience it in different ways.
- We exist in time at an embodied level.
- We exist in space, and space and time are inextricably linked.
- We exist in time at a neurological level.
- Our sense of self depends on the experience of continuity.
- Our identity inevitably changes as we move through different life-stages and there are generally judgements, comparisons and stories behind this.
- Because we exist in time we face certain existential challenges.

We exist in time. This is an inescapable fact. Every breath, every movement, every thought-act has a time contour – a beginning, middle and end. We exist in micro-time. For instance, we know that the brain can react to a stimulus in nanoseconds, much faster than we can think. But we also exist in longer time spans – the cycles of night and day, of the year, the different life-stages we go through between birth and death. Then beyond this we exist within the context of history – our family history, the history of our country, our social group, of mankind, the planet and the universe. which stretches back billions of years. As I pause a moment, I am struck with the magnitude of this, of the knowledge that my own seemingly so important life is no more than a flash in these bigger time spans. I am also struck by the myriad ways that we try to escape being in time and affected by it. We try to buy time, make time, reverse its effects, prolong our lives and avoid thinking about finitude and our mortality. Paradoxically, all this effort makes us even more conscious of time and its duration.

Although we exist in time, we experience it in different ways. There is a difference between experience as measured and formalised and experience as lived and embedded in socio-cultural patterns, and this is certainly true when it comes to time. Chronos, objective and measurable time, frames everything we do within its regular beat and forward direction. It brings uniformity into our interactions with others. It standardises and homogenises life. It is also seen as a scarce and limited resource and therefore of economic and political use. Kairos speaks a different language. It is a rich and nuanced language informed by what we sense in our bodies, our state of well-being and arousal, by feelings and by the level and focus of our attention. Our phenomenological experience of time can include moments of timelessness after which we can be surprised to discover how long something has taken, as well as moments when time seems to race past. There are also periods when we are acutely aware of the passing minutes and rail against their speed or slowness. Sometimes time stands still. Sometimes it appears to repeat itself, the feeling of *déjà vu*. When we focus on clock time the left hemisphere is dominant. Meanwhile our subjective experience of time is a property of the right brain.

Within the therapeutic context, one of the paradoxes is that we can experience seemingly timeless or time-expanded moments at the same time that the clicking clock lets us know that Chronos is ever present. How often has someone said, "Is it really time? It feels as if I've only been here five minutes"? And how often have you experienced the time dragging? For one of my clients the first half often feels long. He is anxious about finding something to say and being judged. But then the second half rushes past, his anxiety mounting because then he will have to leave and be on his own again. Another client often remarks with surprise that it feels a long time since we last met or conversely that it feels as if she was only here yesterday. In each case the actual gap is exactly the same. However, I have noticed that what has been going on in her life during the week and whether it was distressing or not plays a part in her felt sense of the interval. We could probably all find examples when personal and clock time were at odds. But one only has to read accounts of people influenced by certain drugs or with conditions like Tourette's Syndrome and Parkinson's Disease for evidence how the two can diverge in more striking ways. Studies also suggest that when caught in a life-threatening situation thought speeds up, but time appears to slow down dramatically. As William James speculated, our judgement of time may depend on how many "events" we can perceive in a given unit of time (Sacks, 2017, pp. 35, 38, 48).

Not only do we have very idiosyncratic experiences of duration, but each of us will have personal associations to certain dates and times of day. Anniversaries have meaning for us, positive and negative. The feel of summer or winter, early morning or evening, may be coloured by much earlier experiences at these times. They evoke memory states in unconscious ways so that past and present become linked. We also move between different time-frames in our thoughts – constantly shifting between an awareness of the present moment and thinking about or reliving a past event, be it five minutes or five years ago, or anticipating something in the future. Thus, time loops backwards and forwards.

Time also has socio-cultural meanings. As Karsten pointed out, social time is "the hub of culture", and if we were unaware that socio-cultural patterns demarcate our ways of dealing with time, we might be surprised to find shops closed on the Sabbath if visiting an orthodox Jewish community, or that a friend employed by a Middle Eastern company has to deal with business calls on a Sunday (2017, p. 320). We take social time for granted because it is so bound up in our norms, values and implicit ways of relating, and need to remind ourselves that people from other cultures shape their lives according to different social temporalities. This goes deeper than how the week or year is organised. It involves people's implicit attitudes to time and how they conduct their lives within it. As Karsten emphasised, although clock time became standardised across the world in the nineteenth century, it does not obliterate the "rich sources of local, idiosyncratic and context-dependent time awareness which are rooted in the social and organic rhythms of everyday life" (pp. 27, 363). For example, in some cultures "event time" is more significant than clock time. Event time depends on nature-related patterns and activities that occur in cycles. It focuses more on the interpersonal relationships between people and is characterised by local customs, practices and traditions. In cultures where event time is prevalent, the pace of life is generally slower and events start when people arrive and end when they leave. This contrasts with societies dominated by clock time which are characterised by schedules, deadlines, punctuality, notions of efficient time-use and a faster pace of life in which interactions between people tend to be brief and swift (pp. 332–4). Being aware of the relational implications of these two time-modes may be important when working with people from different cultural backgrounds.

My third proposition is that we exist in time at an embodied level. Writing in 1960, Ronald Laing compared the embodied and unembodied self. The former has a sense of personal continuity in time "and an experience of his body as being a base from which he can be a person with other human beings" (1965, p. 67).

The unembodied self feels divorced from his body (p. 74). Since Laing's day much has been written about the importance of our bodily and sensory experiences in the foundation of a sense of self. This is the "core self" described by Stern. We learn about self and other through moving and being moved, touching and being touched. And it is through the body that we will have our initial encounters with both the patterning of time and the dimensions of space. In the womb the baby will feel the music of his mother's bodily rhythms. His body-self will "dance" with them. After birth his own inner rhythms form the fore- and background of his experience as will the cyclical pattern of need, action, satisfaction and rest.[1] He will become familiar with the punctuation of a range of experiences with stops and starts, accelerations, pauses and fadings away, Stern's "vitality affects" (1985). And the daily repetition of many of these sequences leads to a sense of predictability and ongoingness.

Our cognitive life is embedded in our somatic experience and also in time. "Thinking is movement of the brain". "Every thought has a beginning, a middle and an end" said one neuroscientist (BBC Radio 4, 10 December 2016). Thinking is also recursive. The same thought keeps popping up, with new variations as in a piece of music. Some thoughts don't feel completed. Something else intervenes. Our thoughts can race. They can be sluggish, and it is interesting to notice the temporal adjectives used to describe thinking. I imagine too, that were I with a neuroscientist he or she would be telling me about the rapid sequence of neural events that occur during any thought-act. These are the micro-experiences of our temporality which occur alongside our experience of macro-time.

Our bodily/emotional life is grounded in the micro-experiences of the present moment and in an ongoing, forward moving process, whereas thinking disconnects us from the present moment. As Sletvold said, "thoughts and fantasies can take great leaps forwards and backwards in time, and sideways as well". Our imaginings can be about anything at any time (2015). In therapy, although we are mindful of how the past influences the present and although a lot of what is communicated verbally concerns past events and future concerns, we have a much greater appreciation now of the fact that change occurs in "now moments" and in our ability to reflect on and discuss what goes on in subjectively experienced micro-moments during sessions.

Turning to the fourth proposition: *We exist in space.* Space is the other dimension which shapes our identity, and space and time are inextricably linked. They are linked linguistically – for instance, in phrases like "he finished everything in the space of twenty minutes" or "man's allotted span" – experientially we routinely gauge duration in terms of movement across a certain space. Meanwhile from a developmental perspective, whilst the infant is becoming familiar with the patterning of time, he is also beginning to negotiate space. As babies we initially learn to move in the horizontal plane – expanding outwards and contracting; rolling from side to side and front to back. In this plane we scan the world. Our eyes dart left and right. We search for Mum's face. We watch and hang onto objects visually as a means of self-regulation if she is absent too long and we are in need of comfort. Then we learn to crawl which takes us into the sagittal plane. Reaching for Mum and for objects is also sagittal. Mastering the vertical, the third stage, is a significant achievement. When a toddler stands, he is saying "here I am" and psychologically he can begin to "take a stand" and assert his will. According to Rudolph Laban, an influential figure in the world of movement analysis in the mid-twentieth century, the horizontal plane is related to space. It is about *where* we are – and to communication. The sagittal plane is related to time, to *when* we are – and decision making. We rush forwards or we hold back. We move quickly and decisively or in a sustained way, lingering, pausing, hesitating. Meanwhile, Laban argued that the vertical dimension is associated with *who* we are and the presentation of the self. We can hold ourselves tall or we might slump in despair or make ourselves smaller to avoid being noticed. When tuning into non-verbal communication it can be informative to pay attention to how a client inhabits and moves in each dimension as well as to the pacing and rhythms of their movements and how these change in response to what is being said.

My fifth proposition is that we *exist in time at a neurological level*. Whilst I balk at reducing my identity to something as mechanistic as neural processes, nonetheless I am fascinated to read what neuroscientists have to say about consciousness, identity and the brain. For instance, according to the neuroscientist Susan Greenfield, as a result of plasticity the many repeated events and happenstances of our lives set up personalised neuronal connections along with a personalised conceptual framework. This, for Greenfield, is what constitutes the mind, our neuronal idiom if you like, and our unique identity (2008, p. 203). She explains that the development of the personalised brain is a slow process involving experiencing, learning, repetition and numerous "first-hand unique adventures" in the real world (p. 201). As the brain matures, and in particular with the advent of language, we start to evaluate the world in terms of what has gone before. Whereas infancy is characterised by a "booming, buzzing confusion" when we experience a deluge of disconnected sensory events, there is now a two-way street between the outside and our personal memories. Experiences begin to have meaning for us personally and we start to see things and people in the light of previous events. This enables us to navigate the world, not as a passive recipient of sensations, but in a constant dialogue between our brains and the outside world. We begin to see ourselves, the rest of the world and our life story as a connected chain, a narrative. We form an ongoing frame of reference out of the accumulation of a morass of events – our personal narrative, and a personalised, coherent sense of self, a first-person consciousness – our unique identity (Greenfield, 2008, pp. 115, 117). Both of these support us in planning for and evaluating whatever comes along next.

In his reflections on consciousness and the brain, Oliver Sacks gave a vivid example which illustrates that the interaction of perception, self-consciousness, explicit memory and a sense of the future is what gives a thematic and personal continuity to the consciousness of every individual. "As I write", he explained, "I am sitting at a café on Seventh Avenue, watching the world go by. My attention and focus dart to and fro: a girl in a red dress goes by, a man walking a funny dog, the sun (at last!) emerging from the clouds. These are all events which catch my attention for a moment as they happen. Why, out of a thousand possible perceptions, are these the ones I seize upon? Reflections, memories, associations lie behind them. For consciousness is always active and selective – charged with feelings and meanings uniquely our own, informing our choices and interfusing our perceptions. So, it is not just Seventh Avenue that I see, but *my* Seventh Avenue, marked by my own selfhood and identity" (2017, p. 182). "*Consciousness is always active and selective – charged with feelings and meanings uniquely our own, informing our choices … ".* I am struck by these words. Perhaps one day it might be possible to programme a robot to learn from its past experiences – a "robotic personalised brain" or incentivised system. But would the robot's subsequent actions be informed by personal feelings and meanings? Could a robot ever have the capacity to be aware of and mentally represent the subjective experience of past, present and future? I doubt it. And could a robot have visions of the future? Or contemplate its existence and actions at a time in the future? Again unlikely.

Our capacity to consider our extended existence across time is something uniquely human, and my sixth proposition, linked with the fifth, is that *our sense of self depends on the experience of continuity.* There is something fundamentally important about the concept of permanence and of being able to trust in the ongoingness of ourselves as well as of others and of places to which we are attached. Our identity is shored up by a sense of our history, our going-on-being over time and by having a verbal, autobiographical self, capable of constructing a narrative of our life (Winnicott, 1968; Stern, 1985). As the sociologist Anthony Giddens pointed out, "a person's identity is not to be found in behaviour, nor – important though it is – in the reactions of others, but in the capacity to keep a particular narrative going". In other words, we continually integrate new experiences and sort them into a sequential, personalised narrative (1991, pp. 51, 54). Even though every moment the neurons in the brain are being effected by and responding to new input in an endless and spectacular way, "there is none the less usually a reassuringly consistent theme that is *you*: your identity", "an irrefutable sense that you are a unique and continuous first-person consciousness". This identity is the most basic assumption for going through life and interacting with others (Greenfield, 2008, pp. 114, 117).

Our identity as coherent beings is shaped by our earliest attachment experiences. With good enough care between birth and 18 months, the period when Erikson believed our task is to deal with the conflict between trust and mistrust and to form the basis of a sense of identity (Erikson, 1965, p. 241), we learn to trust in the reliability, predictability and responsiveness of others. In the language of object-relations we develop an internal good object and this serves as a secure platform for trust in our own ongoingness and for autonomy and optimism. A psychotherapist who intuitively grasped the idea of ongoingness, and what is needed relationally for this to develop, was Donald Winnicott. He viewed a sense of continuity and of finite time as a developmental achievement, a process that depends on repeated complex sequences, many being intersubjective, involving moving, sensing, being responded to and the many predictable events experienced at a sensory level which pattern the day of a young child. Winnicott also recognised that we gain a sense of continuity by transmitting things from generation to generation (1968, p. 173). Whether this is through handing things on to children and grandchildren or through creating something that will live on after our death – a work of art, a building, a theory or a business – it forms a bridge leading from the past into the future. Linking our personal story with the histories of others – our family, social group, religious community or country contributes to a sense of ongoingness. Their stories become one of the strands in how we define ourselves. Sometimes, I have wondered whether having no children has given an additional edge to my own wish to write, so that there is something I can leave behind. And in currently re-connecting with aspects of my past I am also focussing on the other end of that bridge which, as Winnicott said, is vital too. Connecting with our individual history and the history of mankind is vital because our culture depends on experience. Without tradition, paradoxically, it is impossible to be original.

Annihilation is the antithesis of continuity. In Winnicott's writing this was captured by his reference to the primitive anxieties of "falling forever" and "going to pieces". At a cultural level meanwhile, it was exemplified by what was a real fear for Winnicott and his generation: world annihilation by the atom bomb. The end of the world would not only mean the end of me and you, but of all the accumulated riches of the world built up by generation after generation. Perhaps that is why the news this century of the bulldozing of places like Palmyra and Nimrud in Iraq or the destruction of Buddhist statues in Bamiyam evoked so much horror and outrage. Or why the fire at Notre-Dame in 2019 had such an impact.[2] It shocks and horrifies us to think of there being no more – an absolute end. Death is something different. If through our generativity we can pass something on, then in this sense death is not a discontinuity. It implies that we have experienced life with a place in continuous time (Winnicott, 1968, p. 174).

Laing used the term ontological security to describe personal ongoingness. The ontologically secure person has "a sense of his presence in the world as a real, alive, whole, and, in a temporal sense, continuous person, and experiences others as equally real, alive, whole, and continuous" (1965, p. 39). Like others, Laing argued that this security generally begins from birth, although his account lacks any reference to the interpersonal world in which this occurs. By contrast, without this basic sense of ongoingness the individual may feel more unreal and dead than real and alive. So precariously differentiated is he from the rest of the world that his identity and autonomy is always in question. He lacks the experience of temporal continuity and of personal consistency and cohesiveness. He feels insubstantial and profoundly split off from his body. In consequence, life poses a continual threat. It is the experience of people whose caregivers were terrifyingly absent, or who are dissociative or haunted by ghosts from the past. It is also the experience of people trapped in psychosis. One woman I worked with often talked about the void she lived in and about how unreal she felt. "Nothing speaks to me", she would often say. And if we are split off from our bodies how can the world "speak" as it were, because so much of it is experienced through our senses? For a long time, Marcie seemed unaware of things around her. She clung to a few precarious absolutes. But in time I noticed how she became aware of and interested in things in my room or noticed on the journey to therapy – the flowers, my large pot plant, the familiar passengers on the bus. Marcie's acutely depressed mother was not able to provide the attuned reliability she needed to develop a sense of trust in the ongoingness of herself and others. During her long therapeutic journey, I believe she was able to take in that I held her in mind, and in the brief contact she maintained for some years after we ended she clearly valued the fact that I could still remember the history of her journey.

My seventh proposition is that *our identity inevitably changes as we move through different life-stages*. Giddens pointed out that in traditional cultures where things stayed more or less the same from generation to generation, attributes relevant to identity such as lineage, gender and social status were all relatively fixed, and transitions between one life-stage and another were governed by institutional processes (1991, p. 74). In the modern world, by contrast, "the altered self has to be explored and constructed as part of a reflexive process of connecting personal and social change" (p. 74). Accompanying any life-stage transition there are generally judgements, comparisons and stories. What individual and cultural judgements, for instance, lie behind the fact that in early censuses there was a tendency for people to claim to be older than they were, whereas during the twentieth century people started to understate their age? We appear to privilege youth rather than, as in past centuries, revere the old. Or as Atul Gawande argued, is it that independence and autonomy are revered? (2015, pp. 17–22). Teenagers can't wait to be adults and independent. People in their fifties can't wait to retire and be free from bureaucratic, rule-based workplaces. To be free to do as one pleases! An illusion of course. But then a point comes for increasing numbers when a free, enjoyable later-life slips into one of increasing frailty and dependency, and it is impossible to ignore the passage of time.

This takes me to my final proposition, that *because we exist in time, we face certain existential challenges:*

- Our time is limited.
- We are insignificant in the context of vast, 'deep time'.
- We live in an increasingly time-compressed, decontextualised world.[3]

Human beings have been aware of the first challenge for as long as we have records, and perhaps earlier, and this has generated specific beliefs and practices surrounding death. However, it is only over the last two centuries that we have grasped the incredible age of the planet and the universe and what Sacks described as the "glacially slow process of evolution" (Sacks, 1997, p. 242). In pre-modern times, scholars believed their universe was no more than 4000 or so years old and that the end of the world was imminent. Contrast that with our current age. We have to face our insignificance as individuals, as a planet, even as a galaxy in the context of "deep time" – a universe that is billions of years old with millions of galaxies at vast distances from our own. We all face the awareness of tremendous forces of destruction – nature, climate change and the brutality of mankind itself; aware that we or those we love or the homes and possessions that matter to us can be swiped away at a stroke. Our lives are fragile. And the fear of becoming insignificant and irrelevant in other ways is something we often hear about in our work, expressed by people who have lost or never found a sense of purpose, who believe they have nothing to contribute and are of no value to others. Meanwhile, the third challenge has only emerged in the last 30 or 40 years, although without the invention and increasingly widespread use of what Charles Dickens aptly named the "deadly statistical clock" and then of the computer, plus all the changes brought about by urbanisation, industrialisation and globalisation, things might have been rather different (Dickens, 1995; Karsten, 2017). We live in a world where time no longer has the same meanings as it did for someone living 100 years ago. It is also a world faced with the fragmentation of social bonds and erosion of structures of meaning that supported us in the past. I will say more about these challenges in Chapter 4.

A guide to the journey ahead

In this chapter I have tried to give a flavour of the many contexts in which our relationship with time is embedded: the context of the body, of our intersubjective experiences, of our individual culture and wider socio-cultural patterns, of history and geological dramas. These contextual themes will be expanded upon as the book proceeds through the lens of psychotherapy and also with reference to ideas from other disciplines including history, science, sociology and anthropology. In the chapters that follow I want to think about the dialectic between our ever-changing self and our ongoing self – about when we are firmly in time and about states of being when we become a "self-out-of-time". Another strand I will pursue is that of identity and meaning. As beings constantly faced with the existential challenges of living in time, how do we make sense of our experiences in a world which can sometimes feel meaningless?

Let me explain what I mean by a "self-in or out-of-time". As I became increasingly curious about my own temporal phenomenology and that of the people I work with, I began to notice how in certain situations there is a dissonance between "real" time and our lived experience of time that impacts our sense of self. From this came the idea that we can be both selves-in-time, and selves-out-of-time. The former implies an awareness of time's structure, its duration, and of the boundaries between past, present and future. We can take for granted that others share our experience and conceptualisation of time. We feel embodied, grounded in time. By contrast, to be a self-out-of-time implies that we have lost this anchoring and that time has become strange, uncanny, meaningless and no longer a shared given. Georg Simmel's idea of the adventure provided me with a metaphorical way of thinking about our in-and-out of time-ness. He argued that ordinary life is continuous, meaning that a consistent process runs through the individual components of life, however distinct they may be. By contrast, an adventure involves a momentary "dropping out of the continuity of life", and the beginning and end are "much sharper than those to be discovered in other forms of our experiences" (1971, p. 188). It "stands in contrast to that interlocking of life-links, to that feeling that those countercurrents, turnings and knots still, after all, spin forth a continuous thread". Although certainly a part of our existence, it "lacks that reciprocal interpenetration with the adjacent parts of life which constitutes life-as-a-whole." "It is like an island in life" (p. 189), or to use another metaphor I find helpful, it is an event in parentheses. We could argue that a traumatic event has some of the properties of an adventure, except that it is terrifying rather than exciting. It also entails a temporary dropping out of the continuity of life. The same applies to life crises such as a period of critical illness or the events surrounding and following the death of a loved one. When we lose touch with the continuity of life, my contention is that we become for a while a self-out-of-time. I will say more about this at later points in the book.

The book is divided into three parts. In the first section the focus is on our existence as individuals in time. Chapter 2 expands on my argument that we need a sense of ongoingness in order to feel real and explores the paradox that the Self is both continuous and fluid, for we are constantly shifting state in micro-time and across longer time spans. The dialectic between our ever-changing self and our ongoing self is a theme continued in other chapters. The second half of Chapter 2 considers our past, present and future selves and how we can become fixed in one of these three time-frames rather than fluidly moving between them as interlocking modes of time. For instance, the past or the imagined future can be where we locate our self-concept and become the context that conditions how we think and act. In Chapter 3, I ask how we acquire a sense of temporality and what goes on in the brain that enables us to notice and gauge the passing of time. I delve into the complex subject of memory, its different systems and why memory is important to our sense of self. Chapter 4 moves away from the individual to the context in which we exist and focuses on the third existential challenge of living in time. I put forward the argument that we are living in an Age of Meaninglessness, challenged by the dominance of Chronos, increasingly cut off from former communal structures and traditions that used to support us and from deep connections with others and ourselves. I then consider some of the implications of this in our work as psychotherapists. The discussion is aimed to provide a wider context for the subsequent focus on the time-related issues people bring to therapy and on the impact of experiences that take us out of time such as trauma, serious illness and traumatic loss in Chapters 9 and 11.

In the second part of the book the focus narrows to the consulting room. Chapter 5 looks at "therapy time" – its structure, routine and boundaries and the different arrangements that exist for determining the length of sessions and the overall time-frame. One of my questions here is how can we be sensitive to our clients' needs as we try to manage the time-frame and the balance between therapeutic flexibility and holding? The next two chapters focus on the time-related issues that can emerge, either explicitly or implicitly, in therapy and their impact on the individual's sense of self. I am particularly interested in the themes that can emerge at different life-stages and at transitional points. After a general discussion about life-stage transitions, the individual and cultural expectations associated with them and at what supports people as they move from one stage to the next, Chapter 6 looks at early adulthood and the tasks and challenges of "growing up" in the modern world. In Chapter 7, I turn to the late life transition and how that links with the first existential challenge of living in time. I hope that the material in these chapters will help clinicians to be curious about when their client's relationship to time might be in the field and inspire thought about how to bring this into the conversation. Narrative plays a significant role in all therapies and this is the theme for Chapter 8. I discuss the functions and attributes of story-telling and in particular how they play a part in shaping us as selves-in-time. I then focus more specifically on the place of narrative in psychotherapy and how it is related to the change process.

In the third part of the book I focus on the impact of trauma and other crises on our existence in time. Here, my basic premise is that certain experiences drastically alter our sense of temporality and our anchoring in consensual time. In turn this affects our identity and often leads to a loss of meaning. Chapter 9 illustrates how trauma stops or distorts time and can fundamentally alter our relationship to past, present and future. Chapter 10 returns to the place of narrative in psychotherapy by asking whether telling the story is essential in order to heal after trauma and when it might be re-traumatising. I look at different views and ways of working with trauma, as well as outlining my own integrative approach. In Chapter 11, I explore the impact of other life crises on our identity and structures of meaning, such as acute or chronic illness and bereavement and loss. Chapter 12 draws together some of the book's key themes and considers the implications for practice by focussing on the question: "what is it that we do that leads to change?" And lastly, by way of an epilogue I invite my readers to join me in an appreciation of time. As Carlo Rovelli said, "we inhabit time as fish live in water. Time is at one level such an ordinary, easy to define thing and at the same time deeply mysterious. It challenges us, stresses us and puzzles us, and it brings us gifts if we are willing to look for them (2018, p. 1).

Notes

1 The cycles of the body, most occurring outside our awareness unless something goes wrong, constitute another aspect of our existence in micro-time. Throughout the body there are systems like the autonomic, endocrine and immune systems that are linked in a balanced, rhythmical, cyclical equilibrium. These rhythmical cycles go on in the background of our experience, maintaining homeostasis in the face of internal changes and environmental challenges. We are more aware of other cycles, for instance hormonal cycles or the cycles of tiredness and rest, hunger and eating.

2 Commenting on the latter, Simon Schama said, "in a disposable world we cling to things that endure" (BBC interview, 19 April 2019). Historic buildings have gone through many evolutions and metamorphoses as earlier generations have repaired or updated them. Our great cathedrals and national monuments also hold stories and bind communities, and in this way they connect us across time.

3 I am using the term decontextualisation to capture how in the modern world the trend is for things to be separated from their natural, traditional and relational contexts, contexts which used to offer support. I have drawn on Giddens' (1991) use of the term in his study of modernisation and globalisation, but more broadly to capture fundamental psychological and interpersonal changes. In particular it is a concept that speaks of fragmentation and a severing of ties and of abstract, impersonal social structures rather than ones that individualise and connect.

References

Dickens, C. 1995[1854]. *Hard Times*. Ware, Hertfordshire: Wordsworth Editions.

Erikson, E. 1965. *Childhood and Society*. Harmondsworth: Penguin Books (1st edition, 1950. New York: W. W. Norton & Co.).

Gawande, A. 2015. *Being Mortal: Illness, Medicine and what Matters in the End*. London: Profile Books.

Giddens, A. 1991. *Modernity and Self-identity: Self and Society in the Late Modern Age*. Cambridge: Polity Press.

Gilbert, P. 2005. *Compassion: Conceptualisations, Research and Use in Psychotherapy*. London: Routledge.

Greenfield, S. 2008. *ID: The Quest for Meaning in the 21st Century*. London: Sceptre.

Karsten, L. 2017. *Globalisation and Time*. London: Routledge.

Laing, R. 1965. *The Divided Self*. London: Penguin. (1st edition, 1960. London: Tavistock Publications).

Rovelli, C. 2018. *The Order of Time*. London: Allen Lane.

Sacks, O. 1997. *The Island of the Colour Blind*. New York: Alfred A. Knopf.

Sacks, O. 2015b. *On the Move: A Life*. London: Picador.

Sacks, O. 2017. *The River of Consciousness*. London: Picador.

Simmel, G. 1971. *On Individuality and Social Forms*. Chicago: University of Chicago Press.

Stern, D. N. 1985. *The Interpersonal World of the Infant*. New York: Basic Books.

Svetvold, J. 2015. *Embodied Approaches to Psychotherapy*. Confer Online Module.

Waddell, M. 1998. *Inside Lives: Psychoanalysis and the Growth of the Personality*. London: Duckworth.

Watts, A. 1992. *The Wisdom of Insecurity: A Message for an Age of Anxiety*. London: Rider. (1st edition, 1951, Pantheon Books).

Whitrow, G. 1988. *Time in History*. Oxford: Oxford University Press.

Winnicott, D. 1968. *The Maturational Process and the Facilitating Environment*. London: Hogarth Press.

2

BEING A "SELF-IN-TIME"

You have to begin to lose your memory, if only in bits and pieces, to realise that memory is what makes our lives. Life without memory is no life at all …. Our memory is our coherence, our reason, our feelings, even our action. Without it we are nothing.

(Buñuel, cited in Sacks, 2015a, p. 25)

I don't know the context that informed Buñuel's words. But when I read them, I immediately imagined him or someone close to him caught in a nightmare of slowly losing their memory. I felt a chill to think of living with no sense of a past to refer back to – a past that helps to define me, explain me and the world, give me clues about how to respond now and in the future. Without the anchoring of memory, I would become a self-out-of-time. In Chapter 1, I noted the importance of being able to trust in the ongoingness of ourselves, as well as of others and of places to which we are attached, and discussed how our earliest attachment experiences support our identity as coherent, continuous beings. I intend to expand on this by exploring what goes on in the brain to give us this sense of coherent ongoingness. I will explore the paradox that although our experience is smoothed over by an illusory sense of continuity, the Self changes and is transformed continually over time (Mitchell, 1993). I also consider what life must be like for people who, for various reasons, don't experience themselves as existing in an interlocking sequence of past, present and future and find it hard to construct an ongoing narrative of their lives. Without a temporal frame of reference, what is their experience of Self? In my attempt to address these issues I have delved into the writings of scientists, neuroscientists and developmental psychologists as well as psychotherapists.

What do we mean by self?

Any discussion about the Self begs the question, what do we mean by this concept, or by the word identity?[1] Bollas pointed out how fiendishly difficult it is to define the Self, and even if we could, how can we know whether other people sense their selves in the same way that we do? (1995, p. 167). We have a sense of our own being. We feel we are here. We refer to the self as an object, for instance, in saying "I talk to myself", or "I'm not myself today". But we don't have tangible, sensory evidence of the self. It is not something we can touch or see (p. 163). It is "a place where we just seem to live our life" and although unknowable, this self-knowing helps us feel we are the authors of our existence (pp. 179, 166). Bollas is one of many writers since antiquity who have tried to define the Self. I do not intend to engage in detail here with that debate but will mention some ideas that have informed my thinking about being a self-in-time. Certain points stand out:

1. The first is the dynamic nature of the self. Stern speculated that an infant experiences life as a sequence of moments strung together, unique moments of feelings-in-motion during which time his feelings and perceptions rapidly change (1998, p. 14). This is also true of how we experience the Self, our inner "weatherscape". It is constituted by a sequence of moments strung together, "many thousand experiential episodes" that create our essential idiom. It is a "moving or dynamic inner presence" (Bollas, 1995, pp. 148, 152). According to Mitchell, another writer from the analytic tradition, "selves are what people do and experience over time rather than something that exists in some place. Self refers to the subjective organisation of meanings one creates as one moves through time, doing things, such as having ideas and feelings", and our selves "change and are transformed continually over time" (1993, p. 101). As we enter a new environment, for example, this stimulates a different state of mind and body. Even very ordinary transitions, between home and work, for example, call out a different self. We "change hats" and generally do it seamlessly, without losing touch completely with our other roles or identities.[2] This is because in order to negotiate the complex world we live in we maintain "a repertoire of identities that we activate as required by specific situations and circumstances" (Putnam, 2016, p. 138). We might spend most of our time "inhabiting a restricted set of states of being" that encompass our day-to-day activities and roles (p. 164). But in a different context we might feel, think and act very differently to our habitual self. Moreover, our different selves are constantly evolving "within the changing contexts in which we live and function" (p. 160).

2. Despite its dynamic, changeable nature, most people experience the Self as continuous and cohesive. Even though our emotional and physical states are constantly shifting, as James comfortingly said, "I am the same I that I was yesterday" (Meares, 2012, p. 107). I will mention some exceptions to this later. There is a sense of familiarity about my Self – "the me-ness of me" as one client aptly put it, or my personal idiom to use Bollas's term. Haynes gave a beautiful

account of how children can know themselves in a sensory, bodily way. She described how her young granddaughter asked if she liked the smell of herself and then, unashamedly, talked about smelling her finger after putting it in her bottom. She liked doing this "because it smells like me" (2007, p. 210). Haynes reflected that she was communicating "in uncensored language, that her body was herself". She continued, and her words echo those of Mitchell and Bollas: "My own wrestling with attempts to define what I mean by the self have led me to understand that ineffable energy, which we call the self, as an invisible reservoir of meaning-making which contains the potential for each of us to create a unique sense of being and becoming … a self that continues to evolve throughout a lifetime. I understand the self to evolve through repeated experiences of the act of becoming: an approximation of self which is being not yet born, and which is never a fulfilment but always an approach, or search for form" (p. 211).

3. Self-continuity depends on a constant dialogue between past, present and the anticipated future. "We have to have a notion of how we have become, and of where we are going" in order to have a sense of who we are (Giddens, 1991, p. 54). And because of this "dialogue with time", each of us constructs and lives a 'narrative', and this narrative is our identity. "Each of us is a singular narrative, which is constructed, continually, unconsciously by, through, and in us through our perceptions, our feelings, our thoughts, our actions, and not least, our discourse, our spoken narrative" (Sacks, 2015a, p. 117).

4. A sense of Self depends, therefore, on the capacity for introspection. There is "a known and a knower" explained William James, an observing ego that engages in "a stream of consciousness" – James's much used phrase capturing the fluidity of Self (Meares, 2012, p. 86). We are continually reflecting on external happenings and our inner world, a "flux of images, sensations, feelings, memories, imaginings", and integrating them into the ongoing story of the Self (Meares, 2012, p. 42; Giddens, 1991, p. 54). In Chapter 3, I will come back to the capacity for introspection, or autonoetic consciousness, when discussing memory.

5. There is a distinction between self and identity. The latter is our public reality, our social self, how others see and define us. The Self is private, unknowable in its fullness to anyone else, and yet shaped by interactions with others. As Meares said, "the experience of self cannot be distinguished from the state of relatedness in which the individual is engaged at that moment" (2012, p. 158). It is a paradox that something so private, so internal as our sense of self is so infused with what is outer – the place we are in, its "climate" or atmosphere, the time of day and year, and most important the interpersonal climate. I am a different self with that person in that place than I am with someone else or the same person in a different mood and context. It is understandable then that the customary states of relatedness in which the child dwells have a deep influence on the formation of self.

The ongoing self

To sum up: The self is unique, fluid, richly textured, referred to as an object and yet indescribable because it can only be felt or experienced, not directly perceived. It is ever-changing, yet continuous; cohesive, yet potentially fragmented. This brings me back to my sixth proposition, that our sense of self depends on the experience of continuity and of knowing our past selves and conceptualising ourselves as future beings. Freud touched on this when he argued that to be constantly brought up against the impossibility of the new abolishes something essential to our identity, "all those unfulfilled but possible futures to which we cling in phantasy ..." (Cox Cameron, 2007, p. 264). Clinical observation and research in neurophysiology and child development highlights how the self as a coherent being existing across time is shaped as a result of the interaction of embodied experiences, particularly during early childhood, the development of the mind-brain and our interpersonal experience. In what follows, I intend to focus on how the brain supports temporal cohesion.

In a fascinating paper arguing that neural structures give coherence to perception and consciousness, Oliver Sacks opened with the question "Is the time we live in, or live by, continuous like (a) river? Or is it more comparable to a chain or a train, a succession of discrete moments like beads on a string?" (2017, p. 161). His question piqued my interest because it resonated with my own emerging questions about the nature of time and how we relate to it. James argued that to its possessor, consciousness seems to be always continuous, "without breach, crack, or divisions", never "chopped into bits" (Sacks, 2017, p. 161). But is the continuity really an illusion? And what implications might such an illusion have for our identity?

Sacks' discussion reminded me of Mitchell and Bromberg's emphasis on "normal" multiplicity. They argued that we are all multiple selves and in their clinical examples illustrate how we are constantly shifting between different self-states (Mitchell, 1993; Bromberg, 2001). But to yoke all this together our experience is smoothed over by an illusory sense of continuity. As Bromberg pointed out, we need a feeling of coherence in order to override the awareness of discontinuity caused by constant shifts in state. These repeated state changes in response to internal and external context are generally difficult to perceive. They are in the background of our experience. "The developmental process that eases the transitions across states of consciousness", Bromberg explained, "typically results in a healthy person being able to smooth out awareness of the changes" (pp. 182, 244, 260). We are therefore able, most of the time, to sense ourselves as unified selves. Without an irrefutable sense of selfhood, our identity would be incredibly fragile and existing in the world would be a frightening challenge. Yet this is the experience of some people, for instance, who have experienced extreme trauma, or who because of brain injury, dementia or other neurological conditions effectively "lose their minds" and with it their core identity.

Sacks' "last hippie" is an example. As a result of a brain tumour Greg became amnesic, confined "to a single moment – the present – uninformed by any sense of a past (or a future)" and, as Sacks pointed out, whereas ordinarily "some sense of on-going, of 'next' is always with us", Greg lacked this sense of movement, of happening. "He seemed immured, without knowing it, in a timeless moment." Sacks mused that, "given this radical lack of connection and continuity in his inner life, I got the feeling, indeed, that he might not have an inner life to speak of, that he lacked the constant dialogue of past and present, of experience and meaning, which constitutes consciousness and inner life for the rest of us. He seemed to have no sense of 'next' and to lack the eager and anxious tension and anticipation, of intention that normally drives us through life" (1995, p. 46). In this, as in other clinical tales, Sacks gets to the heart of what it is to be human and to have a self, that our self is constantly being formed by an ongoing dialogue of past, present and future and by keeping a narrative going which we charge with feelings and meanings.

Sacks drew on the work of scientists like Gerald Edelman and Francis Crick as well as observations from his work with people with neurological disorders. My non-scientist's interpretation of his conclusions goes as follows: In order to explore the neurobiological basis of consciousness, scientists have studied visual perception. It appears that we take in the visual environment in brief, static frames then fuse these to give visual awareness its normal movement and continuity. However, during migraine attacks, certain seizures, hallucinogenic trips and motion blindness some people see a flickering set of stills rather than visual flow. Crick and Koch suggested that the fusion of stills is the result of neurons in many cortical areas cooperating together in some form of global activity. The neurons in some areas process colour, in others form, motion and orientation. "Our experience of perceptual unity thus suggests that the brain in some way binds together, in a mutually coherent way, all those neurons actively responding to different aspects of a perceived object" or, as Sacks said, "the sense of continuity results from the continuous overlapping of successive perceptual moments" (2017, p. 180).

Having put the case that the fusing of discrete visual snapshots is a prerequisite for continuity, Sacks continued: "if a flowing dynamic consciousness allows at the lowest level, a continuous, active, scanning or looking, it allows at a higher level, the interaction of perception and memory, of past and present"[3] (p. 181). According to Edelman this "primary consciousness" is highly adaptive in the struggle for life. It makes it possible to integrate the present scene with the animal's past history and then to discriminate and plan in the light of past events. Such integration has survival value. From simple, primary consciousness "we leap to human consciousness, with the advent of language and self-consciousness and an explicit sense of the past and the future. And it is this which gives a *thematic and personal continuity* to the consciousness of every individual" (Sacks, 2017, p. 182). "Consciousness is always active and selective, charged with feelings and meanings uniquely our own, informing our choices and interfusing our perceptions". In other words, this higher consciousness is crucial for our sense of self. James captures this more poetically: "Our passing thoughts … do not wander around like wild cattle. Each one is owned, our own, and bears the brand of this ownership, transmitting whatever it realized as its Self to its own later proprietor" (p. 183). Our ongoing sense of self then, is rather like a river consisting entirely of a collection of moments which flow into one another but which we yoke together through a thematic self-narrative.

What Sacks did not consider is when something happens, internally or externally, to create a disconnection between two moments so that we can literally feel a different self from the "me" a moment before, a shifting between self-states or parts of self when something shocks, surprises or triggers us. We all experience these hiatuses or ruptures in continuity, probably many times during the day in subtle ways. Our somatic-affective state can go through many shifts during the course of a few moments in response to our ever-changing context. This is especially true of our interpersonal context, for our reactions to others often occur on a micro-temporal scale. However, most of us, to use Bromberg's words, can "stand in the spaces between different realities without losing any of them" and "feel like one self while being many" (2001, p. 274). But for people who have experienced ongoing trauma during childhood, the shifts or switches can take a much more dramatic form. As Bromberg said, "when the illusion of unity is too dangerous to be maintained because of being overwhelmed by input that cannot be processed, there is then a return to the simplicity of dissociation" (p. 273). I will say more about such dissociative switching and the unitary self in Chapter 9.

Coherence and identity: a psychological perspective

To continue my exploration of how a sense of coherent ongoingness is sustained I turn to the work of two men who straddle the disciplines of psychotherapy, psychology and science. In *The Developing Mind* (1999), Daniel Siegel talked about different types of integration – neural, spatiotemporal, synchronic and diachronic. The first refers to the coordination of neural activity in a range of circuits across different domains in the brain – vertical, dorso-lateral and lateral. Siegel's account of neural integration, which he argued is fundamental to self-organisation and the capacity of the brain to create a sense of self, accords with Crick and Koch's observations about the cooperation between neurons in many cortical areas in some form of global activity (1999, p. 302). It also links with what I will say later about the functions of both hemispheres and autonoetic consciousness.

Spatiotemporal integration is an interactive process between neural circuits involving space-time patterns. It suggests that "the brain is capable of representing, in the moment, patterns of activity in which direct influences from the past are encoded". It also functions as an "anticipation machine" able to represent the future. "Such anticipatory mechanisms directly shape the way in which linkages may be made across various processes and across time." The value of this process is that it enables us to act adaptively in an environment that changes across time and space and this obviously enhances our chances of survival (p. 305). Siegel then put forward the view that the essence of integrative capacity is to achieve coherence of the self (p. 310). Some people, and in my experience this is often people whose early experiences of care were grossly inadequate or traumatic, are unable "to find the emotional well-being in integrating multiple self-states into a coherent experience of self". For them there may be cohesive functioning within a given state. But across the self-states, spatiotemporal integration may not be possible.

The idea of self-cohesion and coherence brings us to the concepts of synchronic and diachronic integration. The former creates a cohesive mental state as information processing across widely distributed neural circuits is integrated at any given moment. The latter refers to the way that the flow of our states of mind across time are linked together to facilitate flexible and adaptive functioning. Both cohesion in the moment and coherence across time are important and support self-regulation and our sense of going-on-being as unitary selves. Without these integrating processes we risk feeling fragmented, disoriented and are liable to experience others as confusingly inconsistent.

Daniel Stern took a more intersubjective and developmental approach to self-coherence. He speculated that five invariant properties of interpersonal experience give us a sense of me as a single, coherent, bounded physical entity, in other words a core self, as distinct from you – another coherent identity. Of these five invariants, coherence of temporal structure is most relevant to my theme.[4] Time, said Stern, "provides an organising structure that helps identify different entities". Visual, auditory, tactile and proprioceptive stimuli emanating from the self share a common temporal structure and different parts of the body move in synchrony. There is *"self-synchrony"*. The temporal patterns of someone else will be different. Four-month-old infants recognise things with a similar temporal structure and can detect temporal incongruities – for instance, between sights and sounds that are expected to be paired such as lip movements and speech. They act as though two events sharing the same temporal structure belong together and are selectively inattentive to competing visual events with a different time structure. These capacities assist in differentiating self from other and this other from that other (1985, pp. 83–6).

Reading this I recalled working with a young woman with autism. Tina did not speak and seemed to exist in a sensory world, some sensory experiences evidently evoking pleasure, but others triggering distress and self-harm. At the time, I practised as a dance movement therapist and Tina seemed to enjoy the experience of moving together in time to music. If I copied her exactly all was well. When some part of my body was not in synchrony with Tina's movements she protested. Sometimes I took her out walking, an activity she loved. She would grab my hand and march forwards at speed. If I did something with my other hand, such as scratch my nose, her free hand would reach out and push my arm down. At the time I surmised that Tina viewed me as an extension of her body. My gestures would therefore have been disconcerting as they were not under her volition. In the light of Stern's discussion on temporal coherence it could be hypothesised that Tina, and perhaps other people with severe autism, are unable to determine temporal structures in the same way as most people, perhaps because of deficits in the neurological fusing of different perceptual data. Their use of their own bodies and objects in perseverative movement and sound raises other questions about the perception of temporal contours in people with autism. But this is beyond the scope of my survey.

To sum up my argument so far: Perception, memory and their continual integration across many regions of the brain are all essential for giving us a sense of Self. Integration involves both linkage and differentiation. With temporal coherence, both synchronic and diachronic integration being important, we are able to differentiate self from other, same and different, what is continuous from what is "out of synch", discordant and incoherent. In addition, because we are far more than mechanistic brains, the capacities for language and reflection help us to fashion coherent, emotionally-hued thematic stories about our lives, and it is this that gives us our unique identities – identities which are both enduring and ever-evolving. I will discuss the significance of creating a narrative of our lives in more detail in Chapter 8.

Identity, place and history

Our sense of going-on-being is as dependent on connections to place as on temporal ones. Remember my proposition that *we exist in space*. As McGilchrist said, attachment to place runs deep inside us and "where I am 'at home' implies a sense of permanence"[5] (2009, p. 390). The need to feel at home and belong to a social group is important whatever our age, and at a time when thousands of people across the world have had to flee their homes and are desperately seeking safety, it stands out even more as a crucial human need. Without the anchoring of a stable home our identity can become incredibly fragile. Denise Inge made some interesting points about our attachment to place. She pointed out that a common practice these days is to request that our ashes be scattered somewhere that might be meaningful to us. This contrasts with older practices where people were buried somewhere they called "home", often near relatives. The latter provided a lasting memorial, somewhere that future generations might visit, whereas the scattering of ashes reflects a more fragmented sense of ourselves in the modern world. Inge continued by observing that not only are we physically more mobile than our ancestors, but we are also spiritually more eclectic, picking and mixing from a range of philosophies and beliefs. "Added to this is a kind of social looseness – through social mobility and through social networking, we scatter our seeds of friendship more widely than ever before. We may belong less profoundly to any one place, but we visit a wider variety of places; we may not belong to any one person for a lifetime, but in the tabulation of virtual friends many belong to us" (2014, p. 172). Inge then questioned whether the scattering of ashes is one expression of these scattered lives. "Is this I wonder, because we haven't stayed in one place long enough to feel that we belong there deeply? Does place no longer spell out belonging? Or is it simply that length and depth are not the same thing – that we may feel deeply drawn to places with which we have no lengthy connection" (p. 172). Her questions are worth reflecting on.

Isca Salzberger-Wittenberg, writing in her late eighties, also commented on the importance of feeling that we belong and are part of something that extends beyond our individual lives. From her work with a group of people in their seventies and eighties she noticed a shared interest in tracing their roots – perhaps by constructing family trees, visiting their parents' old homes, or writing family stories. "All these activities", she wrote, "seemed to indicate an urge to place oneself within the generational chain, to know about one's forebears, internalise the past, and the wish to preserve such knowledge for the coming generation" (2013, p. 158). The need to preserve a connection with past generations can also be present at earlier life-stages. For instance, Salzberger-Wittenberg speculated that part of the motivation behind starting a family is an "awareness of being part of a lifeline which stretches from past generations and makes us wish to continue it" (p. 103). It is a form of investment in a future beyond our lifespan, a hope, she suggested, that "by having offspring, a part of us remains alive – is immortal". Another analyst used the term "genetic immortality" (Raphael-Leff, 2012, p. 209). This drive might also include wanting to preserve or pass on qualities we value in our parents, grandparents or partner, in effect to keep them alive. Preserving lineage and ensuring that the estate or family business stays in the family is the stuff of many nineteenth-century novels. But is this such a preoccupation today I wonder? Especially with so many broken marriages and complex family formations. Perhaps it becomes more figural for men and women who are unable to give birth. When someone well-meaningly said "but you can always adopt" to one young woman struggling with infertility problems she was angry. "I want to be pregnant", she said. "I want my genes to be carried on. Adopting just wouldn't be the same". For her and others like her there was a risk of feeling disconnected, not just from friends with children, but from past and future generations – what Raphael-Leff described as the loss of an ongoing hope of an "eternal linkage from past to future generations" (p. 209).

Being a self-out-of-time, a "no-being"

In our work we see people who have little sense of a coherent, ongoing, firmly embedded in time Self. They have lost or never found themselves. And we see others who are stuck in more rigid, limiting definitions of self. People with conditions such as psychosis, Borderline Personality Disorder (BPD) or Emotionally Unstable Personality Disorder (EUPD) as it is now known, and dissociative disorders often lack a core self, the result in many cases of early attachment failure and traumatic experiences. There are also people who lack an ongoing sense of self because of neurological conditions, brain injury or dementia.

Meares' research on Borderline Personality Disorder has helped in my thinking about what it is to be a Self, although I should state my preference for avoiding this label.[6] Meares concluded that the core of BPD is a painful sense of personal incoherence, unreality and lack of continuity accompanied by a fear that personal existence would end if a close relationship were lost[7] (2012, pp. 36, 43). People with this diagnosis often complain of "a sense of hollowness in living, an emptiness, a feeling that nothing is happening, and that in some way … an element of self-hood is lacking" (p. 87). They lack the inner sense of self that goes with a stream of consciousness. To understand this absence of self and experience of inner emptiness we need to look to their earliest relationships. As Meares argued, "the sense of self depends upon, and arises with, a sense of other: where self is fragile, so also is the sense of other" (p. 38). Hobson eloquently captured this when he said: "Beneath a chaos of disconnected fragments lies an abyss of nothingness. The odd sentence 'I have no being' carries with it the implication 'no one is there'. I have no sense of contact with another person who might confirm that 'I am me' with an identity separate from the world of people and things 'out there'" – and I would add to this, a "me" that is ongoing (1985, p. 270). In no-being, Hobson wrote, "there are no fantasies, no thoughts, no ideas". "No-being is dimly expressed in the terrible paradox: 'I am no one'. There are no images that I can call 'me', 'mine', or 'my own'" (pp. 269, 270).

Hobson's description fits the experience of a number of people I have worked with. For example, one man, Ezra, told me he felt like a chameleon. He observed the people around him and copied what they did or echoed their choices and opinions. In one setting he would act one way. With another group he might be very different. But Ezra had no idea who he was. Nor did Marcie whom I mentioned in Chapter 1. She often lamented that nothing spoke to her. "There is no feedback", and she complained of a void inside. Marcie spoke of this in a flat, rather numb way. It fitted what I thought of as a one-dimensional self (Wright, 2009). For Bree, however, the loss of self was experienced as far more frightening. I sat with her on many occasions whilst agitated, desperate and sobbing, she described the terror of annihilation and of "ceasing to be", and she had a recurrent nightmare of being left alone in her cot and floating off into space because of nothing to hold her. Hobson's concept of no-being reminds me too of Lucianne, also mentioned in Chapter 1, although her loss of self was more fleeting than that of Marcie or Bree – a temporary occurrence at a point when she was feeling acutely alienated from others. She felt terrifyingly alone, and this echoed repeated moments during childhood. For example, one day Lucianne said, "I'm scared of losing myself". I sensed she meant much more than losing touch with her coping, adult self and that it was a fear of no longer existing and later, when in a very distressed, dysregulated, childlike state she repeated the phrase "I'm nothing" several times, it meant more than "I'm worthless or insignificant". It spoke of an absence of self. Reading what Hobson says about loneliness helped me to make sense of this (1985, pp. 268–9). He distinguished between two modes of loneliness, "no-being" and "cut-offness", and associated them with two types of anxiety: basic or existential anxiety and separation anxiety. "In infancy", he wrote, "the sense of 'I' is at first transient or evanescent. The 'I am' comes and goes; it seems to be established, then it is lost. If early mothering is defective the sense of 'I' remains tenuous and a terror of ceasing to be persists throughout life. It is experienced as the loneliness of no-being, the heart of darkness".[8] "We need other persons who are reliably there, who can be with us", wrote Hobson. "We need basic trust. If we are threatened by abandonment, the sudden and unpredictable loss of contact with a human body, then we are constantly faced with the horror of no-being. No-body is there"[9] (p. 268).

"No-body" was reliably there for the clients I have mentioned in the early years so crucial for the development of a sense of self – an "I am" that does not come and go. Marcie's mother was chronically depressed and, I suspect, dissociative. Lucianne's mother was either frightening and abusive, or frightened and childlike. Moreover, in the present Lucianne kept encountering the painful reality of no-body being there to hold her when she was distressed. Many is the time when she said, "I just want someone to hold me. I want someone strong who'll say, 'it's OK. I'll deal with it'". Meanwhile, my impression from what I learned of Bree's mother is that she found her little girl's emotional needs too triggering. She spent as little time as possible with her daughter, her musical career providing a convenient excuse, and according to Bree was always ready to hand her over to someone else.

Another, but causally different, aspect of Bree's lack of self is captured in her belief that her essential self or spirit died very early in her life. The message she was given by her parents, a message encountered on many occasions as she worked through childhood memories, was "you can exist, but only on our terms". "I had to fit in", she said, "to know my place". Hers was a predefined, packaged self – stultified and unable to evolve freely over time. Or it would have been, had a part of her not rebelled against the limiting narrative imposed upon her by becoming a problem child. Ezra, the chameleon, also came with a packaged, predefined self. The family myth was that he would be the one to save his parent's marriage, cheer up his depressed mother and amuse his intolerant father. To this original "mission"[10] other roles were added later: the bright boy who would go to university; the helpful child who politely distributed prayer books in his father's church and made tea for parishioners who called at the vicarage. Ezra communicated these earlier scripts through the language of psychosis when, aged 17, he became obsessed with a mission to save the world. Meanwhile his parents struggled to face the loss of the son they had imagined him becoming.

To exist we need to be recognised as a subject, a unique being in our own right, and for an inner narrative or stream of consciousness we need someone to have reflected us back to ourselves. In the conversational play between mothers and babies, for instance, the mother "plays out an embryonic me in relation to the baby as I ... in her quasi-imitative behaviours she shows the baby who is me" (Meares, 1998, p. 177). Going back to Haynes' contention that the self evolves through repeated acts of becoming, we also need an other who "dreams" us into being, who can imagine us, even before we are born, as the child and teenager and adult we could become, and who keeps dreaming a future on our behalf. In effect, parents oscillate in time to support our evolving self. They carry our history, reflect back our current experience, and encourage our potential self. But some caregivers are unable to do this. I remember one session with Bree when, in a state of sleepy reverie, I caught myself "dreaming her" as an elegant, vivacious person in the future – a model with a self that was represented in amazing photographs. Why this image? Why a model? There could be many meanings: I was seeing her in scenes where she was fully alive, so unlike the familiar wish to die Bree often felt when caught in the terror of empty, no-being. The "others" looking at the pictures recognised and communicated that she was special, which her parents never did. The third association to my daydream, is that portraits immortalise a self that can be remembered and carried forward into the future.

Having considered some intersubjective factors underlying the lack of an ongoing sense of self, I want to turn to another group of people who lack an ongoing sense of self – people suffering from amnesia because of brain injury, dementia and other neurological conditions, who not only lose their past, but lose their Self. Reading Sacks' vivid depictions of patients who lost their temporal frame of reference and his searching questions about their lived experience has helped me to appreciate what I take for granted – my own past-present-future flow. It has also aided my understanding of the phenomenology of clients with dissociative conditions whose memory for certain periods in their lives eludes them, and of other people who cannot conceive a future and are stuck in an unbearable present. When people lose their memory, and my opening quotation speaks of this, they don't just lose their past, and with it the feeling of continuity and being connected with others across time, they lose their Self. They also lose a future horizon with its sense of a "next" to anticipate and move towards. And without these two ends of the temporal "bridge" who are we? "What sort of a life (if any)", asked Sacks, "what sort of a world, what sort of a self, can be preserved in a man who has lost the greater part of his memory and, with this, his past, and his moorings in time?" (2015a, p. 25). What would go on in the privacy of our thoughts if we had no awareness of time? Would our thoughts move along? Or flash in and out of consciousness like random, contextless shooting stars? Or would they play recursively like the snatch of a tune we can't shake out of our mind? Thoughts that can't be thought about?

Some of Sacks' patients had Korsakoff's Syndrome, a condition caused by alcoholism that causes neuronal damage and has a severe impact on memory functioning. In particular, patients with this syndrome typically lose the memory of recent events. Sacks described how one man, Jimmie, seemed "isolated in a single moment of being, with a moat or lacuna of forgetting all round him … He is a man without a past (or future) stuck in a constantly changing, meaningless moment" (1995, p. 31). For another man, anything in his surroundings that had changed since 1978, the point at which his retrograde amnesia began caused him immense distress. Changes that Stephen's wife had made to their home in the succeeding years; new buildings in the neighbourhood; friends who looked older confused and alarmed him. Sacks concluded, "such patients, fossilised in the past, can only be at home, oriented, in the past. Time, for them, has come to a stop … Never have I known a patient so confronted, so tormented, by an anachronism" (2015a, p. 45). Similar phenomena can be observed as a result of certain cerebral tumours. For instance, Greg, mentioned earlier, who was "confined in effect to a single moment – the present – uninformed by any sense of a past or a future" (1995, pp. 37, 46). Greg was effectively imprisoned; with people, yet very alone, because in our inner world we are repeatedly going over or imagining events involving others. I am struck by the horrifying thought of being stuck in a constantly changing, meaningless moment. As Sacks emphasised, the present is given meaning and depth by the past, hence it becomes the "remembered present" to use Edelman's term. It is also "given potential and tension by the future". But for the men cited, and perhaps too for people afflicted by advanced dementia, the present was "flat and (in its meagre way) incomplete" (p. 46).

Our past, present and future self

I can think of a number of people who, for different reasons, might also describe their present as flat and meaningless and who would probably agree if asked whether they felt stuck in a prison or if they no longer knew who they were. In some cases, this is because the legacy of the past still haunts them, colonising the present and making it hard to envisage a different future. In others, it is because the challenge of surviving each day, perhaps due to being immersed in a chronic physical or mental illness, has severed their contact with their past and potential future selves. This takes me to the chapter's final theme. I have emphasised how selfhood is founded on a sense of ongoingness and how this is entwined with trust in the ongoingness of others. It is also linked with the ability to construct a chronological story of our lives, and to establish connections with past and future generations. I have commented too on the evolutionary advantage of being able to think ahead and look back in order to generalise from past experiences. Now I want to explore our relationship to past, present and future by considering people who become immersed in one time-frame to the exclusion of the other two. It is a rather "Alice in Wonderland-ish" question to ask: "Where are you? In the past, the here-and-now, or the future?" Everyone, I am sure, is familiar with the experience of not being fully present because of thinking about a past event or what may or may not happen in the future. We frequently engage in mental time-travel. And at certain periods in our lives our primary focus might naturally be on our future or on the past. For instance, I would expect teenagers and young adults to orient to the future, planning their career, finding a partner and creating a home; while looking back is typical in the later stages of life. But this does not mean losing touch with the present or with our former or potential selves. However, some people seem to be permanently stuck in one time-zone. Phenomenologically, that is where their Self resides.

In what follows, I draw on Charmaz's detailed study of people experiencing chronic illness and expand on her ideas by referring to other writers and my own clinical work. Chronic illness, especially when involving considerable pain and fatigue or, in the case of mental illness, ongoing depression or crippling anxiety, limits what people can do. Like trauma and periods of critical illness, enduring illness entails a dropping out of the continuity of ordinary life, and in some cases the loss of what gave purpose to their lives. To use Stolorow's term, the onset of a severe illness or disabling condition "shatters our absolutisms" – the trusted, taken-for-granted aspects of life (2007, p. 18). And as Charmaz discovered by interviewing people with chronic physical conditions for periods of between five and eleven years, it represents a radical disjuncture in their life story. Like trauma, chronic illness can also call into question how people see themselves and their relationships. Charmaz made the interesting point that "time serves as a container for locating the self" (1991, p. 231). More specifically she noticed a variety of ways in which her respondents located themselves, or rather their self-concept, in the past, present or future. In defining the term, Charmaz explained that sociologists view the self-concept as "embedded in and emerging from relationships". However, "those relationships develop during specific periods in a person's life; and all relationships exist within socially constructed times as well as within social structures". With this temporal perspective, she viewed the self-concept as providing "meanings that people attribute to themselves and unifies subjective experience over time" and she highlighted how circumstances influence the extent to which we locate the Self in a particular time-frame (p. 230). Following Charmaz's example, I have become curious about where my own clients locate themselves. I will begin with the present:

The self in the present

There are different ways of anchoring oneself in the present and, according to Charmaz, they are distinguished by the number, pacing and quality of events.[11] For example, she observed how some people with chronic illness cram their days, or at least their "good days", with activities and events. She called this the *filled present*. By contrast, in the *slowed down present* people deliberately scale down their lives and reduce the number, pace and intensity of events. For some of her interviewees, slowed down time often felt empty. As one man said: "it is space to fill before the period of sleep" (p. 243). Other people felt more in control when they slowed down and were able to savour quiet moments. Charmaz's third category of presentness, in which the quality not the number or speed of events is most important, is the *intense present*. She described how a sense of passion, authenticity, and involvement distinguishes this mode. It is also characterised by inner work, a reflective engagement with time's finitude, an acceptance of the possibility of death, a review and re-evaluation of one's life and one's priorities. "With the intense present comes a sense of urgency – urgency to act, to experience, and to bond with other people" (p. 246).

In a moving account of how his relationship to time altered during treatment for cancer, Jim Pye spoke of his heightened appreciation of the beauty of the ordinary. "Cancer makes being alive urgently wonderful" (2017). In similar vein, the writer Susan Sontag said that thinking about death had "added a fierce intensity to my life … having cancer does put things into perspective" (Charmaz, 1991, p. 247). An intensity in present-moment experiencing can also occur when reprieve follows an illness that has put life on hold. This can also be true after other life crises. For a while at least, people approach and savour life with vigour. They notice and deeply appreciate things usually taken for granted. I am sure we have all experienced this occasionally. Even after a short period of ill health or pain, having energy and joints that move freely can feel glorious. Life feels fresher, new, remarkable. Then, as we fall back into the busy pattern of our days – our personal filled present or preoccupation with the future – the intensity fades and good intentions are forgotten.

In addition to Charmaz's three categories I should like to add two more. The first fits Charmaz's concept of the *intense present* and occurs when we are engaged in something that drops us out of the usual continuity of life. Here I am thinking about Simmel's notion of the "adventure". In a situation distinct from the familiar continuous thread of life, our identity changes, or rather it can assume a different shape. As long as it is safe, we can "play" at being someone different. Think how on holiday we can do crazy things we "wouldn't usually be seen dead doing". We spend time with people we might not normally associate with. We risk challenging ourselves. And sometimes we come back from a holiday with romantic ideas of moving, changing course, of really living a different self, and can resent being swiftly pulled back into time's usual course. A love affair is another example of an adventure in which, when they slip out of the continuity of their usual routines, people can act in ways very discrepant from their usual selves. Time can slow down, speed up or seem not to exist when with or contemplating the "beloved". They can "lose their heads", the self-monitoring, self-reflective part of the mind, and do things that later, back in humdrum ordinary time, they regret. An "adventure" can also take the form of a retreat – a period of "time out" in order to be with oneself in a way that can feel impossible when we are caught up in the busy, daily round. Presentness is the dominant time-mode during an adventure, and that is for two reasons. We often work out what to do as we go along. We may not be able to rely on plans made before the adventure started, nor on how we have done things in the past. So we play it by ear. Our focus is very much on now and what happens next. The other reason is that what we are engaged in often absorbs us – true also of a love affair. It has a sense of passion and involvement, Charmaz noticed.

My second example of the Self in the present is very different. This is the "constricted or confined present". Again the "last hippie" comes to mind and Sacks' description of him being confined to a single moment, a man whose present was flat and incomplete because of amnesia (1995, p. 46). It also reminds me of the plight of an adolescent discussed by Bollas who had a terrifying absence of self and did not know what the term meant. As Bollas said, "his internal conversations were not with some seemingly knowable thing called self but with a kind of empty space". He preoccupied himself writing lists and "going over what he would do in the next week, the next twelve hours, the next five hours, the next hour". "And that is all there is to me. I don't have anything back. I just think and think about what I am going to do, where I am going to do it, and whether I can proceed to do it". Bollas commented that "he lived in a perpetual present, with no past, and a future made up only of projected present moments linked by the agenda he set" (1995, p. 159). This was also someone with little reflective capacity, which as argued earlier, is important in order to have a sense of self. Somehow neither he nor Greg had any touchstones: past moments to go back to, future scenarios to be imagined as possible, lived realities, situations they could think themselves back or forwards into and relate to their current thoughts, feelings and desires. The self-in-time in the constricted present has a one-dimensional character different, I would argue, from the experience of someone whose life feels flat and stuck in a more depressed way.

The self in the past

To understand how and why people come to locate themselves in the past we need to discover what the past means to them. In some cases, it is associated with confusion and unresolved issues and generates endless questioning – lots of "why did?" and "what if?" questions – in an attempt to make sense of whatever happened, understand the present and predict the future. When people are stuck in what Charmaz called the past as *a tangled web*, they keep questioning their part in events. In the case of her interviewees the questions tended to relate to their illness, for example "did I do it to myself?"; "what if I had had less stress" (1991, p. 231). For some of my clients the questions are: "why did that happen to me and not the others?", "what did I do that made Dad leave?", or even "why was I born?" Lurking behind such questions is often a shame Self who feels intrinsically bad and flawed. Although seeking answers is an attempt to free themselves from its legacy, their questioning keeps them tied to the past. Paradoxically there is also a future imperative in such rumination, an implicit hope that finding answers might help them to avoid repeating what happened before. It provides an illusion of control.

Charmaz also noted that people tend to locate themselves in the past when they sense a radical disjuncture between a familiar past and an inexplicable, alien present – the case for many people who suddenly find themselves undergoing tests and treatments for a body that is acting strangely. To see oneself in the *familiar past* is comforting for it is predictable. It can also serve as a psychic retreat when the self in the present is felt to be untenable or unacceptable (1991, p. 233). Another situation is to seek refuge in a rosy or *reconstructed past* by reliving the "good old days". It is a nostalgic refuge described by Pye as a "slow falsifying decoration of memory" (2017). In the case of the chronically ill, Charmaz explained that they reject being identified by their lived present and when a dark, empty future looms ahead the value of a past self increases (1991, p. 235). Such people often regale others with stories of things they used to do and places and people they knew. Perhaps it gives them a sense of vitality if they feel stuck in an empty present or serves to distract from physical and emotional pain. Perhaps it puts them in touch with a "preferred self". It reminds them of a time when they had more agency and felt valued. The past can certainly become a retreat for many older people, their memories sometimes becoming more real than present day events.

In an interesting chapter on older people and narrative, Bruce noted how it used to be thought that living in the past was pathological and professionals tried to distract the elderly with activities (1999, p. 182). These days reminiscence is viewed more positively. "The process of creating a coherent story and sharing it with a respectful listener has a new value as a route by which people in later life may adjust to inevitable losses and come to face death with equanimity" (p. 184). It is a way to find continuities between now and then. It can help in settling unresolved conflicts. Moreover, reminiscence narratives sometimes rework the past to create a good story, thus enabling the older person to hold on to self-esteem in the face of decline (pp. 186–7). However, for younger people who seek refuge from their chronic health problems in the reconstructed past there are disadvantages. They may already have curtailed former activities, including stopping work, and begun to lose touch with friends – all important in shaping their pre-illness identity. Everyone else appears to be moving forwards, whilst their lives become even more constricted as they find themselves "out of step" with others and with less and less to share. The lines between past and present blur, and their belief in a self that keeps evolving fades (Charmaz, 1991, p. 237).

There is another group of people whose self-concept is anchored in the past, the survivors of severe trauma. Many of the people I work with are trapped by the past. It haunts the present. We could name this the "relived past". Like the group in Charmaz's book, for many the present is felt to be untenable or unacceptable. But there is no rosy past to retreat to in their minds. For them, the past is either full of gaps or a chamber of remembered horrors. Despite evolving a range of strategies to escape the past, until they can process and grieve for what has happened, it is impossible to live fully in the present. Some get stuck trying to make sense of what has happened to them, echoing what Charmaz noticed, or in fantasising the enactment of some form of revenge or that those who hurt them will one day apologise and say they love them. Others are endlessly, albeit unconsciously, searching for the care they never received in current relationships. But it never comes, and they find themselves in the same story over and over again: a story of being let down, rejected and abused; a story that intensifies the question, "why me?" These are the stories that emerge in the therapy room, drawing us with the client into the relived past. I will say more about this later in the book.

The self in the future

We all need to be able to envisage potential selves, to see ourselves in the future and work towards certain goals. Life would have no meaning without this prospective thinking. In describing the "man with the shattered world", Luria made the telling point that when robbed of any possibility of a future we lose "precisely what it is that makes a person human" (1972, p. 34).[12] However, it can be problematic if our self-concept is always located in tomorrow. To return to Charmaz's framework: One category she noticed was of a group who located themselves in the *improved future*. For them, what they did now was seen as a step towards a preferred or ideal self in the future, or living or working somewhere much better (1991, p. 251). They pinned their self-concept to how they imagined they could be. Another category was the *taken-for-granted future*. In this time-mode their self-concepts are cast into the future. That is where reality lies, and even though the future could include difficult times, the focus again is on what people do being in the service of something later. It provides a reason for working hard and in some cases for living (pp. 253–4). Charmaz's third category, the *everlasting future*, is particularly interesting as it relates to the first challenge of living in time and to our quest for meaning. In this mode, people cling to the illusion of an immortal self. They are consoled by the thought of an afterlife or of peace and relief if they feel trapped by their circumstances, locked in a failing body, stuck in a limited life, or plagued by mental health problems. Charmaz also mentioned the notion of "symbolic immortality" (p. 255). She described this as the urge to leave something behind that preserves our identity – children, a record of our life history, a work of art, a book, an invention, a business. We want to be remembered and to feel that our life has made a difference. It had a purpose. It is, as said earlier, about our need for a sense of ongoingness and to pass things on to future generations.

Again, with my own clients in mind, I can think of people who locate themselves in a "dreaded future". They wait with terror or resignation for the future they are certain will come: being hurt and humiliated again; being rejected and finding themselves alone; failing at whatever they try to achieve. These are the scripts held by the survivors of early abuse and neglect; of childhoods when they were the odd ones out and the victims of bullying throughout school; of relationships which never worked. Such people hyper-orient to the future, always on the lookout for warning signs of the dreaded fate. They find it impossible to envisage something different occurring, to entertain options, to form an intention, to know it's OK to change their minds. It is as if their minds are closed to difference and novelty, and to learning or trying something new. It feels too unsafe to explore new possibilities and so they cling to the familiar known. And when we encounter someone who is caught in such a "closed system", our agenda for change – and I think however much we embrace unconditional acceptance and the premise of following the client, it is inevitable that we have agendas – often leads to rifts and impasses.

There are other reasons too why people fail to develop the capacity to imagine, dream and play with future possibilities. Ordinarily, the sense of having a future Self develops in childhood, prospective thinking being an important dimension in normal play, and parents can assist in this process of development or obstruct it. As Alvarez said, they "carry for the child not only a sense of the baby that he once was and in part still is, but also a sense of the man or woman that he will become, and *is* becoming" (2012, pp. 178, 183). In her work with deprived, abused and severely depressed children she encountered children who had very little sense of a future. They were "too despairing to imagine that (they) could ever be like an admired or idealised figure" (p. 184). Such children "may see closed doors and grey skies everywhere. Eight stretching to twelve may seem an impossible dream. They often see themselves as very stupid or very ugly" (p. 186). What they need is someone to believe in them and carry hope for them. Like Bree, and perhaps like Bollas's client, they need to be "dreamed into being".

Conclusions

Let me go back to my Alice in Wonderland question: "Where are you? In the past, the here-and-now, or the future?" It can be useful, in terms of our own temporal phenomenology, to check now and then where we are most in our preoccupations. And it can be revealing to think about the question when reflecting on the individuals we work with. Where do they locate their self-concept and why? And intersubjectively, how might that be adaptive? Then more generally, can we identify whether certain time-frames tend to be focal for specific groups? Is it linked to life-stage? To circumstances? To something else?

Another researcher, Laura Carsensten, studied the contrasting time priorities of the young and old. Perhaps not unexpectedly, she found that young adults seek a life of growth and self-fulfilment. They search for new experiences and are willing to invest in their futures and delay gratification for future goals. As people grow older their priorities change. They focus on "being rather than doing and on the present more than the future" (Gawande, 2014, pp. 93, 97). How these groups use their social time also differs. Young adults seek wider social connections and these are often briefer. Older people tend to interact with fewer people and concentrate more on spending time with family and established friends.[13] However, when someone comes face to face with mortality, perhaps because of a near-death experience or diagnosis of a life-threatening illness, their perspectives radically change, and this applies however old they are. With an uncertain future, being in the present and spending time with people and doing things that really matter becomes important. As Carstensen concluded, how we choose to spend our time depends on how much time we perceive we have (p. 97).

Charmaz observed that however her interviewees adapted living in the present and whichever time-mode they prioritised, each response required changing their expectations of self and criteria for self-worth (1991, p. 245). When illness strikes, and the same is true of other crises that interrupt life, a crisis of self can ensue. We start to question who we are and to re-evaluate our relationships. We cling to our pre-crisis self, the old notions of selfhood that defined us and the roles and social identities that formed the currency of our relationships. Alternatively, we might cling to the visions we had about our future self. The surgeon Paul Kalanithi's account of his inner journey after being diagnosed with terminal cancer tells movingly how someone can flip between trying to live as the former self and trying to find a new definition of self and sense of purpose. "The tricky part of illness", he said, "is that, as you go through it, your values are constantly changing. You try to figure out what matters to your, and then you keep figuring it out" (2017, p. 160). Until cancer struck, Kalanithi's self-concept was located in the future. He knew who and what he was. As he said: "Medical training is relentlessly future-oriented, all about delayed gratification; you're always thinking about what you'll be doing five years down the line. But now I don't know what I'll be doing five years down the line. I may be dead. I may not be. I may be healthy. I may be writing. I don't know. And so it's not all that useful to be thinking about the future – that is, beyond lunch" (p. 197). Kalanithi described how "the monolithic uncertainty of my future was deadening; everywhere I turned the shadow of death obscured the meaning of any action" (p. 149). "The way forwards would seem obvious if only I knew how many years or months I had left. Tell me three months, I'd spend time with my family. Tell me one year, I'd write a book. Give me ten years, I'd get back to treating diseases" (pp. 160–62).

Other people were in Kalanithi's mind as he mused on his place in time – colleagues whose lives were still going forwards, his family, as he recalibrated his thoughts about the time he had with them, however long that be, and the possibility of having a child (symbolic immortality?) and nurturing a new life while his faded (p. 139). From a relational perspective, I believe that there are usually others in mind, implicitly at least, when we locate ourselves within a particular time-frame. Indeed, rather than self-concept, perhaps we could think of a self-in-relation-concept. In my experience people preoccupied with figuring out the past do so because how they see themselves now is heavily coloured by how others used to treat them. Meanwhile, inhabiting a rosy past is in some cases because the individual associates it with a version of self more acceptable than the self he imagines others perceive now. Alternately, it might serve to create a feeling of connection with others and, as I discuss in Chapter 8, groups and communities bind around shared myths of heroic or better times. Meanwhile, the self in the future will have the responses of others in mind as he contemplates future goals or thinks with dread about the inevitable replay of the past. So we are both selves-in-relation and selves-in-time, each informing the other.

Notes

1 Although the two terms are not synonymous, I use them interchangeably.
2 Although some transitions, as Salzberger-Wittenberg noted, can cause catastrophic anxiety about not being able to manage on our own, an anxiety that echoes the nameless dread of a baby that feels unheld in something terrifyingly new (2016, pp. 23, 128).

3 It has been speculated that a dynamic consciousness probably first arose in reptiles a quarter of a billion years ago. No such stream of consciousness exists in amphibians like frogs which appear not to visually follow events. They respond automatically to insects if they enter their visual field (Sacks, 2017. p. 181).

4 The other four invariants are unity of locus and coherence of motion, intensity structure and form (Stern, 1985, p. 82). All are important in differentiating self and other.

5 Certain animals bond with their nest sites as much as with their mothers (McGilchrist, 2009, p. 390) and many species return year after year to the same places to hibernate or to breed.

6 I see the characteristics and relational patterns of people with this diagnosis as a manifestation of disorganised attachment and locate the origins in attachment failure and early trauma.

7 Significantly, the first three are also characteristic of dissociative states.

8 Unlike existential anxiety, separation anxiety, the fear of losing a significant other is, expressed in, and defended against, by the loneliness of cut-offness.

9 I am struck by the emphasis on bodily contact here. I exist as a body in relation to other bodies, and early physical contact is important in developing a sense of "me".

10 Here I have in mind Apprey's idea that one aspect of transgenerational trauma is for a child to inherit an errand to heal past wounds in some way (2017).

11 Charmaz's categories are put in italics.

12 Because of a bullet wound that caused extensive brain damage, this former soldier could not conceive of what he would do in the next minute, let alone the next hour or day (1972, p. 34).

13 This echoes the difference between low and high-context cultures which I mention in Chapter 4.

References

Alvarez, A. 2012. *The Thinking Heart: Three Levels of Psychoanalytic Therapy with Disturbed Children*. London: Routledge.

Apprey, M. 2017. "Representing, theorizing and reconfiguring the concept of transgenerational haunting in order to facilitate healing" in S. Grand & J. Salzberg (Eds.) *Trans-generational Trauma and the Other* (pp. 16–37). New York: Routledge.

Bollas, C. 1995. *Cracking Up*. London: Routledge.

Bromberg, P. 2001. *Standing in the Spaces*. Hillsdale, NJ: Analytic Press.

Bruce, E. 1999. "Holding on to the story: older people, narrative, and dementia" in G. Roberts & J. Holmes (Eds.) *Healing Stories: Narrative in Psychiatry and Psychotherapy* (pp. 181–205). Oxford: Oxford University Press.

Charmaz, K. 1991. *Good Days and Bad Days: The Self in Chronic Illness and Time*. New Brunswick, NJ: Rutgers University Press.

Cox Cameron, O. 2007. "Lifetime and deathtime: reflections on Joyce's *Finnegans Wake* and Beckett's *How It Is*" in B. Willock, L. Bohm & R. Curtis (Eds.) *On Death and Endings: Psychoanalysts' Reflections on Finality, Transformations and New Beginnings* (pp. 259–65). New York: Routledge.

Gawande, A. 2015. *Being Mortal: Illness, Medicine and What Matters in the End*. London: Profile Books.

Giddens, A. 1991. *Modernity and Self-identity: Self and Society in the Late Modern Age*. Cambridge: Polity Press.

Haynes, J. 2007. *Who Is It That Can Tell Me Who I Am? The Journal of a Psychotherapist*. Bristol: Cromwell Press.

Hobson, R. 1985. *Forms of Feeling: The Heart of Psychotherapy*. London: Routledge.

Inge, D. 2014. *A Tour of Bones: Facing Fear and Looking for Life*. London: Bloomsbury.

Kalanithi, P. 2017. *When Breath Becomes Air*. London: Vintage.

Luria, A. 1972. *The Man with the Shattered World: A History of a Brain Wound*. Cambridge, MA: Harvard University Press.

McGilchrist, I. 2009. *The Master and his Emissary: The Divided Brain and the Making of the Western World*. New Haven: Yale University Press.

Mariotti, P. (Ed.). 2012. *The Maternal Lineage: Identification, Desire and Transgenerational Issues*. London: Routledge.

Meares, R. 1998. "The self in conversation: On narratives, chronicles and scripts", *Psychoanalytic Dialogues*, 8(6), 875–91.

Meares, R. 2012. *A Dissociation Model of Borderline Personality Disorder*. New York: W. W. Norton & Co.

Mitchell, S. 1993. *Hope and Dread in Psychoanalysis*. New York: Basic Books.

Putnam, F. 2016. *The Way We Are: How States of Mind Influence our Identities, Personality and Potential for Change*. New York: International Psychoanalytic Books.

Pye, J. 2017. "Full Circle: 'We had the experience but missed the meaning'". Conference Presentation.

Raphael-Leff, J. 2012. "The Baby-makers" in P. Mariotti (Ed.) *The Maternal Lineage: Identification, Desire and Transgenerational Issues* (pp. 205–30). London: Routledge.

Sacks, O. 1995. *An Anthropologist on Mars*. London: Picador.

Sacks, O. 2015a. *The Man who Mistook his Wife for a Hat*. London: Picador Classic. (1st edition. 1985. Duckworth).

Sacks, O. 2017. *The River of Consciousness*. London: Picador.

Salzberger-Wittenberg, I. 2013. *Experiencing Beginnings and Endings*. London: Karnac.

Siegel, D. 1999. *The Developing Mind*. New York: W. W. Norton & Co.

Stern, D. N. 1985. *The Interpersonal World of the Infant*. New York: Basic Books.

Stern, D. N. 1998. *The Diary of a Baby*. New York: Basic Books.

Stolorow, R. 2007. *Trauma and Human Existence*. New York: Routledge.

Wright, S. 2009. "Becoming three dimensional: A clinical exploration of the links between dissociation, disorganised attachment and mentalization". *Attachment: New Directions in Psychotherapy and Relational Psychoanalysis*, 3, 324–39.

3

LIVED TIME, REMEMBERED TIME AND THE BRAIN

> Time is the context that gives meaning to everything in this world. And conversely everything that has meaning for us in this world, everything that has a place in our lives, exists in time.
>
> *(McGilchrist, 2009, p. 75)*

How do we acquire a sense of time?

Our lives unfold in time. It scaffolds and, as McGilchrist pointed out, gives meaning to much of what we do. But how do we acquire a sense of time? How and why did we as a species? And, bearing in mind the principle that ontogeny recapitulates phylogeny, how do children develop this sense? Writers have long debated how man became aware of duration and temporal distinctions which, as far as we can tell, is something that distinguishes us from other species. Animals appear to live in a continual present. We have a sense of both the present moment and the past and future. But is the sense of time an *a priori* condition? A specific sense? Or related to the use of our attention or the nature of our actions? All have been put forward by philosophers from the seventeenth century onwards (Whitrow, 2003, pp. 16–18). My own view is that our sense of time is deeply embodied and that we develop an awareness of periodicity through moving and being moved. We perceive changes through all our senses, and through hearing, touch, vision and proprioception we perceive punctuations in the flow of events, both internal and external. With hearing for instance, we rapidly orient to a new sound or change of rhythm in a voice or background noise. But something more than this is needed for the development of a sense of time. After all, animals also navigate the world according to sensory data. "Time", argued Whitrow, "is not a simple sensation but depends on processes of mental organisation uniting thought and action". Our perception of temporal phenomena is a complex activity which has originated as a product of human evolution and which as individuals we develop by learning (2003, pp. 26, 28). Perhaps to speak of a process of integration of sensory data, awareness and memory would be more accurate, and this goes on in many inter-connected areas of the brain.

If man is the only creature with a sense of time, why would evolution have privileged this? The emergence of *homo sapiens* has been correlated with a strongly increased tendency to look forwards, an obvious advantage for the survival of the species, and anthropologists have hypothesised that the original development of the pre-frontal cortex, the areas of the brain involved in integrating information and planning, may have been intimately associated with the growth of man's power of adjustment to future events (Whitrow, 2003, p. 25). William Irvine's interesting book *On Desire* (2006) supports this thesis. The book is concerned with questions such as how we evolved the capacity to desire and what takes place in the brain when we desire something. Irvine argued that creatures with such a capacity had a greater chance of surviving and reproducing than those that did not (p. 120). However, there is a difference between certain desires being hard-wired and the uniquely human capacity to form elaborate plans for getting what we want. In evolutionary terms, this gives mankind an advantage because we can modify our desires according to changes in our environment. "In a full-fledged case of desire" Irvine said, "a creature is able to form a mental representation of the thing it desires, compare the current state of affairs with the desired state, and initiate action to diminish the difference between these states of affairs" (p. 122). For this a complex brain is required.

Irvine traced three stages in the formation of desire. First comes reflexive beha-viour. A shortcoming of this is that "it is focused on the present and oblivious to the future". It is rapid but does not allow for graded responses and adaptations to changing conditions (p. 124). Next comes incentivised behaviour. An animal has more capacity to adapt to changing circumstances if it feels good to do something and bad not to. For this a rudimentary nervous system is required. An example of the adaptiveness of having what Irvine called a "biologically incentivised system" is that the perception of pain, disgust or fear alerts an animal to avoid something harmful (p. 131). Hence a hen will not sit on her eggs however "good" that feels if a fox is nearby. Negative affect warns her against this. Along with built-in incen-tives to avoid what feels bad and approach what feels good, to survive demands remembering and being able to generalise from past experiences. An organism will be even more successful if it can consider the potential consequences of different options, perhaps turning to a previous experience for information. In other words, the more sophisticated the animal's reasoning ability, the greater its chances of survival. As Irvine concluded, it was the combination of a nervous system that could respond reflexively to stimuli with increased logical ability, the ability to feel good and bad and to remember, that led to the world's first incentivised creatures and perhaps, the first creatures capable of desire. This, he suggested, might have happened between two and three hundred million years ago when animal's brains developed limbic systems (2006, p. 143). Humans, like other creatures, have built-in biological incentive systems. For example, we are incentivised to seek proximity with a trusted caregiver and the subsequent feelings of warmth and safety reinforce attachment behaviours. However, the development of the higher cortex has given us a far more sophisticated capacity to devise strategies for acquiring what feels good and avoiding what feels bad. We can feel motivated, form goals and plan how to reach them. We can learn from past experiences and imagine, and worry about, future ones. We have the capacity to hope and to find meaning and purpose in our lives. All of these demand an appreciation of time.

How do children develop a sense of time?

Turning now from man as a species to ourselves as individuals: how did we develop a sense of and then a cognitive appreciation of time? We first learn about time through the body, through interoception (sensations coming from inside the body) and exteroception (sensations coming from outside the body). But just as important are the experiences of time that we have in relation to others. We learn in action and in interaction. Let us go back to before we were born, when we were just one cell, and then as that cell divided again and again, more and more increasingly differentiated cells. Verny and Weintraub argued that the biochemical experience of our earliest cells, months before we had brains or even bodies, "form the first precursors of memory – not memory as we think of it in our present-day lives, but an ancient cellular memory from a time when, chrysalis-like, we had a different form". As scientists now appreciate, "environmental factors that shape cellular functions in the present influence cellular response in the future" (Weinstein, 2016, p. 41). Put simply, at a biochemical level our bodies store memories.

Another rudimentary embodied sense of time emerges as the embryo develops. Ruella Frank, in describing the two, interlinked developmental movements of yielding and pushing, said that in the womb as we float in the amniotic fluid there is both a yielding to and a pushing against it, and when the foetus comes up against the walls of the womb again there is a push (2001, pp. 80–83). Pushing and yielding go together as a vibration or pulsation, and reading this made me question: how much of foetal experience is about pulsations? Well before birth we are exposed to repeated vibrations that have a temporal contour: regular patterns such as our mother's heartbeat; stop/start rhythms – the echoes of her gut and her voice vibrating through the body fluids. And the mother's voice, by echoing through those fluids, will be experienced by the foetus through the whole body. It constitutes what Maeillo called a "sound object" which alternates between moments of presence and absence. Interestingly, she believed that "the maternal voice introduces an element of discontinuity in an environment that is otherwise characterised by continuity", and that this could be seen as a proto-experience of absence and loss (1995, pp. 26–7).

The process of birth, itself entailing considerable discontinuity and loss, will inevitably interrupt the temporal patterns that have become familiar. Then, after birth, how might we experience a sense of temporality? Initially, a baby gains a sense of rhythm as he sucks and pauses, looks and pauses, over and over again. His earliest "conversations" with his mother, "proto-conversation", also provide important encounters with time with its turn-taking, moments of speeding up, pauses and repetition (Alvarez, 2012, pp. 56, 43). Daniel Stern described how in the first two months of life the infant is in a state of undifferentiation, but experiencing affect and tension changes. He argued that the baby is in a process of emerging organisation, of "yoking" different aspects of experience, hence describing the self at that stage as the "emergent self" (1985, pp. 45–7). At this point, perception is presumed to be amodal, something experienced with one sense being potentially yoked with another. Sights, sounds and touches are experienced as shapes, intensities and temporal patterns and can be described in dynamic, kinetic terms – which Stern called "vitality effects", such as "surging, fading away, fleeting, explosive, crescendo, decrescendo, bursting, drawn out and so on" (1985, p. 54). These vitality affects are linked with levels of arousal and are experienced as dynamic shifts or patterned changes and can be described in terms of intensity of sensation as a function of time. "Whether an object is encountered with the eye or the touch or perhaps even the ear, it would produce the same overall pattern or activation contour" (p. 59).

In *The Diary of a Baby*, Stern used another term, "feelings-in-motion", which I think is a more graspable way of describing vitality affects (1998, p. 14). When trying to express how the baby, "Joey", might have experienced things when he was four months old, Stern suggested that we call moments of experience "weatherscapes" which consist of unique moments of feelings-in-motion. These are not static like a photograph. They have duration like a chord or musical phrase and can last for a split second or many seconds. Thus "during the time that fills a moment Joey's feelings and perceptions change together. Each moment has its own sequence of feelings-in-motion: a sudden increase in interest; a rising, then a falling wave of hunger pain; an ebbing of pleasure. It is as a sequence of these moments strung together that Joey experiences life" (p. 14). Stern also argued that "the social world experienced by the infant is primarily one of vitality affects before it is a world of formal acts". Rather than perceiving overt acts as adults do, such as reaching for a bottle, he perceives and categorises acts in terms of the vitality affects they express (1985, p. 57). Before the advent of language, which introduces formal categorisation – things have names, he inhabits a richly amodal world.

The perception and yoking of the dynamic shapes of different sensory experiences is fundamental to our acquisition of a sense of ongoing time and the periodicity of our world. But could we speculate that for a short while, until contingent happenings are bound together, the newborn experiences a very fragmented, discordant environment in contrast to the known sensory world of the womb? Frank described such a baby when discussing her first encounters with a mother and her 14-week-old son. She noticed that Alex was very stressed when making a transition between one event and another, and his mother confirmed that he had difficulty moving from wakefulness to sleep, sleeping to waking, playing to nursing, or in being placed down or picked up. Indeed, he became increasingly frustrated and incredibly hard to soothe. Frank surmised that Alex was very sensitive to external and internal stimulation and that between them mother and child were finding it hard to flexibly merge and separate. As she said, "the experience of opening and closing, the ebb and flow in the process of relating, was losing its resiliency and becoming fixed" (2001, pp. 22–31).

The ebb and flow of relating and of things coming and going, stopping and starting, all contribute to a growing felt sense of ongoingness. As Winnicott stressed, and for me he is the theorist who captures this so well, our sense of "going-on-being" is facilitated by being "held" through time, and he speculated about a baby's experience of being separated from his mother for too long. For a short while, he can hang onto the illusion of the "wished for mother" and so "in x + y minutes the baby has not become altered. But in x + y + z minutes the baby has become traumatized ... trauma [implying] that the baby has experienced a break in life's continuity" (1990, p. 97). And perhaps, in the example above, something in his mother's responses when he was distressed led to Alex experiencing a break in his still-forming sense of continuity. Because of her own history she was not able to consistently do what an attuned caregiver does, namely, help her baby to gradually tolerate gaps and things that have a changing dynamic form in time and learn how to shape the curves of his attention (Alvarez, 2012, p. 62).

As the infant learns to survive delays and moments of absence, he has his first significant experiences of duration, something as intrinsic to our sense of time as an awareness of the differences between past, present and future (Whitrow, 1988, p. 7). Moreover, these early experiences of the flow and punctuation of time offer a foundation for the acquisition of thought and language. Indeed, it has been argued that a prior condition for their development is separation and the experience of distance. As Bion argued, without absence there is no thought and without thought there is no language (Maeillo, 1995, p. 26). After all, why would we need a mental representation of a caregiver if she was always present and always the same?

Alvarez is another therapist who, like Stern, argued that the temporal shaping of reality is something we learn about from early infancy onwards. However, her perspective is a more relational one. Infants discover that "objects", by which she meant people as well as inanimate objects, have "temporal forms". They come and go in rhythmic patterns. Sometimes these comings and goings startle and distress the baby and, like Alex, he needs support if he is to tolerate their changing temporal form. Alvarez also stressed the importance of pauses to digest and recover from experiences. We need time to process, think and reflect as well as time to forget and empty the mind (2012, p. 141). We need rests for the brain and body to develop coherence and integrate experience, something that is a challenge in today's fast-paced, stimulus-rich world.

Alvarez was also interested in the temporal elements in thinking, talking and walking and the links between them. Based on her work with autistic and disturbed children, she observed that some children, and some adults too, struggle to think clearly because they cannot pause or slow down. Thinking is a process that takes time to carry out and it requires being able to manage sequences (2012, p. 58). We need to be able to think one thought at a time. Thoughts have to take their turn, and this entails suppressing distractions. We also need to be able to follow a train of thought. Most of us take this for granted. But some children don't feel they have time to think, often because their caregivers never gave them time. As Alvarez said, "if the patient thinks of pauses as an end of the world, and of his mind, he dare not pause". He finds it hard to appreciate that it is possible to have two things or two thoughts in a sequence. For different reasons, autistic children can find it impossible to wait and have difficulty with the punctuation of their experience. Others have also noticed that autistic children have difficulties with notions of space and time. Meanwhile, when someone is in a psychotic state, thoughts often get on top of each other, they are crowded together and cannot take their place in a sequence (pp. 58, 61, 141).

As noted earlier, proto-conversation with its turn-taking, moments of speeding up, pauses and repetition provides one of our first encounters with time, and managing pauses and turn-taking supports the later use of language. The processes by which we master walking provide further embodied experiences of time. Moving forwards, whether on all fours or walking, involves a swinging, to and fro process – in effect another example of turn-taking – and interestingly Alvarez observed that children who find turn-taking difficult also have problems with the dynamic flow involved in the alternating movement required for walking (pp. 43, 56). It also involves mastering stopping and starting, the psychological correlates of which, managing ending and beginning, we often encounter in our work.

Language and the appreciation of past, present and future

The next stage in the emergence of our sense of time is the acquisition of a language to describe time. As is becoming clear, our conceptual appreciation of temporality is not the same as our felt sense of time and its contours, and develops through learning and the progressive maturation of the brain. We learn in action and in interaction and our language emerges out of a social and an embodied context. So why does man need a language that includes tenses and temporal concepts? What adaptive functions might that serve? Having such a language is fundamental to us as social animals because it provides referents or markers with which we can share our experiences. We can think about, compare and speak about different time-frames, and because language enables us to transcend reality, we can refer back to and sometimes distort the past in our minds and envisage different futures.

Turning to our individual development of an appreciation of past, present and future and the acquisition of increasingly refined words for time, the development of memory plays a significant part. The temporal world of an infant is all present as far as we can judge, although I would dispute the idea of early childhood being a "blissfully" timeless state (Molnos, 1995, p. 4). As Stern pointed out, an infant "experiences events as loosely or not at all connected in time" (1998, p. 78). When he is absorbed in something then in those moments "there is only one long present moment". When his attention is broken and wanders here and there "he will experience time as more fractured and incoherent". If he is inwardly focussed on a sensory image of something that has happened it is not *known* to be a memory. It is just another form of experience or mental event. It feels very alive and therefore present (p. 78). By twelve months the child has a more developed memory and can recall things that are not currently present. This is illustrated by the fact that he will now look for a hidden object (Stern, 1985, p. 85). Towards the middle of the second year, children begin to use signs and symbols to imagine or represent things in their minds. They can communicate about things that are not present and imitate something observed some time after the event. These new capacities, Stern speculated, rest on several things including being able to encode things in long-term memory and to retrieve them; to go back and forth between different versions of reality and to coordinate mental schemas with operations existing externally in actions and words. Equally important is realising that it is possible to share one's own mental landscape with someone else (p. 164).

Language divides experience into sharper and more distinct categories and marks the timeline of events clearly into past, present and future (Stern, 1985, p. 113). Generally, children first learn time-related nouns such as bedtime and dinner-time, which are more about occasions which punctuate the day than words indicating an appreciation of time and, slightly more contextual, words like now, then, tomorrow and yesterday. Comparative terms denoting duration come a little later – for example, soon, later, before and after, and then the grammar of the different tenses. This language becomes richer because of a growing ability to recall and to narrate memories. As Stern said, in the second year of life a child can "experience a subjective present that is a patchwork of times and places as an adult's is" (1998, p. 123). He can now refer to something that happened earlier in the day and appears to be able to think ahead of something he plans to do and comment on its success or failure – for example, build a tower of bricks and say "there" as he completes it or "uh oh" if it falls down (Wilde Astington, 1994, p. 51). In the third year, children start to grasp more complex rules of grammar using the present participle (e.g. "where Mummy going?") and future-oriented words. Past tenses come later (Whitrow, 1988, p. 6). The capacity to weave together an auto-biographical narrative that takes place in a historical context also emerges around the age of three. This highlights the child's growing capacity for intersubjectivity and for seeing and interpreting the world in terms of "story plots" with a beginning, middle and end (Stern, 1998, p. 131). The final step in the child's evolving sense of temporality is the development of a unified concept of time as something abstract and separate from the self. As Whitrow pointed out, initially, when children begin to recognise temporal sequences, time depends primarily on their own activities. However, they gradually begin to appreciate that there are histories beyond their own history and lived experience and to grasp the idea of a single common time in which all events happen (1988, p. 6). Once again, the principle that ontogeny recapitulates phylogeny is relevant because over the centuries mankind has gradually developed a historical sensibility.

Lived time and autonoetic consciousness

> "Young Master, the days are passing slowly".
>
> "Yes, they are", I said, "They're barely creeping by."
>
> "Young Master, what are you talking about? Time is passing much faster than before. So many unimaginable things have happened. In the past it would have taken at least five hundred years for all of them to happen. Are you aware of that? My dear young master, even five hundred years might not be enough, and here you are saying that time is passing too slowly."
>
> *(Alai, 2002, p. 310)*

This debate between the historian, the young master, and the steward in Alai's novel *Red Poppies* captures the vagaries of Kairos.[1] Lived time can creep by or speed past. On occasions it stands still. It loops back on itself. It concertinas so that it feels as if we are rapidly travelling between different periods in our lives. Stern made an important point: that without subjective time "we could not link the many sequential happenings that occur in the present moment into a whole coherent experience. Life would be discontinuous and chaotic". If all we had was Chronos, then the present moment, Stern argued, would simply be a "moving point in time headed only towards a future and leaving past in its wake". Effectively there would be no present (2004, p. 5). Our sense of self would also be discontinuous and chaotic. To be a self-in-time, a "going-on being", depends on the appreciation of duration and being able to integrate our felt sense and cognitive appreciation of the passage of time. It also depends on being able to access memories, including memories of former states of self, to track our present moment experience and to project ourselves into an imagined future. In other words, we have to be able to oscillate in time and to reflect on those experiences.

What makes all this possible? In what follows, I discuss what goes on in the brain that enables us to notice and gauge the passing of time and what gives coherence to the myriad of disparate things we perceive moment by moment. I delve into the complex subject of memory, its different systems and why memory is important to our sense of self. In order to appreciate why overwhelming, traumatic events often lead to disturbances of time the chapter ends by discussing trauma and the survival-seeking brain.

Let me start with what supports the two different, but complementary modes of relating to time – measuring and experiencing it. The lateralisation of the brain is important here and the interplay between neural circuits across regions of the brain. Taking lateralisation first, when we focus on linear time the left hemisphere is dominant. This hemisphere is good at serial processing and likes to break things up into units or static points. It deals with the sequencing of time or moments of interruption of temporal flow by ordering and measuring it. It re-presents time.[2]

Meanwhile, as McGilchrist pointed out, "virtually all aspects of an appreciation of time, in the sense of something lived through, with a past, present and future, are dependent on the right hemisphere, principally the right prefrontal and parietal cortex" (2010, p. 76). The right hemisphere also helps us when sustained monitoring of temporal information is required and deals with spatial relationships like the degree of distance and duration. It appreciates flow over time and, crucially, is responsible for maintaining a coherent, continuous and unified sense of self, a self with a narrative, and a continuous existence over time (p. 88). Significantly if someone suffers damage to the right hemisphere the sense of permanency is lost. Not only is his sense of past and future severely impaired, but it impairs his sense of self over time – a self with a narrative. As Oliver Sacks commented, "each of us constructs and lives a narrative and is defined by this narrative", citing a patient with amnesia due to Korsakoff's Syndrome "who had to make himself and his world up every moment" (2015a, p. 272). Imagine what that would be like. How disorienting, how hard to make meaningful decisions or sustain relationships, which are inevitably embedded in past experiences and future expectations.

Our sense of identity and personal continuity also depends on communication between the hemispheres and the coordination of neural activity across the vertical domains of the brain. The orbitofrontal cortex is one of the structures or systems that integrate disparate happenings into something coherent. Because of its central location, lying as it does behind the eyes, this system integrates information from the brain stem, limbic system and other parts of the cortex. Amongst other crucial functions the orbitofrontal system is a central mechanism for affect regulation and generating self-awareness and processing self-related material (Schore, 2003, pp. 121, 240). Moreover, it is able to access memory functions and contributes to the integration of past, present and future experiences. Wheeler, Stuss and Tulving coined the term *autonoetic consciousness* for the capacity to become aware of and mentally represent the subjective experience of past, present and future. In their words, the right prefrontal cortex "empowers healthy human adults with the capacity to consider the self's extended existence throughout time. The most complete expression of this capacity, autonoetic awareness, occurs whenever one consciously recollects or re-experiences a happening from a specific time in the past, attends directly to one's present or online experiences, or contemplates one's existence and conduct at a time in the future" (Schore, 2003, p. 122).

The uniquely human capacities to mentally travel through time and to self-reflect come online at about eighteen months, the time of orbitofrontal maturation. The maturation of the left hemisphere during the second and third years of life supports further developments and in particular, the use of language and explicit or declarative memory. So too does the development of the hippocampus, which I discuss later (Siegel, 2010, p. 154; Wilkinson, 2006, p. 20), and from this point, we enter the territory of naming and measuring the passage of time and being able to draw on past experiences in order to make sense of the present or plan the future. Stern describes vividly how language opens new worlds for a child. "He is now able to go to places unimagined before, farther back into the past or ahead into the future". It also restructures the child's world by "dividing nonverbal experience into different and sharper categories". He becomes a measurer of his experience. "It marks the time line of events clearly into past, present, and future. It allows a wider network of associations. It transcends reality with greater ease. It stands outside the lived experience it reflects, as something separate that can be viewed or reviewed." On the flip side, Stern pointed out that language creates a gulf between the hitherto familiar non-verbal world of rich, global experiences and the world of words (1998, pp. 113–14). We lose some of the directness of experiencing and perhaps some of the joys of living without awareness of time.

Memory and time

> Memory is a seamstress, and a capricious one at that. Memory runs her needle in and out, up and down, hither and thither. We know not what comes next or what follows after. Thus, the most ordinary movement in the world, such as sitting down at a table and pulling the inkstand towards one, may agitate a thousand odd, disconnected fragments, now bright, now dim, hanging and bobbing and dipping and flaunting, like the underlinen of a family of fourteen on a line in a gale of wind.
>
> *(Woolf, 1977, p. 49)*

The ability to contemplate our extended existence in time would be impossible without being able to remember former states of self. In other words, we rely on a sense of continuous memory in order, using the words of William James, to be able to say, "I am the same I, that I was yesterday" (Putnam, 2016, p. 129; Meares, 2012, p. 106). Memory anchors us in time and helps us weave experiences together into a more coherent whole – our life story, the narrative by which we live. Using the brain's capacity to register a piece of sensory data then rapidly scan our memories for relevant previous information, guides how we respond in the present and anticipate the future (Cozolino, 2016, p. 6). Yet memory is also capricious with its frustrating gaps, its errors, its distressing persistence in repeatedly bringing certain things to mind. It plays tricks on us, making us doubt what we thought we knew. It contributes to the strangeness of time. It has the capacity to rapidly alter our present state of mind and body and, as Woolf's depiction highlights, we don't know which memories are going to be pulled from their files nor what additional fragments will be agitated. But what exactly is memory?

We generally think of memory as something verbal and in everyday conversations talk about remembering facts and figures or relate stories about situations with a beginning, middle and end and about which we said, did and felt various things. These "declarative" (factual) and "episodic" (autobiographical) memories are part of our explicit memory system. But we have other forms of memory: sensory, emotional and procedural, and these belong to the implicit memory system. Our different memory systems depend on coordination between and within different regions of the brain and develop hierarchically, the most sophisticated involving the most connections and developing last.

The implicit memory system comes online before birth and harnesses the brain's capacity to generalise from experience and prime us to respond to events in certain automatic ways (Siegel, 2010, p. 150). Implicit memories are of three types – procedural, sensorimotor or emotional. Procedural memories include sensory data, motor skills, instinctual defence strategies (fight, flight, freeze), and approach/ avoidance patterns, as well as learned "procedures" for being with others which emerge in the context of our earliest attachment relationships. These are the internal working models that continue to shape our expectational field – a knowing *how* to be with others that exists outside of reflective awareness (Wallin, 2007, p. 118). Sensorimotor memory includes memories of former sensations, physical states and actions. Emotional memories flag and encode important experiences that can later prompt protective actions.

The explicit memory system can be sub-divided into two categories. Semantic or declarative memories are next in the developmental hierarchy and emerge around the age of two when children begin to acquire language and start to recall facts about their sensory environment. Episodic, or what we usually call auto-biographical memory, develops last. This is connected with the child's discovery of the experience of self and capacity for introspection around the age of four. He can now conjure up episodes from the past in his mind's eye. He becomes in this sense a "self-in-time". To use Tulving's term, he has autonoetic consciousness, and at the same time he is starting to have some insight into the psychological world of others. "This state of mind", Meares pointed out, "is larger than earlier states. The individual is now able, figuratively speaking, to roam around in the mind through scenes brought up at will in memory and imagination" (2012, p. 53). He can draw on memory to link and compare different events and fashion coherent narratives to make sense of his experiences. Because episodic memories help us to orient in time and space, he can also make use of past learning to predict and enhance the future (Levine, 2015, p. 20).

I like the image of roaming through time in our minds as we weave together our personal stories. It suggests something playful, creative, a narrative freedom which contrasts with the fixed, rigid and limiting narratives that some people live by. It is the stuff of our private inner worlds. Yet whilst this is going on, we are also driven by procedural memories lying out of conscious awareness. To appreciate why, we need to know about the neural structures associated with each type of memory. Explicit memory depends on the hippocampus and higher cortical structures that mature during the first decades of life from roughly the age of three (Cozolino, 2016, pp. 70–74). Siegel described the hippocampus as "the brain's master puzzle piece assembler" (2010, p. 154). Its job is to encode memories, thus tagging them in time and place, and later to retrieve them by drawing together separate pieces of stored data into the assembled pictures of factual and auto-biographical memory. On the left hemisphere it builds our factual and linguistic knowledge; on the right, it organises the building blocks of our life story according to time and topic. This assembling, integrative process is possible because the hippocampus has many connections with the cortex and limbic regions of the brain.

The encoding of implicit memories operates very differently and depends on more primitive structures such as the amygdala, the thalamus and middle portions of the frontal cortex. The amygdala, our body's early warning system, is particularly important. It retains the imprint of traumatic and very early experiences, experiences we had before the hippocampus came online. These somatic markers are experienced in the body as physical sensations and can be triggered by features in the present which echo the past, such as sensory details, similar types and intensities of emotion or being treated in ways that remind us how we were responded to in the past. This could be of being welcomed and attuned to and will generate a sense of safety and confidence. However, for someone with a history of neglect and trauma, it could be of being abandoned, humiliated or hurt (Levine, 2015, p. 22).

Trauma, time and the survival seeking brain

> Memory is like a shadow on water. Falling across the flow of life it undulates, broadening and narrowing on the water's surface. The water moves but the shadow remains, a marker.
>
> *(Inge, 2014, p. 128)*

Our memories, the shadows of earlier experiences, provide a thread of continuity linking past, present and future. Sometimes we are conscious of these shadows falling across the flow of life. At other times we are unaware how much they colour our feelings, thoughts and actions and how they can shape our choices in beneficial and in harmful, limiting ways. This is especially true when they mark highly distressing, humiliating, painful and traumatic events. "The choices our bodies make on their own, without our awareness, when we are under threat are not always the choices we might have made in a calmer state of mind" and that, Fogel explained, is because "under threat embodied and conceptual self-awareness go offline as the more primal parts of the brain activate an ancient trove of wisdom that has assured the continuation of life on earth for millions of years" (Fogel, 2009, p. 152).

An awareness of the areas of the brain affected by traumatic experiences and how traumatic memories differ from other memories can help us to understand the distortion of time long after these experiences and why exposure to traumatic events often leaves people at risk of repeated re-traumatisation. Van der Kolk pointed out that, "trauma results in a fundamental reorganisation of the way the mind and brain manage perception. It changes not only how we think and what we think about, but also our very capacity to think" (2014, p. 21). During terrifying situations certain regions of the brain shut down. Although we can think of this as a survival response to prevent us from being utterly overwhelmed, it brings unintended consequences. One is that these systems can keep going offline when something triggers memories of earlier experiences of fear, rejection, shame or pain. Another is that, unlike ordinary memories, the memories are never fully integrated. The survivor may not have a clear chronological record of what happened but be left with a legacy of symptoms and reactions with no context that identifies them as memories (Fisher, 2017, p. 20). The neural networks in question include the medial prefrontal cortex (MPFC); the dorsolateral prefrontal cortex (DLPFC); the thalamus which integrates incoming sensory data into our auto-biographical memory, and Broca's area, the region necessary to put feelings into words. And these are the regions that need to be bought back online in order to heal from trauma (Van der Kolk, 2014, pp. 62, 71, 73).

The medial prefrontal cortex, or brain's "watchtower" as Van der Kolk called it, is important in executive functioning and impulse control. It helps to modulate and regulate the automatic responses of the limbic system or "emotional/survival brain". When it is online it enables us to observe and have an overview of what is happening, see things from different perspectives and make predictions about what might happen if we act in particular ways. In PTSD the balance between the MPFC and the amygdala, our body's "smoke alarm", changes radically and this makes it much harder to control emotions and impulses (Van der Kolk, 2014, p. 62). Also important is the dorsolateral prefrontal cortex, the brain's "time keeper", which normally informs us how present experiences relate to the past and how they may affect the future. When the DLPFC is deactivated "people lose their sense of time and become trapped in the moment, without a sense of past, present or future" (p. 69). Meanwhile, when Broca's area shuts down, and this can be both during a traumatic experience or when reliving it, we lose our ability to speak or think clearly. We can be speechless with fear. The functioning of the left hemi-sphere, the side of the brain that gives things words and organises events sequen-tially, can also be compromised, and "without sequencing we can't identify cause and effect, grasp the long-term effects of our actions, or create coherent plans for the future" (p. 44).

As I said, these important neural structures often shut down when something triggers a memory of past trauma. The more primal parts of the brain, our "survival brain", kick in and react as if it was still happening. I have often observed people suddenly become paralysed with fear or very agitated and restless as if about to run. Overwhelming emotions and sensations flood them, horrific images flash through their minds, and for a while they are not able to take in what I am saying or even to see me for who I am. Instead I might become a persecutory or shaming figure from the past, someone likely to hurt or shout at them at any moment. Fay described such triggering as leading a parallel life when past and present overlap (2007, p. 69). The intrusive memories that evoke such strong reactions are like "time capsules" filled with thoughts, feelings, impulses and memories that don't fit the present context, and what most people don't realise is that what floods and incapacitates them, is memory.

Let me give an example of an amygdala-driven response. Deborah could not understand why talking to a particular customer on the phone made her feel incredibly agitated and unable to concentrate afterwards until we identified that the customer's voice reminded her of her abusive stepbrother. Explaining that her threat system had been activated but that it was a "false alarm" and listing things she could do to stay present helped. Deborah decided to stick a notice on her desk saying, "I'm here now, not back there". "It will remind the scared part of me that I never have to see my stepbrother again." The problem with implicit memories is that whilst we don't consciously remember them, we never forget them (Cozolino, 2016, p. 5). To put this another way, they are resistant to change and this is one reason why people react to triggers in the same way as they reacted long ago. Whenever a sensory detail echoes the traumatic past, like the man's voice, it can quickly evoke the same emotions, body sensations, impulses and thoughts accompanying the original experience. A term sometimes used for this is state dependent memory. This is what was going on when Deborah heard that particular voice. Positive experiences can also evoke state dependent memory. It is what Woolf described when she referred to drawing the inkstand towards her. It is also what happened when Proust tasted a madeleine, the smell and taste transporting him back to childhood and his grandmother's kitchen. This transposition of past experience into the present in such a live way explains why we sometimes feel inexplicably sad, or younger than our true age or compelled to react in a way that, logically, seems over the top. But we rarely appreciate when we are being influenced by past memories, or at least not in the moment.

Disruptions in the continuity and consistency of our behaviour across different settings and times can feel like inhabiting a different identity, and this highlights the inextricable connection between memory and identity. Changes in one go with changes in the other. As Putnam explained, because of the complex world we live in and our various roles, we have to maintain "a repertoire of identities" to meet the demands of specific circumstances (2016, pp. 129, 138). In each identity we will think, feel and behave in slightly different ways. Despite this, we are usually able to sustain a sense of our core identity. However, in emotionally charged situations, and especially if traumatic events have coloured our lives, because of the powerful affects and sensations evoked by state dependent memory, we can lose that reassuringly consistent theme of being "me" discussed in Chapter 2. Whatever impulses we feel, and the beliefs that arise, even if they are a replay of the past, they feel compellingly real right now. And this can be incredibly unsettling and unnerving. So, when Deborah's threat system was activated, and this used to occur on a regular basis, she lost touch with her competent, adult self. In the moment she felt younger and scared. And afterwards she was confused and anxious about what was going on. "It's like I keep losing myself and I don't know why. Am I going mad?". When I first met Deborah, the loss of her ongoingness could persist for weeks at a time. It took committed work on her part to become able, in Bromberg's words, to "stand in the spaces" between her different selves (1996, p. 274).

State dependent memory can also activate other long-forgotten memories of previous trauma and create a "domino effect", and this keeps interfering with recovery (Van der Kolk, 1997, p. 9). To make things worse, the brain can become increasingly conditioned by procedural memory, meaning that over time the neural circuits associated with traumatic memories become more sensitive to further exposure to matching or similar stimuli. Each time the original events are relived during flashbacks or nightmares, the re-release of stress hormones further kindles or strengthens the memory imprint. An additional problem is that the amygdala can pair any stimulus with anxiety and fear. For example, if we keep having nightmares, we might become phobic of the room where they occur and try to delay going to bed as long as possible. Or, hypothetically, had Deborah not mentioned the dysregulating telephone calls or done a lot of work already on strategies to calm herself, she might have begun to panic whenever the phone rang, experienced mounting anxiety even thinking about going to work and eventually resigned with the belief that her job was the problem and that she was a failure.

Explicit memories are more malleable and open to updating than implicit ones. As we talk or think about them, we integrate them with new links and meanings. They therefore change and become woven into the continuous, textured flow of our experience (Levine, 2015, p. 6). Loewald used the term "memorial activity" for this. In his view, memory is not a *fait accompli* "leaving traces on a wax tablet brain". As a result of memorial activity, we link "what would otherwise be disparate bits into a nexus which has meaning and gives meaning to each element by subjective virtue of the reciprocal relationship created between them". We make our history (and thereby shape our identity) by virtue of this memorial activity "in which past-present-future are created as mutually interacting modes of time" (1972, p. 409). Writing about the malleability of explicit memory Van der Kolk said, "the mind cannot but make meaning out of what it knows, and the meaning we make of our lives changes how and what we remember" (2014, p. 191). This has been verified by studying what happens biochemically when conditioned memories in rats are accessed. Within the brain it appears that "every time we reflect upon the past, we are delicately transforming its cellular representation in the brain, changing its underlying neural circuitry" (Levine, 2015, p. 141). Commenting on this statement by Lehrer, Levine pointed out that "the very act of recall is to provide the molecular opportunity to update the memory based upon new information". In other words, "the present has the potentiality of changing the past".

"Change in psychotherapy", argued Cozolino, "is all about memory: the exploration of past memory, the impact of the past on the present, and the ability to modify what is stored in memory to affect changes in thoughts, feelings, and behaviors" (2016, p. 68). In a sense we need to have a "dialogue with time" (Giddens, 1991, p. 72). The challenge for us as therapists is to discover what is needed for each client, not only to link and make sense of disparate bits of conscious memory, but to update traumatic implicit memories with more recent information in order to reduce their rigid, limiting grip.[3] In recent decades a range of therapeutic approaches have evolved which help do just that. I will mention some of these in Chapter 10. But let me return to Deborah and an example from later in our work. It illustrates how a new experience can alter our present experience of our memories at affective, somatic and cognitive levels, and sometimes in ways that surprise and amaze us.

A dialogue with time

Deborah had been thrown back into familiar fears, self-loathing and old self-harming strategies. This made her hate herself even more. Her abusive stepbrother had cancer and was unlikely to survive. She felt pressurised by the rest of the family to visit him. Her mother was distraught and kept telephoning Deborah for support. Each time his name was mentioned, she was flooded with horrific memories. Despite feeling loath to do so, she agreed to accompany her mother to the hospital. To support Deborah, we explored ways to regulate herself during the visits, and we worked on the memories that were being triggered. On one occasion a dialogue emerged between her adult self and the child self that held the memories. I will call that part "Debs". During this dialogue it became clear how angry Debs was with Deborah for making her go. She felt betrayed. She was also angry that everyone else cared about her stepbrother and was saying nice things about him. I asked how often she felt angry in the past when he was the centre of attention? "All the time!" she exclaimed vehemently. "I hated him always being the special one and that no one noticed me". Deborah seemed surprised by the strength of her feelings, her tendency being to suppress anger, but explained that she hated seeing him too. But it was for her Mum because she cared about her and because she wanted closure. "I want an end to this fear." I checked how Debs felt hearing that. She wanted that too, but was desperately scared. Deborah added, "I don't want her to feel so frightened". I asked how Debs felt knowing that her adult self was concerned about her. "Good", she replied, "but what's making me so scared? I can't stop it. It feels like he's still winning." I explained simply that we can respond to a present experience with the same feelings, thoughts and body as in the past. Then I invited Deborah to name what was similar now and different. As a child, and thinking about visiting her stepbrother, she felt very afraid, alone and helpless. But our discussion helped her to appreciate that, rather than being alone, there were a lot of supportive, caring people in her life now; that instead of being helpless she had strengths and options unavailable to her as a child; and that although sometimes scared, she was strong. "I'm strong now!" she exclaimed. "And he's weak. He can't hurt me anymore." Hearing this I asked how that felt in her body. She said, "bigger, alive, excited." "And how does Debs feel knowing all this and that you understand her?" "She wants to show him she doesn't care. She knows we can do it together." And Deborah smiled!

The "dialogue with time" in this session had two aspects to it. One was cognitive, the level of the top brain, as Deborah made sense of why she had become so dysregulated. Meanwhile at the level of the survival brain, directly accessing the memories and feelings of the child and interspersing them with current information was what really facilitated change.

Notes

1 It also highlights that in the pre-industrial world significant change tended to be evolutionary, meaning something innovative could take decades to emerge and become widespread. The mechanical clock, which has had a profound effect on life, is a case in

point. Compare this with the revolutionary advances we see today in technology and IT which make it hard to keep abreast with new ideas and ways of doing things.

2 Interesting in this context, is the fact that the word "time" is derived from an Indo-European root, *di* or *dai*, meaning to divide (Rovelli, 2018, p. 53).

3 As an example of beliefs that need to be updated, in some self-states someone who experienced childhood trauma seems unable to realise that she is grown up now, or does not live there any more or that someone who badly hurt her is dead, or that her body can move rather than feeling trapped and frozen.

References

Alai, Sylvia Li-Chun Lin. 2002. *Red Poppies*. London: Methuen.

Alvarez, A. 2012. *The Thinking Heart: Three Levels of Psychoanalytic Therapy with Disturbed Children*. London: Routledge.

Cozolino, L. 2016. *Why Psychotherapy Works*. New York: W. W. Norton & Co.

Eliot, T. S. 1969. *The Complete Poems and Plays of T. S. Eliot*. London: Faber & Faber.

Fay, D. 2007. *Becoming Safely Embodied*. Somerville, MA: Heart Full Life Publishing.

Fisher, J. 2017. *Healing the Fragmented Selves of Trauma Survivors*. New York: Routledge.

Fogel, A. 2009. *Body Sense: The Practice of Embodied Self-Awareness*. New York: W. W. Norton & Co.

Frank, R. 2001. *Body of Awareness: A Somatic and Developmental Approach to Psychotherapy*. Cambridge, MA: Gestalt Press.

Giddens, A. 1991. *Modernity and Self-identity: Self and Society in the Late Modern Age*. Cambridge: Polity Press.

Inge, D. 2014. *A Tour of Bones: Facing Fear and Looking for Life*. London: Bloomsbury.

Irvine, W. 2006. *On Desire: Why We Want What We Want*. Oxford: Oxford University Press.

Levine, P. 2015. *Trauma and Memory: Brain and Body in a Search for the Living Past*. Berkeley, CA: North Atlantic Books.

Loewald, H. 1972. "The experience of time". *The Psychoanalytic Study of the Child*, 27, 401–410.

Maeillo, S. 1995. "The Sound-object: A hypothesis about prenatal auditory experience and memory". *Journal of Child Psychotherapy*, 21(11), 23–41.

McGilchrist, I. 2009. *The Master and his Emissary: The Divided Brain and the Making of the Western World*. New Haven: Yale University Press.

Meares, R. 2012. *A Dissociation Model of Borderline Personality Disorder*. New York: W. W. Norton & Co.

Molnos, A. 1995. *A Question of Time: Essentials of Brief Dynamic Psychotherapy*. London: Karnac.

Putnam, F. 2016. *The Way We Are: How States of Mind Influence our Identities, Personality and Potential for Change*. New York: International Psychoanalytic Books.

Rovelli, C. 2018. *The Order of Time*. London: Allen Lane.

Sacks, O. 2015a. *The Man who Mistook his Wife for a Hat*. London: Picador Classics (1st edition, 1985. London: Duckworth).

Schore, A. 2003. *Affect Regulation and the Repair of the Self*. New York: W. W. Norton & Co.

Siegel, D. 2010. *Mindsight*. London: Oneworld Publications.

Stern, D. N. 1985. *The Interpersonal World of the Infant*. New York: Basic Books.

Stern, D. N. 1998. *The Diary of a Baby*. New York: Basic Books.

Stern, D. N. 2004. *The Present Moment in Psychotherapy and Everyday Life*. New York: W. W. Norton & Co.

Van der Kolk, B. 2014. *The Body Keeps the Score*. London: Penguin.

Wallin, D. 2007. *Attachment in Psychotherapy*. New York: Guilford Press.

Weinstein, A. 2016. *Prenatal Development and Parent's Lived Experiences*. New York: W. W. Norton & Co.

Whitrow, G. 1988. *Time in History*. Oxford: Oxford University Press.

Whitrow, 2003. *What is Time?* Oxford: Oxford University Press. (1st edition, 1971. New York: Oxford University Press.

Wilde Astington, J. 1994. *The Child's Discovery of Mind*. London: Fontana.

Wilkinson, M. 2006. *Coming into Mind: The Mind-brain Relationship: A Jungian Clinical Perspective*. London: Routledge.

Winnicott, D. 1990. *Playing and Reality*. London: Routledge (1st edition, 1971. London: Tavistock Publications).

Woolf, V. 1977. *Orlando*. London: Grafton Books (1st edition, 1928. London: Hogarth Press).

4

OUR QUEST FOR MEANING AND THE AGE OF MEANINGLESSNESS

He put this engine to his ears, which made an incessant noise, like that of a water-mill and we conjecture it is either some unknown animal, or the god he worships: but we are more inclined to the latter opinion, because he assured us ... that he seldom did anything without consulting it. He called it his oracle, and said it pointed out the time for every action of his life.

(Karsten, 2017, p. 356)

The dominance of Chronos

God? Oracle? Judge? Master? Time has been personified in many ways over the ages and this wonderful description by Jonathan Swift of what the Lilliputians made of Gulliver's pocket watch speaks of our enslavement to the clock and the dominance of Chronos over our lives. But how did we get to this place? In this chapter, I am going to move away from the individual to the context in which we exist and want to focus on the third existential challenge of living in time, that we live in an increasingly time-compressed, decontextualised world. To explain why, I need to don my historian's hat and tell the story of two technological innovations that dramatically altered our relationship to time, the mechanical clock and the computer, and the revolutions with which they are associated. The first, the Horological Revolution, took place in the context of urbanisation, the expansion of overseas trade, industrialisation and the erosion of traditional forms of social cohesion; the second, the Digital Revolution, in the context of globalisation and what has been described as the "Age of Meaninglessness". Lest this seem a digression, I want to reiterate the importance of knowing our context, and that includes our origins. Maté wrote, "whatever problem we are hoping to resolve or prevent – be it terrorism, economic inequality, a marriage in trouble, climate change or addiction – the way we see its origins will largely determine our course of action"

(2008, p. 202). We need to take care lest our "preference for a simple and *quickly* understood explanation" and "tendency to look for one-to one causations for almost everything" gets in the way and we miss engaging with the complexity of our interactions with our world and ourselves (p. 201). By taking a journey into history I hope to contextualise some of the major changes in how we think about and live in time that have come about because of economical, political and religious changes since the Middle Ages. It will also provide a wider context for the subsequent focus on the time-related issues people bring to therapy and on the impact of experiences that take us out of time such as trauma, serious illness and traumatic loss in Chapters 9 and 11.

The horological revolution

It has been argued that the invention of the mechanical clock in the fourteenth century was "the single most important practical innovation of the entire Middle Ages, both scientifically and socially" (Karsten, 2017, p. 8). This was because of what mechanical clocks did compared to earlier time-keepers – they powered themselves rather than being dependent on the sun or water like sundials, natural shadow clocks or water clocks, and, crucially they were far more accurate – and because of their rapid adoption. As more accurate, compact, portable timepieces were designed and clock use spread in the next three or four hundred years from churches, town halls and mansions to factories and the ordinary person's home, the mechanical clock bought precision and uniformity into people's lives. At the same time the pace of life began to change radically as society moved from an economy governed by agrarian rhythms which was free of haste and concern about exactitude and productivity, to a new commercial economy that depended on adherence to clock time to ensure maximum productivity and the smooth running of business and trade (p. 78).

The mechanical clock objectified time. It "dissociated time from human events and helped create belief in an independent world of mathematically measurable sequences: the special world of science" (Whitrow, 1988, p. 127). People's temporal world could now be thought of in terms of a "continuum of linear, infinitely divisible moments", moments that were uniform, regular, precise and measurable. "Years were divided into equal days, days into equal hours, hours into equal minutes, and minutes into equal seconds" (Karsten, 2017, p. 356). We take for granted that an hour lasts for sixty minutes whatever the time of day or year and that our watches synchronise with those of people in other parts of the country. Not so for people in the centuries before the mechanical clock. Because the practice was to define an hour as the twelfth part of the day or of the night, in summer the daylight hours would be much longer than those at night, in winter the reverse (Cohen, 2010, p. 369). Time reckoning was also "local", meaning that the exact hour depended upon latitude.

Meanwhile, at a symbolic level the mechanical clock gave us a neutral, self-sufficient concept of time (Karsten, 2017, p. 90). It emptied time of its symbolic meaning. The rich symbols of time as part of the natural order of the universe, the planets and the gods, and man's life cycle as linked to heavenly cycles – symbols that were commonplace in ancient and early modern societies – were stripped away as scientific discoveries challenged longstanding beliefs and religion gave way to secularism. Time no longer reflected natural cycles. The symbolic ways it was used to highlight the social order through a calendar of communally binding, traditional events were also lost. The advance of capitalism played a part in this collapsing of symbolic meaning. The rise of industrial, urbanised societies dislocated people from their traditional contexts, contexts that were primarily determined by concrete time, and re-embedded them in settings dominated by abstract time (p. 27). As economic needs and opportunities intensified mobility, the ties that formerly connected people to their communities and "the value systems that secured people's sense of belonging in the moral and spiritual universe" were weakened (Maté, 2008, p. 261).

Of course, the changes in man's relationship to time from the Middle Ages onwards were certainly not all to do with the "tyrannical two-handed clock" (Dickens 1995, p. 75). Indeed, the very fact that clock time was so widely embraced is because it suited a dramatically changing social context that was fuelled by commercial, political and religious developments. The increasing dominance of Chronos was a manifestation of as well as a contributor to sea-change. Initially the changes associated with the clock were only gradual. As long as most work, including textile production, was carried on at home people had little need to know the exact time. They did not need to coordinate with others and could determine their own timing. So, for a long time old and new practices co-existed. Church bells and the chime of town clocks, if heard, oriented the population to the passing hours. But many people still patterned their days according to the cockerel, the length of daylight and the season. There is also evidence for the use of traditional time markers such as natural sundials long after the introduction of the mechanical clock. The contexts where clocks first became widespread were ones in which uniformity and order was particularly valued. In monasteries, the prevention of idleness as well as the need to standardise times of worship drove clock use. In the armed forces clocks helped synchronise the movement of troops. Lastly, and most importantly, as the West became increasingly urbanised and industrialised, employers began to appreciate that time itself was as an important commodity and that productivity increased when labour time was structured according to the clock (Karsten, 2017, p. 81).

As we move into the Industrial Revolution this became an even more important driver. Having invested in new power-driven machinery that only paid for itself when in use, the early mill owners and industrial entrepreneurs realised that it was imperative to maximise that time. Time is money! Pay was now based on hours of work rather than tasks. Clocks became common throughout factory buildings and workers became tied to the clock in unprecedented ways. By the nineteenth century, struggles between workers and employers became common as the latter tried to impose strict time schedules on the working day, something that leaked out into a control of people's lives more generally. The clock had become a tyrant exemplified in *Hard Times* by Thomas Gradgrind's "deadly statistical clock which measured every beat like a rap on a coffin lid" (Dickens, 1995, p. 75).

The Industrial Revolution was also characterised by the standardisation of time across space. The expansion of trade and development of regional and international transport networks made it imperative to establish common standards for measuring and defining time. The first time-tabled services were developed in Holland to organise canal transport, and in England for the mail coach system. With the development of steam trains, which could travel further and faster than ever before, the fact that individual towns still adhered to local or "sun" time created considerable confusion. From the 1840s it was therefore agreed to adopt a uniform railway time based on Greenwich Mean Time (GMT) and Bradshaw compiled the first railway timetables. An Act of Parliament in 1880 stipulated the adoption of GMT throughout Britain and four years later at the International Meridian Conference it was agreed that universal time should be based on the Greenwich meridian. A time-zone system was also set up throughout the world to improve the coordination of transportation and communication across long distances (Whitrow, 1988, pp. 160–65).

The digital revolution and its unintended consequences

If the mechanical clock led to profound changes in man's relationship to time, even more revolutionary has been the impact of the computer. Computers have speeded up processes to a staggering extent. Information can be processed in nanoseconds. "Duration has been compressed to zero" and because we can now exchange and respond to information anywhere almost instantaneously, time and space have become separated and emptied yet further of meanings (Karsten, 2017, p. 325; Giddens, 1991, pp. 2, 5, 16). In consequence, social relations, which in pre-modern times were essentially linked through place, have become disembedded. The new discourse in the twenty-first century is of "timeless time" and, as Giddens warned, ultimately this disruption of space and time destroys individual identity and creates a fragmented world of "decontextualisation" where things are separated from their context and people from the uniqueness of place (McGilchrist, 2009, p. 390).

Notwithstanding the advantages of modern technology, these trends have their costs. As Susan Greenfield points out, twenty-first-century technologies are altering our lives in staggeringly fast and revolutionary ways. They are "challenging the most basic compartments by which we have made sense of our environment and lived as individuals within it". As a neuroscientist she is particularly interested in how information, nano- and biotechnologies are blurring boundaries between the cyber and the real world and the body and outside (2008, p. 12). My interest is on the increasing permeability of the boundaries which define the temporal spaces within which we live and interact. We have found ways to ignore the boundaries between night and day and the different seasons. As a result, we are becoming increasingly disconnected from nature's rhythms and ever more decontextualised and estranged from the natural world around us, other people and our bodies. We also face the progressive loss of the "occasions" that used to punctuate life, mark transitions and hold important cultural and individual meanings. Lastly in our pursuit of immediacy we are losing touch with our embeddedness within the context of past, present and future. In what follows I intend to go into more detail about the losses that come from living in a time-compressed, decontextualised world and will then consider how these trends are contributing to the "Age of Meaninglessness".

Taking the loss of boundaries first: Modern technology has given us the capacity to communicate 24/7 and to work when and wherever we choose be it at home, in the car or sitting on a beach. In Castells' words, the natural borders of day and night have "been pushed to the point of disappearance" and what used to be private, free time – our evenings and weekends – has been "colonised" (Karsten, 2017, p. 325). It is as if we live in an envelope of "timeless time". Meanwhile modern transport systems enable us to buy foods all year round and this contributes to the blurring of the seasons. When we override the borders between night and day, we risk losing the ability to register and respond to internal sensations, those sensations that tell us that we need to sleep or that it is time to get up, or when we are hungry or full. We risk losing natural boundaries that contribute to our well-being and heighten our appreciation of what we have. We protest in horror to learn that victims of torture are routinely deprived of sleep, locked in tiny cells with no windows to gauge the passage of time, or wakened regularly in the middle of the night and deprived of anything that supports their natural rhythms. Instinctively we understand that this level of deprivation, if endured too long, could lead to madness. Yet we fail to protest at the insidious deprivation that we all face in our time-compressed world. We are affluent, but sensually and spiritually deprived.

Boundaries, which signify limits and finitude, help us to appreciate what we have. They also contribute to the rhythmicity of our lives. "Rhythm permeates our universe" (Hoppenwasser, 2018, p. 51), and sensing and living in rhythm is one of the attributes of being human. But it is largely in the background of our experience. Judy Ryde described this as "like a ground bass over which a melody is played", and in the past that ground bass would have been in harmony with the predictable rhythms of night and day, the seasons, meal times, work and leisure, sleeping and waking (2017).[1] Our ancestors could only work during the hours of daylight and as much as the tools at their disposal, their hands, horse and water power, allowed. The same was true of travel. They could only walk or ride so far in a day. The bounds of space and time were therefore limited, and maybe that protected people psychologically? As Ryde emphasised, there is something intrinsically regulating about natural rhythms, and if all goes well this rhythmicity begins from birth onwards or even before it. As she pointed out, "our earliest experiences include the regular sound of our mother's heart heard from within the womb and after birth we are rhythmically rocked in her arms. Food and sleep come at regular

intervals. These things hold and soothe us, keeping anxiety at bay in their predictable rhythms", and it is not just their predictability that is soothing. It is because
rhythmic cycles, whether biological, physiological or interpersonal rhythms, are
"a here-and-now, in-the-moment experience" (Hoppenwasser, 2018, p. 53).[2]
They help anchor us in the present. Of course, some children never experience
being held by interpersonal rhythms and the security of predictable routines –
when there is birth trauma, the need for intensive care, parental illness or if they
are brought up in chaotic or abusive homes or a war zone. And interestingly, some
of them turn to perseverative movements in order to self-soothe such as rocking,
chewing, or fiddling distractedly with objects.

Rhythm not only calms or energises us but, as Sacks pointed out, it "binds
together the individual nervous systems of a human community" (2007, p. 247).
When I read this, I thought how music can unite groups and inspire and coordinate people whilst working or engaged in something challenging. I recall how
singing catchy songs kept a small group of us going on a long canoeing trip in
Canada, and how song can also help on long walks. In societies in the past it was,
and in some parts of the world still is, customary to accompany demanding work
tasks with singing and chanting – sailors hauling ropes, loggers felling trees,
labourers in the fields. Watch the film *Once a Slave* for some powerful examples of
this, the united voices of the slaves representing an act of defiance as well as spur-
ring them on. And closer to home, I think of the chants at protest marches and
football matches. Music more than any other art form connects people. It is a
leveller, and in every culture people sing and dance together, or they used to. But
these days, rather than being active participants in something creative and expressive, we are more likely to be listeners and spectators, our brains and bodies
certainly resonating, yet no longer as involved as our ancestors used to be. The
spectator has a "one body" experience rather than a "many body" and hence more
deeply communal experience. Instead of the time-space boundaries of a live per-
formance we can access music when and where we want, and I think this is also
linked with or another example of what I am calling the loss of "occasions".

What do I mean by occasions? To continue the musical analogy, they constitute
the melody over the ground bass, the moments in the daily or weekly round that
punctuate working life as well as events traditionally held on specific days of the
year. Our pursuit of timelessness is depriving us of occasions and in particular ones
involving others. In the past, the calendar was punctuated by a host of religious and
secular rituals and feasts, many linked with the liturgical calendar, but others
marking key points in the agricultural or urban year. These occasions were a fundamental part of life's rhythmical pattern. They provided pauses in the working
schedule rather than our current relentless pattern of "beginning, middle, next",
and they involved many of the attributes that support health and well-being: social
engagement, music, dancing, being in nature, having fun and a chance to rest.
Moreover, traditional time-bound activities supported social cohesion for they
were opportunities for the communal sharing of food and the coming together of
young and old, rich and poor. Turning to smaller time-frames, the day's occasions,

or what we could call the "rituals of daily life", used to include regular breaks for meals. During my childhood, days were punctuated by three meals at set times and consumed together at the kitchen table. These breaks made morning, afternoon and evening more distinct somehow, more clearly defined than they are today. In the past, the days of the week were also more sharply differentiated than they are now by activities specific to each: Monday for laundry, another day earmarked for shopping, Friday for being paid, and Friday, Saturday or Sunday, according to faith, for religious observance, being with family and rest. How different from today when it can feel as if one day merges into the next with little differentiation.

The final loss in our time-compressed world is that we have become so caught up in the pursuit of immediacy that we are losing the boundaries between past, present and future. The past, as Meyerhoff said, is being "ground to pieces" by the mill of inexorable, incomprehensible change (Whitrow, 1988, p. 183). We have lost touch with our rootedness in tradition and tend to dismiss rather than value things from the past, a trend Giddens called "detraditionalisation". The rapid pace of change, social fragmentation, the erosion of old structures of meaning, along with exposure to new cultures and ideas mean that traditional ways of doing things are increasingly questioned. On the positive side it means we have more freedom to choose the aspects of cultural practices that suit our values and way of life so that culture is becoming more fluid and "more open to debate and to adaptations by individuals than ever before". On the negative side, detraditionalisation has consequences for our sense of stability and our identity. In pre-modern societies tradition played a key role in guiding people's actions, organising social life and in linking the generations as social norms were passed down (Giddens, 1991, pp. 48, 145). Meanwhile in our want-it-now culture, it feels as if we cannot wait for the future. We cannot let tomorrow rest in our minds as something to imagine, anticipate and work towards. For the must-have-now self, gaps and delays feel increasingly intolerable. Yet to exist in time demands an appreciation of duration and, as noted before, the capacity to contemplate possible futures, in other words to have a "potential self". Moreover, our psychological well-being and capacity to learn depend on being able to tolerate frustration and delay.

Again, electronic globalisation is playing a significant part in the effective reduction of time to the immediate present, although it is by no means the only cause. Our expectations of ourselves, others and the mediums we interact with have altered dramatically with modern technology. We seek instant gratification and have found ways to stay busier and do more and more things simultaneously. Armed with a plethora of electronic gadgets and computerised systems we expect things to be done easily and rapidly and become impatient when something holds us up. Goals supersede process, "immediate effects supersede thoughtfulness" and "getting the job done is often more important than considering what the job is and how it gets done" (Benton, 2014, pp. 25–6).

As Young wryly put it, a new species is emerging – "*homo accelerands*", victimised by time, "harassed at work and away from it, even though [we] are able to spend a great deal of money on the fruitless task of trying to save time" (Karsten, 2017, p. 358). Is it any wonder that many people today lack the kind of emotional resilience that enables us to tolerate frustration and sit with discomfort? The computer can feel maddening as it warms up when we want to send a quick email. If we are pressed for time, slow traffic generates impatience and sometimes road rage. In our want-it-now culture if we feel hungry, we grab something from a shop, often consuming it whilst walking. Fast food has supplanted cooking and eating as a process, and crucially an interactive one. We can buy pots brimming with flowers rather than engage in the satisfying, but slow and never certain process of growing them by seed, and as Haynes pointed out, the media bombards us with possibilities of quasi-transformations and encourages us to "seek out pills, or a quick fix, for the ills of the body and the psyche". We are "tantalised by the possibility of instant transformations" (2007, p. 204). In the language of the Gestalt Cycle, no sooner have we registered a need than we try to leap to the completion stage thus cutting out planning and action, by which I mean action with care and thought. But each stage in the cycle is significant and so too are the pauses between them. Another way of thinking about this is by referring to our evolutionary-based emotional regulating systems of threat, drive and care/soothing (Gilbert, 2005). We could argue that contemporary Western society is dominated by threat and drive. As well as the very real disasters which periodically threaten us, we have generated a host of man-made threats – the threat of not meeting targets or deadlines, of paying off large debts, of not having a size ten youthful body, of not being liked and many more. Goals and outcomes drive us to work and try harder and harder. We are addictively focussed on doing, getting and how we appear. And the more driven we are, the less and less time we have for activities and experiences that regulate and nourish us. What are the costs?

An addiction-prone world

Jon Kabat-Zinn pointed out that time has become one of our biggest stressors. Time urgency erodes our quality of life and is a fundamental cause of disease in the present era (1990, pp. 352, 353). It is associated with the risk of heart disease, high blood pressure, chronic anxiety and digestive problems. Concerning too is the way we transmit time urgency to children. We urge them to hurry up and get ready. We repeatedly say, "I haven't got time". We communicate this urgency in the ways we hold a child, in the way our attention rapidly moves somewhere else when they are trying to show us something, through our body language and, because we all have short fuses, through impatience and irritability. Of even more concern is that maternal stress gets passed on to babies in the womb. What are the long-term consequences for children of being "scooped up onto the conveyer belt of their parent's lives and taught to hurry and be time-conscious" rather than allowed to follow their inner rhythms? (p. 355). What happens to their bodies and their brains? What will future generations be like if we keep filling our time with activity and stimulation and ignore the need for periods of rest and quiet with no specific agenda? And what do we do about it? As with so many things, my answer is "start with myself", not easy when living in a world dominated by threat and drive.

The drive for immediacy is contributing to, and also an aspect of a more addiction-prone society. In his writing on addiction and ADHD (attention deficit hyperactivity disorder), and he is open about his own diagnosis of ADHD and addictive tendencies, Gabor Maté spoke about the addict's need for immediate relief. "Drugs have the power to make the painful tolerable and the humdrum worth living for" and "people jeopardise their lives for the sake of making the moment liveable" (2008, pp. 28, 31). He quoted one recovering alcoholic who said: "two things alcoholics hate is work and time. There has to be no effort involved, and you want the results right now". Maté then described his own wish for immediate results: "A sense of urgency also typifies attention deficit disorder … a desperation to have immediately whatever it is that one may desire at that moment, be it an object, an activity or a relationship. If it doesn't happen quickly for me, I feel like bailing, and unless I'm extraordinarily motivated, I often do" (p. 119).

We anaesthetise ourselves with our behavioural or substance addictions and this helps deal with stress and loneliness. We fill ourselves with something in order not to feel or reflect, and our consumer culture intensifies these patterns. Fromm described this as a "consumptive frenzy" behind which lies an inner vacuity (1981). In similar vein, Maté argued that "many of us resemble the drug addict in our ineffectual efforts to fill in the spiritual black hole, the void at the centre, where we have lost touch with our souls, our spirit, with those sources of meaning and value that are not contingent and fleeting. Our consumerist, acquisition-action-and-image-mad culture only serves to deepen the hole, leaving us emptier than before". He added, "the constant, intrusive and meaningless mind-whirl that characterizes the way so many of us experience our silent moments is, itself, a form of addiction – and it serves the same purpose" (2008, p. 259). As Maté stressed, we see addiction as the primary problem. But it is not. In many cases the additive craving for instant gratification, and in particular for something that soothes emotional pain, has its origins in the individual's earliest experiences. For example, extraordinarily high percentages of drug addicts are known to have been exposed to childhood trauma and it is now appreciated that such experiences sabotage brain development. Indeed, the stark truth, wrote Maté, is that "brain development in the uterus and during childhood is the single most important biological factor in determining whether or not a person will be predisposed to substance dependence and to addictive behaviours of any sort" (pp. 180, 192–3). People today are giving birth to and bringing up children in increasingly stressful conditions. If the mother's threat system is online whilst pregnant her stress hormones pass through the blood into the baby and cortisol in particular, is known to cause neuronal destruction. Stressed parents also find it harder to attune to their babies and this has an impact on brain development and in particular the neuronal systems involved in initiating and sustaining addictive behaviours and in self-regulation and dealing with stress[3] (Man Gyllenhaal, 2015; Maté, 2008).

We understand more now about the relational factors that contribute to addiction proneness, but it is also important to hold in mind the social environment and as I will come to, the other-than-human environment. McGilchrist commented that our high-stimulus society is a response to boredom and that we are caught in "a vicious cycle between feelings of boredom, emptiness and restlessness, on the one hand, and gross stimulation and sensationalism on the other" (2009, p. 400). In similar vein, Greenfield argued that in this century the balance is shifting in favour of having "easy fun", meaning "letting ourselves go" and abandoning ourselves to the thrill of raw, immediate, strong, sensory experiences. Life can be lived in virtual and sensational ways, but can it be truly lived? In her book on identity, Greenfield played with some possible future scenarios. If, for instance, our time continues to be pervaded by screen culture and if we become more and more hooked on the sensory-laden raw feelings generated by playing computer games or hedonistic pursuits, activities that tip the balance of an action from its significance to the action itself, she suggested we could end up then with "yuk-wow" mentalities "characterised by a premium on raw senses and momentary experience, as the chemical landscape of the brain is transformed into one where personalised brain connectivity is far less operational" (2008, pp. 201, 208). Our brains would be maximally receptive to incoming stimuli but with relatively less neuronal net-working to assign any meaning. The emphasis would be more on sensation than cognition. We might thrive on fact-fielding activities, but be less equipped than our predecessors to place isolated events in a context. "In short life would be more comfortable and more fun, but have less meaning" (pp. 279–80).

Given that we are meaning-seeking beings, what impact might that have on our identity? Our being-in-the-world as selves-in-time and selves-in-relation? Green-field's argument is that the thrill of attaining an immediate goal can obliterate that "valuable narrative of personal identity and with it the type of thinking that has a content, a real meaning". Moreover, if current trends continue, we could end up witnessing the breakdown of "the traditional compartments of life, and bringing with it a life that's relatively unchanging from one day to the next, *a life lived out of the context of a sequential narrative: nothing less than the demise of a life story*" (p. 281, my emphasis). This idea evokes in me a sense of horror because having a life story, a sequential personalised narrative is essential to our sense of self. Our self-identity, as Giddens pointed out, presumes continuity across time and space and we interpret that continuity reflectively in an ongoing process of integrating new experiences into our personal story, a process that gives us a sense of being "me" (1991, pp. 51, 54). The words of Socrates, "the unexamined life is not worth living", came to my mind as I contemplated this. It made me think of the lament of someone who says, "I can't remember anything about my childhood", or the plight of people with amnesia caused by brain injury, neurological disorders or dementia who, in con-sequence, have lost or perhaps never had an ongoing story of themselves. Our memories provide a backbone to our existence. In the same way, the societies we live in are as much their history as their present, and a denial of tradition impov-erishes both the present and the future. I shall return to the importance of having a life story in Chapter 8.

The age of meaninglessness

There is, I believe, a link between the social decontextualisation discussed earlier, and an inner severing of context, whether as a result of high-stimulus "now" experiences, dissociation or a neurological condition. The link is the loss of meaning and of structures that bind us. The modern era has been described as the "Age of Meaninglessness" by Paul Tillich, a twentieth-century theologian and existential philosopher. In his view, anxiety about emptiness and the loss of meaning is one of three types of existential anxiety, the other two being of fate and death, or in other words of non-being, and of guilt and condemnation. Although all three can be present simultaneously, Tillich argued that each typi-fied a period of history and were thought of and dealt with according to the narratives in which people understood their existence at the time. The anxiety about fate and death typified the ancient world, a fear "that our story is already written and we are merely passive players" (Inge, 2014, p. 183). It is about knowing the contingency of our temporal and spatial being, that of an individual existing in a specific time and a specific place and no other (Tillich, 1952, p. 44). The Middle Ages represent the Age of Judgement when man's predominant fear was that his actions and intentions were never good enough to appease a wrathful God. To deal with this and avoid hell and damnation people were preoccupied with saving their souls by doing good works, going on pilgrimages and paying for masses to be sung on their behalf. In the Age of Meaninglessness meanwhile, Tillich argued that our deepest anxiety is of emptiness, of the "loss of a meaning which gives meaning to all other meanings" (p. 47). It is a state of doubt, despair, isolation and estrangement. This anxiety emerges when people lose touch with former spiritual beliefs, with traditions or activities that give meaning to everyday life or with their embeddedness in place and the natural world. When structures of meaning are in place, structures that convey a sense of place and continuity with past and future generations, individuals have a way of dealing and over-coming their anxiety. In periods of great change when systems of meaning disintegrate and there are conflicts between the old and the new, this method of assuaging anxiety is no longer adequate (p. 62).

Tillich's ideas about meaninglessness remind me of another mid-twentieth-cen-tury writer, Victor Frankl, who famously said "man is ready and willing to shoulder any suffering as soon and as long as he can see a meaning in it" (2004, p. 117). Having what I have termed an "ethic of meaning" (Wright, 2016, p. 194), was what enabled Frankl to survive the unspeakable horrors of Auschwitz. He was keenly aware of the dire consequences for anyone who lost meaning and purpose and argued that "we needed to stop asking the meaning of life, and instead to think of ourselves as those who were being questioned by life – daily and hourly. Our answer must consist, not in talk and meditation, but in right action and in right conduct. Life ultimately means taking the responsibility to find the right answer to its questions and to fulfil the tasks which it constantly sets for each individual" (2004, p. 85). Frankl believed that man's search for meaning is the primary motivation in his life and commented on the "existential frustration" when our will to meaning is frustrated. In his psychiatric practice he heard many people complaining of a loss of purpose, people who "have enough to live by but nothing to live for" and were "haunted by the experience of inner emptiness, a void within themselves" (p. 142). They were caught in what he called an "existential vacuum", often manifesting as a state of boredom and dealt with by seeking power or immediate pleasure, such as taking drugs to fill the void (p. 111).

Both Tillich and Frankl were writing after the horrors of two world wars and they were certainly not alone in raising questions about the meaning of existence and arguing that the erosion of old traditions that connected people has created an existential vacuum. The trends I have been describing because of industrialisation, globalisation and the digital revolution along with the collapse of the supportive networks of extended families and local communities in the wake of increased mobility have created a world in which nothing can be taken for granted. But are we still in an Age of Meaninglessness, or responding to it as the descendants of those who lived in such an age? Put another way, should this be seen as a state of mind, cultural and individual, specific to the post-war and Cold War era, or linked with and intensifying in a decontextualised world? I think our current age is one of meaninglessness, although the reasons are different to those noted by Tillich and it takes a different shape.

It is understood that repeated trauma and loss can lead to a loss of sustaining beliefs and erode people's sense of meaning, purpose and hope (Herman, 1994, p. 121), and this was certainly the context in which Tillich and Frankl wrote. But the traumas of that age have not gone away. They still haunt the minds of survivors who are still alive and, through transgenerational transmission, the bodies of their children and grandchildren. Moreover, trauma seems endemic in our society. For instance, the Adverse Childhood Experiences Survey revealed that of over 17,000 Americans questioned, 25 per cent had experienced physical abuse, 28 per cent of the women and 16 per cent of the men some form of sexual abuse and 12 per cent had witnessed domestic violence (Van der Kolk, 2014, p. 145). Even if we have not personally experienced traumatic events, we are brought face to face with horror through the media on a daily basis. Moreover, in the short time-span I have been immersed in writing this book, discussions about climate change and the various ways we are destroying our planet, the loss of endangered species, the pollution of our rivers and oceans, and about time running out for life on earth as we know it, have mushroomed. There are more calls to action, debates about our role as psychotherapists, more emphasis on our interconnectedness with the other-than-human world.

Present day meaninglessness comes not just from the loss of structures that used to bind communities or spiritual beliefs and traditions that give meaning to life. Nor is it solely a consequence of unmet relational needs, for instance, of shared, live experiences rather than virtual ones; of being heard, attuned to, encouraged and acknowledged for who we are, moments-of-connection that we know are vital to us as human beings. The epidemic of meaninglessness also comes from the severing of our connections to the natural world, or what Bednarek described as a "catastrophic loss of the attachment to nature". We "carry a deep but silent grief for our diminished sense of community with a world that we see as alive". "We have lost access to the ways of weaving ourselves into the 'web of life'" (2018, p. 11). It comes from an abandonment of our primary satisfactions, satisfactions, as Weller explained, that "evolved over thousands of years and that our brains are wired for such as gathering around communal life, around story, mythology, meaningful relationships, ritual, gathering around fire …. sharing and preparing food, spending time in nature, being fully embodied". Instead, Weller argued, we are surrounding ourselves with secondary satisfactions such as power, prestige, wealth, status, material goods and stimulants – the trappings of the addiction-prone world (Bednarek, 2018, p. 14). And like any drug, we will always want more in order to feel less empty.

What are the implications for our work as psychotherapists?

We often see people who are trapped in despair and appear to have lost any sense of meaning, joy or vitality. I recall a teacher sobbing desperately as she described the difficulties faced by the children in her school and her sense of powerlessness to do anything to change things. Her tears intensified as she added to the list all the horrific things going on in the world. Looking at me bleakly she asked, "what's the point of all this? I'm not sure I want to live in a world like this". Trauma and unmet relational needs played a part in Melanie's distress and sensitivity to the suffering of others. But her anguished observations about the context she, or rather we, live in have been echoed by other people in my room. I can resonate with their concerns and feelings. In response to Melanie on that occasion I acknowledged her despair and lack of hope and shared how sometimes I too slip into despondency and despair. But then I spoke of the beliefs that contribute to and bolster my personal sense of meaning – for we all need sustaining touchstones to anchor and comfort us.

I have written elsewhere about six factors that foster hope and the will to keep going despite life's difficulties (Wright, 2016). The foundations of these "dimensions of hope" are laid down within the matrix of our earliest attachment relationships, but also within those social structures of meaning which Tillich and Frankl appreciated were so important. The family routines and communal traditions that give us a sense of basic trust – a trust that enables us to take things for granted. What strikes me is that without these dimensions, and current trends challenge each of them, we are more at risk of personal meaninglessness and hence more likely to cling to "easy fun" or absolutist beliefs or to slip into loneliness and despair. Let me explain what I mean by taking each dimension in turn.

1. A sense of mastery and agency

We need to feel that we are the authors of our lives and can have an impact on our world. Yet many people lack a sense of agency because, as Giddens pointed out, so many aspects of life today are controlled by large, abstract systems (1991, pp. 201, 222, 242). Although advances in hygiene, medicine and technology have eliminated many of the hazards faced by our ancestors, we face new risks in our "brave new" world, some with potentially devastating, wide-ranging consequences. As individuals we can feel powerless to deal with them. Contrast this with people in pre-modern societies. Certainly, life was highly contingent on possible risks, including natural hazards, accidents and illnesses without the mitigating factors of insurance policies and services like the NHS. Yet most people had some control over what they produced and how and when they worked. They could make their own decisions and had the satisfaction of engaging in a process from start to finish. Without ownership or a voice, it is easy to feel insignificant and disaffected.

2. Something that gives meaning to our experiences

As Frankl said, we can shoulder suffering if we can see meaning in it. We need a narrative, a way to put our experiences into a context, especially those that challenge our assumptive world. This includes suffering and also events that shock or surprise or demand that we do things in very different ways. I have described some dramatic social changes over time and especially during the last fifty years. Such is the staggering pace of change that it becomes increasingly difficult to assimilate the new with the familiar. We can become specialists in increasingly complex areas of knowledge but end up knowing less and less about other things and depending on others or the news to mediate change for us. Also hard to assimilate are the horrifying events which impinge on our consciousness every week and leave us shocked, incredulous and struggling to make sense why such things happen. This is especially true when traumatic events and tragic losses touch us personally. Such events call into question all that previously gave meaning and purpose to life. As Levinas said, "suffering is ungraspable; we cannot dominate it. It breaks down meaning, at least until another responds" (Orange, 2011, p. 69). As noted earlier, in the Age of Fate men made sense of forces beyond their control by referring to fate and recurrent cycles. They believed in an inherent logic to their world. In the Middle Ages, in Judeo-Christian societies at least, man's relationship to his environment was thought of in terms of a complex symbolism reflecting the divine order, and the life of the individual as a linear journey towards judgement and eternal life. External events were frequently ascribed to the hand of God. But in this increasingly secular age we lack belief systems to buttress us and provide consoling answers to our existential questions, a collapse of meaning epitomised in twentieth century existentialist art.

To give an example of experiences that can't be given meaning: When talking about her childhood, Bree often sobbed like an inconsolable child. She would cry in anguish, "Why are they doing this? Why are they like this? Why would they treat me like this?" And in the face of such questions I would reflect back her stunned disbelief and confusion, then say: "I don't know why your Mum and Dad were like that, but I do know you didn't deserve it". Bree had experienced the "trauma of non-recognition" as well as considerable emotional neglect from the moment she was born (Bromberg, 2011, p. 57). She learned that she had to keep quiet, a figure in family photographs expected to "perform" when required, but otherwise not seen or celebrated for the unique being she was. Her parents' unspoken message was "we don't really want you". And this experience was repeated at intervals throughout Bree's life and eventually bought her to therapy. Her last encounter with her narcissistic mother left Bree reeling as if something had shattered inside her. "Nothing will ever be the same again", she said. Except she knew, like me, that this had happened before, long ago. "How could she!" "Why doesn't she see that I'm suffering?" Such expressions of stunned incredulity hang in the air between therapist and client, leaving us as witnesses to the shock of trauma and at a loss for words. They are moments when, to use Orange's words, all we can offer are our "empty hands" (2011, p. 63).

3. Having a sense of purpose

In the second dimension I used the word meaning in the sense of an explanation. Here I am thinking of meaning as purpose. When I observe how many people these days feel lost, disaffected and alienated, living lives that lack meaning, the words of Nietzsche ring true: "He who has a why to live can bear with almost any how" (Frankl, 2004, p. 109). Sometimes the lack of purpose is because it is so hard to find fulfilling work, or any work at all, and for young adults, increasingly difficult to get a foothold on the housing ladder. Often it is because they feel marginalized. Sometimes trauma and loss create a sense of personal meaninglessness. Again, these are issues which emerge regularly in our work. I recall for instance, how one man whose wife and son had been killed in a car accident said, "it feels as if my life has lost all meaning. I'm in a kind of limbo. There's nothing left to live for". Meanwhile Bree often spoke of her sense of something essential being taken from her when she was tiny: "her spirit, her natural hope". "Something inside me died." She became resigned, "sentenced to life", yet one that had no real meaning for her and which she filled by cramming herself with food, drugs and alcohol. Bree defined her experience as an "existential agony" and spoke of the challenge of having to live a life that had been rendered meaningless. It was a challenge that reminded me of Tillich's thesis about the "courage to be" in the face of doubt and despair (1952). And there was an admirable courage in Bree, for she kept trying despite her history of repeated trauma and struggles with addiction. Our own challenge as therapists is to stay with people like Bree in that place of meaninglessness, whilst also supporting them to find a renewed sense of purpose.

4. A sense of future possibilities

The fourth dimension is connected to the third. "The self", as Giddens said, "forms a trajectory of development from the past to the anticipated future", and a key aspect of personal ongoingness is the ability to project ourselves into the future

(1991, p. 75). The foundations of a "potential self", as discussed earlier, lie in childhood. Children need caregivers to dream dreams for them and to support and encourage their tentative strivings. But some parents are unable to do this. If our parents hold anxious or pessimistic views about the future, we may inherit them. "Don't risk! The world out there isn't safe." We can also inherit their unfulfilled dreams and find ourselves following a trajectory that we think is right yet never feels satisfying. I am sure I am not alone as the child of parents who lived during the Second World War in being affected in both these ways. Later experiences can also make us pessimistic about the future. After trauma and repeated failures, illness or losses it is far from easy to believe in a positive future. The same is true for people who have been dislocated from their homes and cultures and who feel alienated from their communities. And with our heightened awareness of the reality of climate change and of the deeply worrying signs of its consequences it is becoming increasingly hard for everyone to conceptualise a positive future.

5. Trust in others and the capacity for meaningful relationships

The capacity to take things for granted is grounded in secure attachments as well as in the psychological supports available in traditional communal settings. Many parents are able to provide safe, loving and supportive relationships. But many can't because of their own attachment history, their traumas, and the "threat/drive" pressures under which they live. Even the most loving parent can find it hard these days to spend emotionally meaningful time with his or her children and to be present with "presence". And children are quickly being initiated into a world of virtual relationships mediated through one-dimensional screens. It has been argued that we are now facing an epidemic of loneliness. More and more people are living on their own, and even though it is possible to contact people anywhere at any time, it is doubtful how emotionally meaningful these contacts are compared with face-to-face, body-to-body relationships. This is especially true in what anthropologists call low-context societies, the norm now in the Western world, which are typified by individualism and relatively short interpersonal relationships. People get straight to the point without wasting time and clock time prevails. By contrast in high-context societies, cultures where tradition plays an important role, people are more socially oriented, cohesive and committed to common goals. Their pace of life is slower and more in tune with natural rhythms and they invest more time in social interactions (Karsten, 2017, pp. 330–33).[4] The pain of loneliness is made worse when you see others enjoying being together. It leads to days that drag and preoccupations about how to find a friend or partner and about how you are seen by others. Such are the enduring themes in many of our client's lives. And if you felt lonely as a child and lonely as an adult then it is hard to feel comfortable being with oneself because, using the language of object relations theory, you have been unable to internalise good objects. Your inner world is not a resource, but a bleak, comfortless place filled with anxiety and self-loathing.

6. Faith in something greater than the self

Frankl spoke of an existential vacuum. We are simultaneously aware of existential insecurities yet have little to offer by way of hope and consolation as religion did in the past. Others have also commented on a demise of belief in the modern world. For example, Inge reflected on the fact that "we have lost so many of our stories", one of the most significant being "our loss of a narrative of meaning which for countless people over many generations was rooted in an overarching story of faith". Instead of understanding ourselves and the transitions of our lives in terms of what holds them and us together, Inge argued that increasingly "we understand ourselves and our transitions in terms of collapse". "We understand the parameters of a marriage at its divorce rather than at its duration, and death as a finality rather than a gateway. Whereas a medieval worldview understood life by how it held together, we who have dissected the tadpole and the atom understand our world by how much it falls apart" (2014, pp. 171, 172). This is a grim thought.

This is not to say that a religious faith is the only way to find meaning or access something greater than ourselves. It is something that connects, that brings us together rather than separating and fragmenting us. It is something transient. We are not aware of it all the time. Such moments of connection can include connecting to the divine, to nature and what is eternal and enduring, to art and beauty, to the power of love or courage. It is hard to define. Yet we know it when we experience it and such moments help us keep going and sustain meaning through life's ordeals. We all need experiences of the "something more than", moments of deep subjectivity when we are caught by and fully enter into a fleeting experience – seeing drops of rain glistening on a tree, hearing the roar of a waterfall or the call of a blackbird, walking in an environment where the landscape evokes a sense of awe. Fully present and most deeply alive, we pause and savour, a "sacred" moment before our attention shifts and we are pulled back into our busy, time-bound lives.

7. Acceptance

To the list of dimensions of hope I want to add a seventh: *acceptance*. It is one of the characteristics of resiliency and transformation after trauma identified by Wilson, meaning "accepting the loss of invulnerability and that much of life is illusory, accepting one's smallness in the face of horrific experiences and the vastness of the universe, and accepting the continuity and discontinuity of life – in other words, change, loss and death" (2006, pp. 406–8). They are existential truths which the pursuit of easy fun tries to avoid. Langan pointed out that all of us face "an idiosyncratic version of the same problem: how to live a life signifying something, however fleeting in the face of oblivion". His own answer is beautifully expressed: that "we rise and fall on waves of onflowing experience in which we can dare to meet, and to find significance through one another … The struts and frets of life matter, because they are the forms in which we find one another" (2014, pp. 174, 175).

Salzberger-Wittenberg made a similar point. We can manage frustrations, dis-appointments and losses better if we feel ourselves to be members of our community and the wider human family and "held within the universe in its rhythm, its cycling ebb and flow, life, death and renewal". Moreover, even if acknowledging our mortality causes us to feel "helpless, infinitely small and unimportant", it can make us conscious that what we do or don't do makes a difference and that it is within our power "to add to or diminish the fund of love, hope and joy in the world" (2013, pp. 13, 152). It is interesting that whilst contemplating our mortality, both these writers are emphasising the bigger ongoing, cyclical context in which we are held as well as the kinship of people, and that both call us to recognise our existential insignificance and *still* to believe that we can contribute something worthwhile. Can we find an ethic of meaning and "the courage to be" in the face of existential uncertainty? In the face of our smallness and all too human vulnerability we need to keep acknowledging that things matter – other people, the planet, our cultural heritage, the terrible things that happen and should not happen and that what *we* do matters. We *need* to have feelings about them.

Let me end with a personal example of allowing people to matter and, I hope, adding to the fund of love and hope in the world that occurred whilst writing about these themes. I had begun the day facing one of my own occasional struggles to find joy and meaning and, hard as I tried to work on this, still felt weighed down. Then, as I walked through the early morning streets, a young man huddled in a shop doorway called out asking if I had any spare change. My first less hospi-table reaction was to give a hasty apology. But I turned back, dug in my purse then, I think more importantly, asked where he had come from. The lad told me a little about his story and his wish to settle in this area. We talked about the diffi-culties facing homeless young people, then departed wishing each other well. Perhaps both of us were enriched by our short conversation? I certainly walked away feeling a sense of warmth, love and reconnection.

"Only connect" said E. M. Forster (1910). Those words have always stuck in my mind as emblematic of deeper truths. If we are to find meaning beyond the bare bones of existence, we need something to live for. As Shabad said, "the notion of a meaningful life that transcends the self is not merely an existential appendage that becomes relevant only after our basic needs are met and biological survival is secured … Living for something or someone other than oneself is fundamental to being human" (2001, pp. 38, 39). Given my argument that the Age of Mean-inglessness is typified by a severing of connections – between peoples, people and place, humans and nature, and intrapsychically a disconnection from ourselves and our emotions, we need to do all we can to foster connections. As therapists we need this if we are to survive repeated exposure to the immensity and intensity of human suffering and horror and avoid slipping into despair and meaninglessness. We also need to foster connection and engagement with our clients and support them to find meaningful connections with others.

Only connect the prose and the passion, and both will be exalted and human love will be seen at its height. Live in fragments no longer. Only connect, and the beast and the monk, robbed of isolation that is life to either, will die.

(Forster, 1970, p. 174)

Notes

1 Rovelli observed that diurnal rhythm, whether this be the rhythm of night following day or the 24-hour rhythm that goes on in the biochemistry of our body's cells, "is an elementary source of our idea of time" (2018, p. 56).
2 This is useful to bear in mind when working with trauma survivors. Because they can be easily dysregulated and lose touch with the present moment when anything triggers memories of the past, to suggest moving in rhythm, for example standing and shifting from foot to foot or walking round or tapping each shoulder alternately can bring them back to the present.
3 It impacts the dopamine-based, drive system and the opioid reward-attachment system, both of which are involved in initiating and sustaining addictive behaviours, and the prefrontal cortex which is crucial for self-regulation and dealing with stress.
4 This is worth bearing in mind if we work with people of different ethnicity. Stretching the metaphor, could we argue that dissociative processes, whether this is because of an autonomic shutdown in the face of trauma, or an endorphin fuelled ecstatic moment, create a "low-context culture" in the brain of fast but weak connections? Meanwhile in activities involving thinking deeply, making associations and contextualising experiences, the brain is operating as in a high-context culture. Many more connections are made, but the pace is slower.

References

Bednarek, S. 2018. "How wide is the field? Gestalt therapy, capitalism and the natural world". *British Gestalt Journal*, 27(2): 8–17.

Benton, J. 2014. "Success and Failure: Cultural and Psychoanalytic Perspectives" in B. Willock, R. Coleman & L. Bohm (Eds.) *Understanding and Coping with Failure: Psychoanalytic Perspectives* (pp. 25–32). New York: Routledge.

Bromberg, P. 2011. *The Shadow of the Tsunami and the Growth of the Relational Mind*. New York: Routledge.

Cohen, R. 2010. *Chasing the Sun: The Epic Story of the Star that Gives Us Life*. London: Simon & Schuster.

Dickens, C. 1995[1854]. *Hard Times*. Ware, Hertfordshire: Wordsworth Editions.

Forster, E. 1970. *Howards End*. London: Penguin (1st edition 1910. London: Edward Arnold).

Frankl, V. 2004. *Man's Search for Meaning*. London: Rider. (1st edition, 1959. London: Random House).

Fromm, E. 1981. *Homo consumens* available at https://www.philosophicalsociety.com/Archives/Homo%20Consumens.htm, accessed 8 December 2017.

Giddens, A. 1991. *Modernity and Self-identity: Self and Society in the Late Modern Age*. Cambridge: Polity Press.

Gilbert, P. 2005. *Compassion: Conceptualisations, Research and Use in Psychotherapy*. London: Routledge.

Greenfield, S. 2008. *ID: The Quest for Meaning in the 21st Century*. London: Sceptre.

Haynes, J. 2007. *Who Is It That Can Tell Me Who I Am? The Journal of a Psychotherapist*. Bristol: Cromwell Press.

Hoppenwasser, K. 2018. "Bearing the unbearable: meditations on being in rhythm", *Attachment: New Directions in Psychotherapy and Relational Psychoanalysis*. 12(2), 48–55.

Inge, D. 2014. *A Tour of Bones: Facing Fear and Looking for Life*. London: Bloomsbury.

Kabat-Zinn, J. 1990. *Full Catastrophe Living: How to Cope with Stress, Pain and Illness Using Mindfulness Meditation*. London: Piatkus Books.

Karsten, L. 2017. *Globalisation and Time*. London: Routledge.

Langan, R. 2014. "Brief Candle" in B. Willock, R. Coleman & L. Bohm (Eds.) *Understanding and Coping with Failure: Psychoanalytic Perspectives* (pp. 172–7). New York: Routledge.

Man Gyllenhaal, K. (Dir.) 2015. *In Utero* (documentary film).

Maté, G. 2008. *In the Realm of the Hungry Ghosts: Close Encounters with Addiction*. Toronto: Vintage Canada.

McCormack, P. 1972. "Kate". *Nursing Mirror*. December 1972.

McGilchrist, I. 2009. *The Master and his Emissary: The Divided Brain and the Making of the Western World*. New Haven: Yale University Press.

Orange, D. 2011. *The Suffering Stranger: Hermeneutics for Everyday Clinical Practice*. New York: Routledge.

Rovelli, C. 2018. *The Order of Time*. London: Allen Lane.

Ryde, J. 2017. "A Fracture in Time". Conference presentation.

Sacks, O. 2007. *Musicophilia*. London: Picador.

Salzberger-Wittenberg, I. 2013. *Experiencing Beginnings and Endings*. London: Karnac.

Shabad, P. 2001. *Despair and the Return of Hope: Echoes of Mourning in Psychotherapy*. Lanham, MD: Jason Aronson.

Tillich, P. 1952. *The Courage to Be*. London: Yale University Press.

Van der Kolk, B. 2014. *The Body Keeps the Score*. London: Penguin.

Whitrow, G. 1988. *Time in History*. Oxford: Oxford University Press.

Wilson, J. 2006. "Trauma and the Epigenesis of Identity" in J. Wilson (Ed.) *The Posttraumatic Self: Restoring Meaning and Wholeness to Personality* (pp. 56–63). New York: Routledge.

Wright, S. 2016. *Dancing between Hope and Despair: Trauma, Attachment and the Therapeutic Relationship*. London: Palgrave.

PART II

The therapeutic journey and its temporal shape

5

TIME IN THE CONSULTING ROOM

This room holds the traces of so many beginnings and endings –
those first hellos with echoes of our first beginnings, yours and mine;
the goodbyes – our ending an anticipated replica
of the previous endings punctuating our lives.

(Wright)

Introduction

Given that we all exist in and face the challenges of living in time how does the relationship to time of both therapist and client play out in the therapeutic relationship? In this chapter I want to think about the practical aspects of therapy time – the domain of Chronos – for instance, about its structure, routine and boundaries and the different arrangements that exist for determining the length of sessions and the overall time-frame. But more important, I want to inspire thought about the dynamic issues that can emerge around the time we have and about what our shared time means to both of us.

Time manifests in therapy in complex ways. Broadly speaking we could group these under the following headings, some of which are more about practice and some about content or process:

- The interplay between Kairos and Chronos.
- The time-frame and how both therapist and client relate to it.
- The temporal contours of the therapeutic relationship.
- The therapeutic journey and its temporal shape.
- Time related themes and issues.
- Our theoretical bias towards past, present or future.

Following the work of Elton-Wilson (1996), I believe that we need to be "time-conscious" therapists and this entails a multi-dimensional approach. We need one eye on the time-frame; another on the links between the client's past, present and future; one eye on our own history and how that might impact the relationship; and a fourth on what I will call the accidents or distortions of time that occur during our interactions. This includes enactments and the interesting and sometimes embarrassing mistakes around timings that can occur, the different ways that we can all – both clients and therapists – try to deny time, and the occasions when we are pulled into roles belonging to earlier time-frames. As time-conscious therapists it is important to consider how we:

- Manage the time-frame.
- Deal with explicit or implicit pulls to offer something outside scheduled appointments.
- Pace the process within each session and overall. For instance, is it appropriate to adopt a phased approach? And with what type of client? And when is there merit in spacing out sessions in a more flexible client-centred way?
- Conceptualise shifts in the working alliance and therapeutic relationship over time.
- Approach beginnings and endings, both in practical terms and in being curious what they mean for each client.

The temporal experience offered by psychotherapy

Psychotherapy offers a particular type of temporal experience. We can think of this in three ways: First, it provides a boundaried temporal space in which the dance between Kairos, our subjective experience of time, and Chronos, clock time, is heightened. This is one of a number of dialectic tensions inherent in therapy time. Secondly, the weekly sessions constitute an "occasion" that punctuates people's lives and in idiosyncratic ways can become hugely important. Thirdly, the rhythms and regularity of therapy create an experience of ongoingness. This is both containing, especially for people whose lives are chaotic, and relationally gives people an experience of being held in mind.

Boundaries and liminal states

Taking the idea of a boundaried temporal space first: Chronos or linear time provides structure. It structures when we meet, for how long, and provides a sense of moving forward in time. As Molnos pointed out, these boundaries carve out a secure psychological space from everyday reality (1995, p. 19). This reminds me of Simmel's concept of the adventure. Like an adventure, a therapy session involves a temporary dropping out of the usual continuity of life, and there is a sharpness to how it begins and ends. When discussing the rituals surrounding travelling to and arriving at therapy with a colleague, she came up with the phrase "book-ends".

They place the therapeutic encounter in parentheses and contribute to its safety. Winnicott's idea of "boundary and space" comes to mind here. To be creative, he argued, we need the security of a boundary, something that creates the "form". "Spontaneity only makes sense in a controlled setting. Content is of no meaning without form" (Davis & Wallbridge, 1981, p. 144). Winnicott was thinking in particular about children's need for safe boundaries before they can play. They can risk being ruthless if they know that the parental environment is indestructible. But he also applied the idea of boundary and space to clinical practice, appreciating that in our context the "form" enables the client to risk being himself in a different way and sharing things that ordinarily he fears would sound foolish, fanciful, even crazy or would be dismissed or criticised.[1] "I don't have to pretend here. I don't have to hide my feelings." "I put stuff on hold in the week that feels too overwhelming to deal with on my own because I know it is safe to let it out here." "This is the one place I feel someone understands me". We could think of this too as a temporal space in which, even though the clicking clock reminds us that Chronos is ever present, its ongoingness and temporary separation from ordinary life takes us into a liminal, timeless state. It offers the chance for a creative type of timelessness that binds past, present and future and has the potential to alter all of them. This is the realm of Kairos where our subjective sense of duration keeps changing and time can turn back on itself or leap forward into imaginary futures. It is the realm of the unconscious and primary process thinking.

The narrative therapists White and Epston noted how in a liminal state we often lose track of time and experience "a sense of *communitas* with the persons who seek therapy". "At such moments", they added, "you are in a threshold state of potential change" (1992, p. 13). Liminal means being at or on both sides of a boundary or threshold – "betwixt and between". In a rite of passage this state includes experiencing disorientation and ambiguity when the participants leave their pre-ritual status but have yet to make the transition to the status they will hold once they re-enter their community. It makes me think how disoriented and scared a client can feel when in the process of letting go old beliefs and unhelpful strategies. It feels very unsettling because of not quite finding or trusting a new way of being.

We tend to associate liminality with mystical and religious occurrences. But there are everyday examples too. For example, the moments between sleep and being fully awake when all sorts of weird and sometimes inspiring thoughts can flit through our mind in no particular order. For me the important thing about liminal states is the sense of possibility, and I have always been intrigued that the Chinese use the same character for the words crisis and opportunity. It is a reminder of the latent opportunity in any crisis. We can learn and grow after adversity, and in a liminal space we are at a border when new possibilities and ways of viewing things emerge. It is a place of wondering, playing with "maybe", and engaging in fantasy.

The term crisis, as McNamee explained, is derived from the Greek *krinein*, which means to separate (McNamee & Gergen, 1992, p. 187). The boundary experience of a crisis can separate us from others and from the continuity of past, present and future. People speak being on a knife-edge or feeling on edge or unattached, floating or unanchored. McNamee's observations made me think of the common use of the term "breakdown" for an emotional/psychological crisis. When I play with this word I think of a breakdown of our psychic and embodied boundaries – the structures that hold us together and contribute to our sense of ongoingness. And without such boundaries we feel as if we are falling apart, falling to bits, cracking up or fragmenting. There is a loss of touch with the core self. Any idea of separation implies a boundary and in some cultures, crises are viewed as integral to life-stage transitions. It marks an opportunity to let go of something we have outgrown or that no longer serves us. The other essential feature about a boundary-as-difference is that it can open our eyes to novelty. Bateson's argument that all information is necessarily "news of difference" and that the perception of difference triggers new responses in all living systems is a core premise of systemic therapy (White & Epston, 1990, pp. 2, 7). Coming back to the idea of boundary and space – in crossing over into a new space, things take on a different perspective. We see things anew. And the difference opens the door to change.

Whilst writing this chapter I had a personal experience of liminality – a remarkable session with a creative woman who was well aware how easily relational events could trigger her. When with people who appeared strong and reliable, she was often hijacked by younger parts of self and their longing to be looked after and this often led to risky relationships. She had recently become preoccupied with an artist. Her "sensible self" knew she would end up being hurt and had to get him out of her mind. She also knew that there was more to this than the relationship. The man had qualities Lisa sought for herself. To explore what he represented, I invited Lisa to imagine a magical process to distil the essence of these qualities into an object she could keep. The visualisation took us on a remarkable imaginary journey in which each of Lisa's younger parts spent time with whatever objects or animals came to her mind. In the process I fell as deeply as she did into an imaginative process, using images and questions that spontaneously came to me. I recall one moment when I had reassured her, or rather the anxious older child, that I would keep an eye on her "baby self" and I slipped into a dreamy state of reverie – realising with my observing mind that this was what attuned mother's do (Bion, 1962, p. 36). At some point I caught sight of the clock and was surprised that it was time to end. It did not feel that we had been together that long. And I was not worried about allowing ten more minutes for gently disengaging from the process and discussing what we both made of it – unusual because sometimes my time-pressured self gets caught in a spin of "how am I going to manage all the things I planned to do before my next appointment?" I felt calm and centred, my mind alert and thoughtful about what had gone on between us. The other curious thing is that my not-quite-being-in-time continued for the rest of the day. I forgot that a colleague was going to call and so was not ready. Then I confused myself about when the appointment after that was starting and so ended our conversation prematurely.

Returning to Epston and White's point about liminal states taking us to the threshold of potential change, how can we understand what began to change for Lisa after this process? Mitchell wrote: "It is precisely the timelessness of the analytic situation that fosters the unravelling (of) and makes learning about and connecting with multiple self configurations possible without having to account for oneself in the way one has to in ordinary life" (1993, p. 115). Here we are back to the idea of the safety to play within holding boundaries. What became clear to us both was that, as a child, Lisa had never felt safe to play spontaneously, and although she longed to engage in creative pursuits now, something always blocked her. I suspect that the "something new" linking the present with memory was that, in taking the role of a m/other who supported and contained how each part of self began to play with the tiny object, I was intuitively providing something Lisa had never experienced as a child. Most important, I communicated that I was holding her in my mind, and this calmed a six-year-old child who suddenly became scared when I sat quietly in dreamy reverie. "Yes, I'm here" I answered, when she anxiously checked. "My mind is floating here and there, but I'm still keeping an eye on the baby and on you." With that reassurance Lisa's six-year-old self felt confident enough to consider going outside to play.

The rhythms and rituals of therapy

Coming back to the significance of the "book- ends", they also give therapy its sense of being an "occasion". As discussed in Chapter 3, in today's world, in part because of our pursuit of immediacy, we are losing many of the occasions or rituals that used to punctuate the calendar or the day and bring people together. This loss contributes to the epidemic of loneliness that we hear more about on the media and is something that our most troubled clients face every day. For many clients, the regular weekly session in longer-term therapy becomes an important occasion – a chance to pause and take stock, and for some people, those for instance, who feel isolated and find it incredibly hard to get through a day let alone a week, it can be an occasion to hold onto in their mind during the week – a point to aim for when perhaps they experience feeling less alone and less scared. Moreover, there are people for whom such weekly appointments are the only regular feature in an otherwise eventless existence, like Hayne's client Thom for whom "holiday breaks were of no interest" … "nor were the days of the week, because his life was unpunctuated by any social intercourse" (2007, p. 71). In today's busy, time-compressed world, Thom is not the only person for whom the missing "occasions" in life are relational ones.

For some people the journey is a hugely important part of the occasion and its rituals. When one woman was reflecting on our work together, itself an incredible journey, in her last session, she said she would miss driving through the woods a few miles from where I work and seeing the landscape through the changing seasons. Other clients have also spoken about the significance of the journey. For instance, Marcie would often talk about the bus trip and stopping for coffee before walking the last half-mile to my house. I did not make that journey with her, but it became part of our shared history. And Eddie reflected how strange it felt when he moved house and had to take a different route to get to therapy. For a short while without the old routine he felt disoriented.

The journey, long or short, becomes part of the therapy, an attachment object somehow. It marks a transition between one way of being, my clients' daily life selves, and another. In this way it echoes the second stage in a traditional rite of passage, a period of abrupt separation from one's community, a liminal phase during which the participants engage in challenging tasks and rituals. Except this "separation ritual" is not so abrupt nor hopefully too challenging for most clients. The exception is for someone with a traumatic history for whom undertaking a journey, sitting with others in a waiting room, risking knocking on the door or passing closed doors on the way to the therapy room can trigger traumatised parts of self. I didn't know until the end of our work that one woman was always scared that I might not open the door, but had sensed that for someone else coming upstairs was frightening; another, anticipating that I would be annoyed to see her and might send her packing, anxiously checked my face as I let her in and often could not settle until we had spent time regulating her. Facing the prospect of leaving is also potentially dysregulating for traumatised people. I have known people get stuck at the door needing reassurance and a few minutes in order to regain contact with their adult and more coping selves. Making enough space for ending in a calm state and supporting re-entry into the daily round can be important. Again, how each dyad does the ending varies, and I am often struck by the different ways people chose to leave and how we co-create the process.

Ongoingness is another important aspect of psychotherapy. The weekly rhythm, the familiar transition rituals and the ways in which we interact are soothing and containing, especially for people whose lives are chaotic. They are part of the ground bass of the therapeutic process over which the melody, which is far more changeable will be played. Thinking of my own timetable I realise that one of the gifts of working as a psychotherapist is that it does shape my week into a familiar pattern. But it is also flexible. In seeing people regularly on certain days, each day has a particular feel to it. "Wednesday is Joe's day" and so on. This is my predictable ground bass, along with the other routine tasks I do. Yet there is flexibility enough for the melody to include variations. We like repetition, perhaps because it feels safe. Think of a young child clamouring for us to read a short story, repeat something funny or tickle them again and again. We keep replaying a track of music that appeals to us. Indeed, the appeal of some music is its repetitive phrases. Our bodies enjoy repetitive actions. We are creatures of habit, instinctively drawn to repetition. The flip side is that life also involves change and we need novelty in order to grow. Indeed, without it we can fall into rigidity. In therapy, as Molnos pointed out, the predictable rhythm of recurrent sessions creates the illusion of eternal return (1995, p. 19). It may be soothing, but we know and have to face that it is not eternal. There is the challenge! Each session has a prescribed endpoint and our relationship will end at some point in the future. Both of us know that, either because a time-limit was stipulated from the outset, or we agreed to negotiate how and when to end when it feels right. But we often choose to avoid knowing and hide in the comfortable timelessness of the unconscious where there is "an unpunctuated continuum that transcends all man-made starts and finishes" (Holmes, 1996, p. 160).

What I think is most important about the ongoingness of a therapeutic relationship, is that it gives people an experience of being held in mind. Over time our clients discover that we remember them and think of them between sessions, and this can be a new and necessary experience. To be held in mind supports the development of a coherent, ongoing sense of self. If our clients can internalise the experience it helps them to hold themselves and others in mind. This is especially important for people who struggle with object constancy and seem unable to "take us away" and remember us between sessions as a resource. These are people whose caregivers had no mental space for the infant, perhaps because of being preoccupied with someone or something else, or depressed or dissociative or who hated the child for what she represented. This was Marcie's story. In an earlier publication (Wright, 2009) I explored the connection between her childhood and the intrapsychic territory she entered when unwell. Marcie's mother suffered from severe depression and appears to have been emotionally absent – a "dead third". Marcie's abiding memory was of sitting silently by her mother's side with nothing to do and nothing to play with, just hours of blankness. Marcie's fragmentary childhood memories and attempts to describe what it was like when she had a psychotic episode, conveyed a world of hostile, fearful or blank faces and internally of vacancy, emptiness, a void. This was the intersubjective landscape of her childhood where we often found ourselves. For Marcie, the familiar rhythms and rituals of our relationship over many years were hugely important – the time and day, the journey, the unchanging things in my room and those that, like her, changed in slow, small ways. For instance, when well, Marcie would often remark on the different flowers on the mantelpiece and how the cheese plant had grown. And these shared experiences clearly mattered to Marcie for she mentioned them in the cards she sent for some years after therapy had ended.

As an example of the significance of the reliable ongoingness of therapy, Ryde pointed out that not only have refugees, a group she works with, endured traumatic experiences, but they have been "torn away from the reassuring rhythms of daily life and thrown upon a new rhythm". She explained that in the UK the "rhythms of life are often very different to those of home – no regular call to prayer for instance, and the usual habits of life like the timings of meals and patterns of work are unfamiliar or non-existent" and so they bring no comfort (2017). Moreover, people forced to flee their countries are also leaving behind the future they had mapped out. This "fracture in time", as Ryde evocatively called it, "leaves people in a terrible limbo, unable to establish the benign and predictable pattern of life they would have expected to live"; "outcasts from the rhythms of life that had sustained them in the past". And the melody now being played is often a discordant one – full of intrusions, jarring and triggering events that take people out of the present right back into the horrific past. These triggering events are the "melody" played out over the ground bass of the usual rhythms of each client's life, perhaps no longer the old, familiar homely ones before the trauma, but a slowly emerging new patterning to the day and the week. And as the moving example of a woman who would come and sit in the waiting room at the time of their usual session if Ryde took a break illustrates, for her refugee clients, a weekly therapy session is often the dominant note in the tune.

Managing the time-frame

Sitting down face to face with someone and talking for an hour, whether the 50-minute hour of traditional psychotherapy or, in my own practice, 60 or 90 minutes, is an unfamiliar experience. How often do we just sit with someone and talk, especially about ourselves, when there are no distractions? We are not sitting with a friend over a drink. We are not talking whilst engaged in a shared activity. Nor are we pulled to respond to something suddenly needing our attention. So, no wonder that anyone coming to counselling for the first time feels at sea, unsure what is expected and self-conscious about being the focus for such a long time.[2] In what follows the invitation is to keep questioning what the time-frame and its boundaries mean to us personally and to each person we work with. Who does it benefit? And when might it be problematic?

From the start of our training, we are taught about the importance of the frame and that upholding the boundaries creates safety. I recall how this left me anxious never to arrive early or to delay leaving by a few moments with my earliest therapists, along with concerns that such time infringements, or alternatively turning up late, might be "analysed away". This was reinforced by a supervisor who used to pack his things and leave the room on the dot and whom I felt would disapprove if I talked beyond that point or showed up early. It also puts me in mind of people I have worked with who became terribly anxious if they were delayed and expected me to be angry and tell them off, and of others who seemed somewhat oblivious to the fact that coming early or engaging in conversation after I had called "time" might not be so convenient for me. What stories lie behind the potential judgements on either side? As trainees we are also taught about contracting and agreeing together an overall time-frame. It could be for a brief piece of work or for something open-ended, an agreement which might not fall into place immediately but be decided on after an agreed number of sessions followed by a review. Elton-Wilson talked about choice points in a client's therapeutic journey and named three such points. The first is at assessment, the second during the first review, perhaps after a short holding arrangement or mini-commitment. The third takes the form of a major review and is usually intended to determine whether to end and return to life without therapy or engage in time-expanded work (1996, p. 13). Of course, we don't always have the freedom to make a choice. We may be constrained by the policies of the agency where we work or by the client's own limitations. Life events can also get in the way so that some therapies end abruptly in ways that can be hard for both parties. In my own practice, and I now have the freedom of working entirely in private practice, I make use of a range of different time models because I realise that what suits one person may not work for someone else. I am also aware that initial plans and expectations about the "shape" of the therapy can change over time.

Duration

I shall talk about flexible arrangements later, but first I want to consider frequency and duration. Barring unforeseen events, how long should or can we work for? How do we know when enough is enough? And why can we make rather hasty judgements about adopting less conventional time-structures? The relative merits of brief and long-term therapies have often been debated and currently there is a lot of discussion about how to offer as much as possible to troubled people in the available 6 to 12 sessions that is the norm now in statutory and agency sessions. I don't intend to go into this in detail here. My interest is more in the meanings of the time-frame to all involved. But I want to mention some of the arguments presently circulating. As an advocate of Brief Dynamic Therapy, Molnos challenged what she saw as a resistance to shortening psychoanalysis and outlined a range of objections and prejudices (1995, pp. 9–20). Perhaps the most important of these, and it applies to therapists and clients alike, is our human difficulty with time's finitude. Like other brief dynamic therapists, she pointed out that one value of time-limited therapy is that "the struggle with the passage of time, with real time, is present from the outset" (1995, p. 19). Although Molnos speaks from a psychodynamic perspective, her book is worth reading by practitioners of all orientations.

Another argument against a long-term relationship between client and therapist is that it fosters dependency. I have certainly heard of counsellors being told, "He/she's becoming too dependent on you", and of clients worried that they are doing something wrong if they admit to liking their counsellor. But why is dependency viewed so negatively? Steele and colleagues presented a cogent argument for depathologising dependency in an article which, whilst focussed primarily on therapy with severely traumatised and dissociative clients, makes points applicable to other client groups. To be independent we need the experience of a secure base and "throughout the life-cycle there is tension between dependency and autonomy" (2001, p. 10). The authors argued for adjusting session length and frequency to what works for the client, meaning "what best supports therapeutic progress that improves the patient's daily life and decreases crisis" (p. 27). They also advocated that session length should not be longer than the individual's tolerance for the work, nor shorter, a view that supports what I say later about flexibility. In the last phase of the therapy frequency generally decreases as people start preparing for ending. Whilst working in a way that is responsive to each individual's tolerance, Steele et al. still emphasised a boundaried position – beginning and ending sessions on time and trying to plan and limit the duration of out-of-session contacts.

We tend to discuss duration from the perspective of our core theories, for example, our bias is influenced by whether we focus primarily on past, present or future, and pragmatics – what is possible in the settings in which we work. But my speculation is that our relational experiences and tendencies also lead to a bias. I admit to a personal preference for working long-term, and Adams, who interviewed therapists trained in different modalities, identified that the majority of her respondents could link their early history with the kind of therapist they became and their choice of model. I like Adams' point that we often "professionalise" our history (2014, pp. 77, 91). Our attachment style can also influence our preference. Holmes observed that an insecure therapist who overemphasises intellectual formulations can get pulled into ending too early, while someone with a tendency to overvalue support and affective resonance might allow the therapy to become protracted and end too late (2010, p. 166). Another reason why we might find it hard to settle for "this is enough right now" is a tendency towards perfectionism. We can fall into a trap of striving for the perfect outcome and always doing just that bit more, and especially if this is also the client's script. And this is often followed by beliefs about failure when our ideals cannot be met.

Preferences aside, I believe that with certain clients, such as the survivors of severe trauma and people with very fragile personalities, there is a strong case for long-term work, and we should be prepared to argue for this. It takes time to build sufficient trust and safety for someone to feel able to face the past and tell her story. And it takes time and sensitive pacing to help people develop new ways to self-regulate, to risk doing things their survival brain has taught them to avoid, and to loosen the grip of old, limiting beliefs. If we only have a limited brief our focus needs to be on stabilisation, what is known as Phase One work by trauma therapists (Van der Hart et al., 2006), and teaching our clients a range of strategies for managing overwhelming feelings and helping them to feel more safely embodied. With a wider window of tolerance, managing daily life and coping with distressing memories becomes easier. We can also hope that the client's psychological journey does not end with us. As Elton-Wilson wisely pointed out, the stages towards psychological growth and healing are not necessarily worked through with one therapist (1996, p. 35).

Knowing our bias and where it comes from and working on our attitude to however long we have, helps us to stay reflective and prevent something being acted out. It is a small part of how we deal with the first challenge of existing in time. As Molnos pointed out, "the therapist has to be confident and convinced that it is possible to use the limited time to maximum effect, that good, productive work can be done within the given time limits". She has to convey that "what makes a difference is not the absolute length of time, but what we do with it" (1995, p. 52). I have never forgotten what I learned from Elton-Wilson about the difference between saying apologetically, "I can only offer ten sessions" or "we can just have ten sessions", compared with "we've got the chance to meet ten times. What would you like to get from that?" What sort of body (posture, facial expression, energy, tone of voice) utters the first two statements? What sort of climate does it create? How would you feel as a client if someone was more upbeat and communicated optimism from the start? I also recall the wisdom of another supervisor when needing to engage young people for whom the time was far too much. When working with someone who really didn't want to come – he had been sent by others – the therapist would say, "I know you don't want to be here. But since you've got to, what shall we do that could be useful or interesting?"

As important as the therapist's attitude to the length of the therapy is that of the people we work with. How they feel about what we can offer will be coloured by their hopes and fears, the reason why they are here, and the extent to which this is for them or driven by the wishes of others. It will be influenced by their culture and previous experiences of or knowledge about counselling. Their attachment style is also relevant. From this perspective, someone with an avoidant/deactivating style is likely to deny any feelings about ending and might find a way to end too early. Someone with a preoccupied/hyperactivating style may well protest if the contract offered is short-term – "It's not going to be enough. What's the point of telling you stuff when you'll shove me out in a few weeks' time" – and to keep finding reasons or crises to show why they cannot possibly end. And as Holmes pointed out, there can be a collusive "fit" between the attachment styles of client and therapist and the risk of an unconscious pull towards either premature or overdue endings.

A client's attitude to the length of the therapy may also be influenced by where they are in the life-cycle. For people in the later stages of life there is the knowledge that time is short. Some older people might not consider counselling at all, with the belief that change is not possible now. Meanwhile, with the exception of those who seek help because of traumatic experiences and/or serious mental health difficulties, younger people often find it hard to commit to something weekly and are more likely to engage in something brief. Some dip in and out of therapy when they feel the need and although we may think that they would benefit from a regular commitment, the open-endedness of being able to call "when I'd like to meet again" can be holding. Such an experience echoes the need for adolescents and young adults to be able to go off and explore the world, then return periodically to a "safe haven". They can trust that a parent, or therapist, is there for them when needed. But the rest of the time they are out there "getting their show on the road".

But there is another factor behind the difficulty in making a commitment and that is the wish for the quick fix. Benton described meeting a young adult who declared, "I don't want to have this problem anymore, and I don't want to spend any time on it. Just fix me" (2014, p. 25). Not everyone will be as explicit as this, but certainly this is sometimes the unvoiced hope. Benton set the young person's pressure to produce change in the context of a world in which technological advances have altered our expectations. We expect to be able to make quick connections and solve certain problems with ease. We have become accustomed to quickly getting information, ordering things and contacting others – the latter usually being in very short, abbreviated and one-person ways[3] – and this is at the cost of tolerance and resiliency. Adolescents and "millennials" are probably most challenged in this way because they have grown up in a digital environment. But the desire for the quick fix is by no means restricted to the young. In our Chronos-driven, time-pressured world, as Benton said, goals are increasingly privileged over process. However, as she told her client, emotional work is just that – work – and it is sometimes frustrating, requiring curiosity and the willingness to try new ideas (pp. 26–7). It also demands being willing to return to an incident, reflect on it, experience one's feelings and be curious about our reactions (p. 28). When this taking stock concerns a rift between therapist and client, it not only facilitates linking present reality to the historical past. It provides a new experience of intimacy, and intimacy surely is something outside of time, outside of and yet, paradoxically, a moment of connection in the present will influence moments and expectations in the future. Emotional work cannot be rushed. "The quickness of efficiency must be weighed up against the slowness of experiencing" (p. 25). And to quote the wise words of Edith Eger, a survivor of Auschwitz, "change can be slow to come, disappointingly slow" (2018, p. 337).

Frequency

Coming now to frequency, we could argue that there is a "classical" or traditional way of managing the time-frame and more creative, flexible approaches. The rhythmicity of the first is of weekly 50-minute sessions with occasional pre-nego-tiated breaks, a rhythm that continues until the final session. It has a regular beat like, for instance, a piece by Haydn. There are undoubted merits to this model. It offers containment and safety – we know where we stand, and it challenges the illusion of endless time. There is another classic framework when a client comes for several sessions each week – a common arrangement in the early days of psycho-analysis, although, except for training purposes, it is far less common these days to have a five-days-a-week analysis. But there other valid, and perhaps more client-centred arrangements. For example, family therapists and couples' counsellors often see a family or couple for a few appointments and then, to support them whilst they work together on a problem or task, at intervals – either as the whole family or a subset. In my own work, I offer a number of options. These arrangements are dependent on individual circumstances and the individual's capacity to manage whatever emerges in the process. Having worked with a lot of people who have had to travel long distances or whose work did not permit a weekly commitment I feel comfortable now in saying, we could meet for a longer session (90 or even 120 minutes) every two, three, or four weeks.

In my experience there are pros and cons to sessions spaced at intervals longer than a week. It could be argued that the therapy is less containing, and when I think that someone is too fragile or their life situation too chaotic, then I would be clear that we needed to meet weekly. Indeed, I have sometimes seen a more troubled client for 90 minutes each week or offered twice-weekly appointments as a holding arrangement during a life-crisis. Another disadvantage is that it is not always easy for either of us to hold things, and perhaps each other, in mind. It can make it hard to follow up something significant from the last session because a lot might happen in the interval. However, when I have worked with someone for a while, the key issues and themes become embedded in my thinking. Moreover, a particular way of being together, a relational and temporal idiom, evolves and it is easy to sink back into this however long it is since we last met. Interestingly, someone who is ambivalent about therapy and has an avoidant attachment style may well begin requesting spaced out sessions – always with a solid practical reason for doing so. It is his or her way of regulating the intensity and pace of the process and the degree of intimacy. On the positive side, I believe that flexibility is more responsive to the individual's circumstances and sense of what he or she needs. Longer sessions give more time to go deeper into a process, as well as to come out of it with sufficient time to regulate the client if it has been challenging, and for the integration of emerging insights and transformative experiences. In Chapter 12 I discuss why this is important. I have also known people who, far from disconnecting from the experience, do a lot of work between sessions, digesting, reflecting and integrating, and then bringing this back to our next conversation. We may underestimate the amount of work that goes on between sessions by both of us, and this moves things along.

When working in a time-expanded way, and I would argue that this is the best arrangement for people who have experienced complex trauma and attachment failure, as we start working towards an ending many people opt to gradually space sessions out. This has the advantage of being something in their control, in itself a reparative experience for anyone who has experienced many sudden endings, and it can facilitate the separation process. If we can offer such an arrangement, to be able to say, "the door is open if something comes up and you'd like a few sessions to explore it", is often valued. Some would argue that this deflects from facing what an ending means – the finitude of time. Yes, in some cases. No, in others. The ending process is an important life-stage to go through in therapy and how it is negotiated and worked on is hugely important. But I also believe there is a place for being able to "touch base", to return "home" having left, in the same way that young adults do. When we have worked with someone for a long time this can be even more important because we have by then become a real figure in their lives as well as an available inner object, and sometimes former clients want to let us know how they are doing and what is going on in their lives. The re-contact, whether it takes the shape of a card, email or actual meeting, is not necessarily because of a crisis or inability to manage independence. And in various ways it often marks the passing of time – reminiscing about how things were and saying, "and things are different now".

Bubbles of contact

Some therapists would disagree about adopting a flexible approach to the time-frame, and sometimes for good reasons. The important thing is that we know what we do and why. I suspect that my earlier career as a Dance Movement Therapist working in day centres for people with learning difficulties and autism is one reason why I am comfortable about being flexible and creative about the time-frame. I could not have had a precise timetable. The men and women referred to me might not be there on my day. They might be about to go out on a trip or prefer to stay doing whatever they were engaged in when I went to find them. Some were adept at communicating non-verbally that they did not want dance today or that after ten minutes together that was enough. Equally, some people would suddenly turn up at my door and if I was free I would invite them in. I recall one lady who never seemed to engage in anything. She went in and out of rooms, spitting out fierce "no"s (one of her few words), if others attempted to draw her in. The other service users did not like her. And yet sometimes she smiled and appeared to be enjoying herself. Although Vera was not meant to attend one of my dance therapy groups, sometimes she came in for a short while, and so I spoke of her as a group member to the others. She never joined our circle. However, Vera seemed to like the music and, at the edge of the room, would briefly do her own dance. I would point this out to the group and say, "shall we try Vera's movement now?" A short moment of connecting, then she would be gone.

At the time I would not have used the term "bubbles of contact". But reading Smethurst's fascinating article on working at St-Martin-in-the Fields in a group for refugees and asylum seekers confirmed my sense that brief moments of conversation, or simply being alongside another person, can be therapeutic. Smethurst explained that when they tried to offer more formal counselling sessions to those who came to the group no-one signed up. Instead, they experimented with simply being available to the guests, "loitering with intent", and being quietly aware of anyone who might welcome an approach. They began to have what they called "bubbles of contact – mini-conversations that were therapeutic but unstructured and impromptu". Slowly the relationships between guests and volunteers were enriched (2017, pp. 28–9). Of relevance to what I said earlier about the containment of the book-ends, the St-Martin-in-the Fields International Group always opened with certain rituals. As Smethurst pointed out, these set ways of doing things created what Bion called "containment in space in time" (p. 30).

We have to capitalise on moments of authentic connection when they emerge, even though sometimes they might be short. In the space of a session too, the dyad shifts between moments of more and less connection to self, each other, emotions, or to a core theme. Like Vera and other so-called "challenging" service users; like a baby making and then withdrawing from eye contact with her caregiver, each person regulates the intensity and timing of contact. This is part of the temporal-affective dance of relationships. With someone who is very withdrawn, often because of intense fears about others or about being seen, the "bubble" might last no more than a minute. Even though, ostensibly, we are together for a full hour, for a long time she might only tolerate fleeting moments of being together. A moment when she looks up or smiles or speaks and then, like a frightened animal, she retreats. Her pace needs to be respected. But a brief shared "hello" can be built on.

Responding with structured flexibility to the "fierce urgency of now"[4]

My next question concerns requests for contact outside our usual time-structure, whatever shape that takes. They can come from an "adult" place, considered, reasonable in the context and open to negotiation. But those that challenge us often come from a place of crisis, panic, and fierce urgency. Let me give an example, but not from work. I noticed a familiar mix of feelings – impatience, worry, despondency – as I listened to the message from my elderly father, his voice full of anxiety, words tumbling out incoherently but communicating panic and urgency. He wanted a doctor – right now! He wanted something to relieve his pain. He wanted me to talk to my mother "because she's in a terrible state!" Of course, urgent calls, whether from family or clients never suit our timing. I had just overrun with a client, who like my father was in teleological mode, wanting someone to do something to get rid of her acutely felt emotional pain and despair, and like him spoke rapidly, full of emotion, recalling times as a child when she had indeed really needed timely, emotional support. I had my own immediate wants too at that point. I was hungry. I had hoped for a short walk and note writing before my first afternoon appointment. My hunger was in "right now!" mode.

The call from my father reminded me of messages from clients when in an emotional crisis – "Sue, can you call me ... I'm ....", or an urgent request for therapy – "could you see me this week. I need to see someone quickly". It can't wait! How can we deal with explicit or implicit pulls to offer something outside the time boundary? The doorknob remark? The email or phone message that communicates panic and, because we are human, makes us anxious about the client's safety or sometimes about what this means about us and our credibility or reputation? How can we respond to the "fierce urgency of now" without urgency? And how can we catch a slower drift into unstructured and potentially risky flexibility so that safety is maintained? I think it is inevitable that sometimes, both briefly and over longer periods, we fall into teleological mode, the proto-mentalising position when only action will do (Bateman & Fonagy, 2004), and although I am suggesting ways in which we can be both flexibly responsive *and* boundaried, I don't always get the balance right.

Perhaps most important if we are flexible about time, is to keep questioning our motivation. For example, am I being pulled into the role of omnipotent rescuer because of my own unresolved issues or by a needy, "attach" part of the client? Am I allowing extra time, either at the end of a session or in contacts between sessions or by suggesting meeting with greater frequency, because I'm finding it hard to contain something that feels overwhelming? Or feeling guilty and over-compensating? Or fearful about a client's safety? Or, can I argue a solid case for the looser arrangement? To guard against drifting into increasing boundary stretching and the risk of something being acted out, we need to "structure" the flexibility by negotiating it. If, for example, we keep overrunning, how about saying "it seems important to have longer at the moment to process everything. How would it be if we agreed on 15 minutes more each week?" Or, "for a while, whilst things are so hard, would it feel more holding to meet twice a week"? And regarding phone or email contacts, can we be clear about the parameters and when we would need to charge extra? I can think of a number of people, all with traumatic backgrounds, who felt more contained knowing that they could get in touch between sessions. But I hold in mind the wisdom of trying to keep the work within the session itself.

Trying to find a focus can also guard against drifting into difficult to end conversations and therapies – Freud's term "analysis interminable" comes to mind. In Sensorimotor Psychotherapy this is called framing, a kind of mini-contracting. It provides a map for us to refer to. Near the start of a session or telephone contact the therapist checks, "is this something you'd like to spend time on today/when we next meet? ... Explore in more detail ... Like to focus on now/on Monday?" We might agree to stay with the current subject or to hold that until another day and focus on something currently troubling the client more. If the subject shifts, we can reframe by saying something like, "that sounds important. Do you want to stay with this and come back to ... later, or shall we hold it for a while?" Another way to retain focus is to ask, "what are you seeking in telling me this?" At the end of the session, the "can I just tell you ..." also challenges the book-ends, and there are many reasons for these doorknob communications. If we can empathically acknowledge what has been said, followed by an invitation to come back to it next week, we create a frame.

The temporal contours of the therapeutic relationship

When discussing the non-verbal aspects of the therapeutic relationship, Beebe and Lachmann pointed out that while the verbal system is usually in the foreground, "simultaneously with the exchanges on the verbal level, patient and analyst are continually altering each other's timing, spatial organization, affect and arousal on a moment-to-moment basis. This is the fundamental nature of social behaviour" (Renn, 2012, p. 120). Our bodies, as Jenner said, can become "locked in a synchronised dance, resonating perfectly with the emotional state of the distressed client in front of us" (2016, p. 29). Our muscles contract to produce movement and our central nervous systems are activated in the same patterns as our clients. There will also be corresponding changes in the autonomic system, for example in heart rate and temperature. Indeed, we literally breathe together if we are in tune, and this is because of the firing of mirror neurons in the brain. Stern saw this synchronised dance as part of how client and therapist position themselves as they establish "a body of implicit knowing about how they work together to get somewhere. They are establishing complicated patterns, unique to them, of how to regulate their intersubjective field" (2004, p. 156).

This gets to the essence of what I mean about the unique temporal contours of the therapeutic relationship. It is co-created over time, something unique to each therapist/client dyad, but not something we are necessarily aware of. It takes the form of implicit relational knowing, and crucially it creates and maintains a "couple window of tolerance". There are of course other dimensions than the temporal to these patterns – how we sit and move in relation to each other, the tone of our voices, who leads when, familiar words, phrases and metaphors that act as shortcut references to shared explicit knowledge and so on. But if we stay with the temporal, I want to return to Stern's concept of vitality affects or "feelings-in-motion" mentioned in Chapter 2. Stern argued that the experiences of an infant, including events in the social world, are not sight, sounds, touches and nameable objects, but the more "global qualities of experience" such as shapes, intensities, and temporal patterns (1985, p. 51). He pointed out that the qualities of feeling that arise in encounters with others don't always fit our existing language of discrete affects. "They are better captured by dynamic, kinetic terms", which convey the intensity of sensation as a function of time, "such as surging, fading away, fleeting, explosive, crescendo, decrescendo, bursting, drawn out and so on" (p. 54). They have a felt quality.

Earlier in the book I mentioned Bree and Lucianne. The emotional, embodied and intersubjective experiences of shared time were very different for these two women and emerged during our meetings. Bree's temporal idiom was characterised by speed. Her movements were strong, sudden and direct; her arrival and departure swift. I was often astonished how she could be deeply immersed processing something overwhelming and full of emotion then, when I warned that we had only a short while left, she would quickly sit up, back in adult, tidying her hair and make insightful comments on what had happened or laugh about something in the immediate present. At times our relationship felt less a to-and-fro dyadic dance, mutually entraining to each other's rhythm, and more a case of me being left a few paces behind, trying to catch up rather than attempt in any way to regulate the pace. The image of a parent breathlessly trying to catch a hyperactive child comes to mind. If I think about vitality affects, the dynamic, kinetic terms on Stern's list that fit Bree are explosive, bursting, surging and crescendo.[5]

With Lucianne, our shared temporal dance was much slower. She took time to arrive and time to speak. Her chronic anxiety led to halting, discontinuous movements, to long pauses and a lack of flow in her speech. And to regulate her I needed to speak slowly and softly and wait patiently for her to communicate. Another feature of Lucianne's temporal idiom was the slow rhythmical movements she made when anxious – small, circular movements with her fingers and feet, or light strokes across her cheeks. I often found myself echoing these rhythms in my own body and sometimes it felt as if I was holding a baby and gently rocking her. Returning to Beebe and Lachmann's point, Lucianne altered my timing, and I hers on a moment-to-moment basis, and this micro-timing echoes what an attuned mother does. She "acts as a modulator to the minute-by-minute line of her child's moods" in order to up or down regulate her (Holmes, 1996, p. 53). In Lucianne's case it was the other way around. She learned to look after her mother when she was distressed but froze in fear when she suddenly erupted with rage. Her body tells that story now with a hypervigilant attention to how I and others look or behave and a tendency to freeze. Lucianne's body also tells the story in the rhythmical soothing movements of a little girl, and probably an infant too, who needed to soothe herself.

I believe that the imprints of early patterns coloured Bree and Lucianne's relationship to time and influenced our temporal dance. For instance, I wondered whether the fact that Bree had a mother who, in her words, "couldn't wait to get away" if she sought her out, meant that from the start she learned to rapidly shift state. A very different early temporal pattern lay behind the sense of rush communicated by another woman when she arrived. Rose was always hurrying from one activity to the next and complained of never having time to put her feet up and look at the books that were piling up in her study. In our work we explored how this stemmed from a childhood when she was expected to keep busy and nagged if she was slow or appeared to be doing nothing. But with Rose I did not get pulled into her pace and it was possible to help her slow down by starting sessions with a visualisation or breathing exercise. Despite her initial hurry, Rose was one of a number of people I have worked with who needed me to sit back and allow them time to find their thoughts, and from what I knew of their childhoods a number of them, like Rose, had experienced the trauma of disconfirmation (Bromberg, 2011, p. 57). When they expressed a feeling or need it was snatched away by a parent who intruded his or her own version of their subjectivity. And to deal with this they learned to rapidly shift state.

"Picking up the cues"

There is research to show that the mothers of securely attached infants pick up their babies more rapidly and frequently than the mothers of insecure children. In other words, their responses are timely and attuned and, as Holmes pointed out, the effective therapist does something similar. She "picks up" the cues of her patient and responds appropriately (1996, p. 53). I find this interesting. It is one of many parallels between what goes on between mothers and babies and therapists and clients. But what do we need to do in order to pick up and use those cues to best effect? Most important is to be aware of our own temporal style and the characteristic dynamic qualities, pace, rhythms and timing of our clients so that we can make conscious use of this. Then we can regulate people when they become hyper- or hypo-aroused and help them to stay present through a rhythmic attunement with their bodies. But as Hoppenwasser emphasised, to sense micro-shifts we have to be grounded in the present ourselves, for we often only have a matter of seconds in which to respond. By minutely tracking our bodies and the person with us we can pick up tiny shifts in their arousal level, rhythm, movements or tone of voice. Then we can alter our own pace and voice to calm or to enliven. "By staying in the present we can prevent the past from becoming a turbulent, rushing river that sweeps us away. We can modulate the current, a kinetic energy of feeling states, and slow the movement, which is often too fast for conscious perception" (2018, p. 54).

Much of this occurs intuitively. But in addition to helping someone who is hyper-aroused return to the window of tolerance, I might deliberately slow things down and be more spacious in the following circumstances:

- To help clients focus on themselves in present time and mindfully notice the details of their experience, their pace needs to be slower and their field of attention to narrow down to a particular aspect of experience (such as emotion, sensation or sensory perception). Reducing how much we attend to is inherently regulating. But it is also useful in a somatic experiment, for example asking someone if he would be willing to repeat an action, but this time in slow motion and to really notice the details.

- When working with someone who communicates urgency and time-pressure it can generate relief if we say slowly, "its OK to take your time" or "we've got lots of time". It is not just our words but our pace and stillness that has impact and for somebody who was always expected to hurry up as a child this can be a new and needed experience. It creates a space to be with themselves and discover what they are feeling or needing. They can "find" themselves.

- Slowing the process also supports the integration of something transformative. I shall say more about this in Chapter 12.

- Another application is when inviting someone into a process involving the imagination and a liminal, transitional state. To do so we need to speak more slowly and softly. Sometimes I start with a short breathing exercise. Then I might use a guided visualisation or ask the client to see what images come to mind when they think of the person or situation we are focussing on, or to see herself, often as a child, and the setting of the distressing or traumatic incident[6]. Through enquiring about the sensory details, we engage state-dependent memory.

- Last but not least, deliberately altering our pace is part of self-care. It helps us to regulate ourselves, and when we are in a state of calm alertness this regulates our clients. For instance, deliberately slowing our breathing can help a client to do the same.

To facilitate a return to ordinary consciousness we do the opposite. I inject more energy into my voice and speak faster. Other situations when I deliberately speed up include:

- To enliven someone who is hypo-aroused. This can also bring people into thinking rather than being immersed in emotion.

- To signal that we need to end soon. The art here is not to communicate haste. Perhaps it is better to describe this not so much as speeding up, but speaking with more energy and directness in contrast to the lulling qualities of sustainment and softness when trying to create an atmosphere of calm.

- My pace and energy generally increase when a client is excited about something. If we think in kinetic terms, excitement is communicated with explosive, surging, crescendo-like dynamics. The cry of "wow, that's wonderful!"; the high five and "well done!"; the "look at that!" Attuning to and amplifying the other's pleasure, wonder or pride calls for emphatic words and gestures.

- When communicating something with emphasis and urgency. For instance, I might want to challenge someone's limiting beliefs or sabotaging intentions, or speak on behalf of the child she once was. "I don't believe that about you!" Or, "I realise that I don't want you to do that and that's because I care!" Or, "I want to shout 'stop' and 'leave her alone!' when I think about him coming to attack you".

Underpinning these interventions is self-awareness. We need to know our own temporal style so that we can "get out of our own way". As a guide take a moment to consider the following questions:

- Are you someone who is often in a hurry? A quick thinker? Or do you take time to consider things?
- Is your preference for movements that are sudden, direct and strong? Or lingering, flexible and light?[7]
- And do you quickly home in on something or have an attention that "meanders", taking in a lot of detail and finding links between many ideas?

I have identified several ways in which we can intervene to influence our clients' physiological and emotional state. Yet there is a paradox here. We cannot rhythmically attune to another if we are engaged in thinking and doing. Thus, with Lucianne, I am certainly conscious of the need to regulate her. But I don't set out to mirror her soothing rhythms. That comes from the place of "witness participation" (Hoppenwasser, 2018, p. 54). Hoppenwasser captured this paradox when she said, "If I am empathically engaged, I cannot clearly see the distinction between sameness and difference. But if I step outside the empathy, I lose the rhythm of connection". Ultimately a "microscopic pendulation between sameness/difference, identification/disidentification", or I might add what Hobson described as aloneness/togetherness, is "the rhythm of the therapeutic relationship" (2018, p. 54; 1985, pp. 193–5). When I read this I immediately thought, yes! That captures what I notice when with someone engaged in a deep process, perhaps moving but not necessarily saying anything, as I sit as witness to the expression of intense emotion or to a liminal process. There are moments when I feel deeply with the other – filled with emotion, or spontaneously moving or saying something as if speaking to the person in the imagined past, or seeing images in my mind, perhaps of the client as a child, that child suffering, or of weird scenarios that at one level have no relationship to the known narrative, but which later prove to have meaning or are the key to something transformational.

Let me conclude with an example of how therapist and client can affect each other unconsciously on a moment-by-moment basis. With Bree I was certainly familiar with a rhythm of engaged/disengaged. There were times when I drifted into dreamy sleepiness, unsure if I was catching something that belonged to her, or becoming a parent who switched off because they could not manage being with her, or struggling with my own capacity to manage something unbearable, or even bored because something stale was being replayed again. I think all were true at different points. But what Hoppenwasser described also makes sense. With very traumatised and dissociative clients, the pendulation is natural and important. Take for instance a session when Bree returned to a familiar theme –feeling that she was falling down an endless tunnel and dying when something triggered memories of rejection and alienation, and in touch with the terror that went with that experience. She knew she had to release something stored in her body and, as she often did, quickly shifted into another state when she moved spontaneously – shaking, tensing, her limbs carving space in different ways. On this occasion the terror shifted into rage, a rage we knew from earlier work did not belong to her. Her movements were sudden, strong, vehement, accompanied by loud out-breaths and growls. And spontaneously I began to shake in time with Bree's actions. It felt as if I too needed to release something physically, and intuitively I used my voice as a soundtrack to our shared "dance" – deep guttural sounds, hisses, rhythmical and discordant. The thought came to me that this was like a shamanic process, not something I have ever experienced, yet I believed belonged to the realms of ritual processing.

Then Bree quietened, curling up, breathing deeply and moving very little apart from an occasional small shuddering. I disengaged. My eye was caught by what a spider was doing with a dead fly on the ground. It moved up and down weaving thread between the fly and a point six inches above on the bookshelf. Up and down, up and down. It was absorbing and hypnotic to watch. And after every few turns the spider's threads pulled the fly closer to the wall – an incredible use of spider engineering! No doubt I was soothed by this. But had I attuned to Bree slipping into a more meditative state? Was I experiencing something she might have done as a child, losing herself watching an insect going about its business? Or did she catch the spider rhythm that I now embodied to make use of for herself? I suspect that there was a mutual resonance, a process of co-regulation, that we both needed after such intensity. The healing calm after the storm. Then, when she was ready, Bree sat up and we talked briefly about what had gone on before, in her familiar rush, she got ready to leave. However, as she stood, she laughed recalling a time when I apparently said, "that's a load of nonsense!" We joked about some other shared moments, then she was off. As I tidied the room, I laughed to myself, "shamanism? Mystical events? A load of nonsense?" Or maybe another example of how, when a client enters an altered state and we join her in that liminal space as an attuned participatory witness, something new and transformative emerges.

Notes

1 In therapy with children, the firmness of the boundary can be especially important so that they can communicate through destructive play and at times by ruthless use of the therapist without things going out of control.

2 This strange experience is especially hard for young people, and I often take a lead in naming the oddness of the situation, inviting them to let me know what it feels like and,

if needs be, I am flexible about our timings. For example, some young people cannot manage a full hour and need us to offer something shorter and hence regulating.

3 By abbreviated and one-person what I mean are the forms of communication when two people are not relating in real time and hence responding to the nuances of non-verbal and verbal communication and negotiating and shaping their interaction moment-by-moment.

4 A phrase used by Martin Luther King in a speech in 1963.

5 Suddenness and discontinuity are hallmarks of shock. Shocks and crises announce themselves in explosive terms. Their rhythm is often staccato – recurrent bursts of bad news, horror and panic, like gunfire punctuating the air in a war zone.

6 In Sensorimotor Psychotherapy this is called "accessing the child".

7 The language I am using here comes from Laban Movement Analysis. It is a language used by Dance Movement Psychotherapists.

References

Adams, M. 2014. *The Myth of the Untroubled Therapist*. London: Routledge.

Bateman, A. & Fonagy, P. 2004. *Psychotherapy for Borderline Personality Disorder: Mentalization-based Treatment*. Oxford: Oxford University Press.

Benton, J. 2014. "Success and Failure: Cultural and Psychoanalytic Perspectives" in B. Willock, R. Coleman & L. Bohm (Eds.) *Understanding and Coping with Failure: Psychoanalytic Perspectives* (pp. 25–32). New York: Routledge.

Bion, W. R. 1962. *Learning from Experience*. London: Maresfield Library.

Bromberg, P. 2011. *The Shadow of the Tsunami and the Growth of the Relational Mind*. New York: Routledge.

Davis, M. & Wallbridge, R. 1981. *Boundary and Space: An Introduction to the Work of Donald Winnicott*. Harmondsworth: Penguin.

Eger, E. 2017. *The Choice*. London: Penguin.

Elton-Wilson, J. 1996. *Time-Conscious Psychological Therapy: A Life Stage to Go Through*. London: Routledge.

Haynes, J. 2007. *Who Is It That Can Tell Me Who I Am? The Journal of a Psychotherapist*. Bristol: Cromwell Press.

Hobson, R. 1985. *Forms of Feeling: The Heart of Psychotherapy*. London: Routledge.

Holmes, J. 1996. *Attachment Theory and Psychoanalysis*. Northvale, NJ: Jason Aronson.

Holmes, J. 2010. *Exploring in Security: Towards an Attachment-informed Psychoanalytic Psychotherapy*. London: Routledge.

Hoppenwasser, K. 2018. "Bearing the unbearable: meditations on being in rhythm", *Attachment: New Directions in Psychotherapy and Relational Psychoanalysis*, 12(2), 48–55.

Jenner, L. 2016. "The high price of empathy", *Therapy Today*, 27(5), 28–30.

McNamee, S. & Gergen, K. (Eds.) 1992. *Therapy as Social Construction*. London: Sage.

Mitchell, S. 1993. *Hope and Dread in Psychoanalysis*. New York: Basic Books.

Molnos, A. 1995. *A Question of Time: Essentials of Brief Dynamic Psychotherapy*. London: Karnac.

Renn, P. 2012. *The Silent Past and the Invisible Present*. London: Routledge.

Ryde, J. 2017. "A Fracture in Time". Conference presentation.

Smethurst, P. 2017. "Borders and Boundaries", *Therapy Today*, June 2017, 28–32.

Steele, K., Van der Hart, O. & Nijenhuis, E. 2001. "Dependency in the treatment of complex post traumatic stress disorder and dissociative disorders", *Journal of Trauma and Dissociation*, 2(4), 79–116.

Stern, D. N. 1985. *The Interpersonal World of the Infant*. New York: Basic Books.

Stern, D. N. 2004. *The Present Moment in Psychotherapy and Everyday Life*. New York: W. W. Norton & Co.

Van der Hart, O., Nijenhuis, E. & Steele, K. 2006. *The Haunted Self: Structural Dissociation of the Personality*. New York: W. W. Norton & Co.

White, M. & Epston, D. 1990. *Narrative Means to Therapeutic Ends*. New York: W. W. Norton & Co.

White, M. & Epston, D. 1992. *Experience, Contradiction, Narrative and Imagination*. Adelaide: Dulwich Centre Publications.

Wright, S. 2009. "Becoming three dimensional: A clinical exploration of the links between dissociation, disorganised attachment and mentalization", *Attachment: New Directions in Psychotherapy and Relational Psychoanalysis*, 3, 324–39.

6

TIME-RELATED THEMES AND ISSUES: LIFE-STAGE TRANSITIONS

Time is our way of situating ourselves in relation to the changing of things.
Time is the measure of change: if nothing changes there is no time.

(Rovelli, 2018, p. 57)

Life-transitions and the self

Rovelli argued that, "the entire evolution of science would suggest that the best grammar for thinking about the world is that of change, not of permanence. Not of being, but becoming". And whilst we can think of the world as made up of 'things', in fact it is made up of events. Of happenings. Of processes. Of something that occurs. "Something that does not last, and that undergoes continual transformation, that is not permanent in time" (2018, p. 86). The same could be said about each of us. Not human beings, but "human becomings", constantly changing in micro- and macro-time, whilst preserving the illusion of a more permanent ongoingness. So how do we, as sentient beings, situate ourselves in relation to the changing of things? My proposition is that it is response to change, or a lack of wished for change, that brings many people to psychotherapy. Some people are prompted by life-stage transitions that raise the theme of their relationship to beginnings and endings. These are the change points that we notice most, and which evoke a multitude of feelings, beliefs and concerns. Some people struggle with "wrong time" events, meaning situations not usually associated with their stage in life, or emerge because their lived experience is not in synchrony with the expectations of their particular age group. Our clients speak directly and indirectly about change: wished for changes, feared change, relative change – "this year I'm doing better/worse than last year or someone else", changes that dramatically alter their lives, concerns about change in others. And at times they reflect on how they are affected by the fast pace of change these days or the changes that are occurring in social, political and ecological spheres in today's world. Whatever is figural, underlying what the client is struggling with are often issues concerning identity and meaning and how he or she relates to the three existential challenges of living in time. And because therapists are also beings-in-time affected by change we can have strong countertransference responses to the time-related issues that emerge.

I intend to focus on life stages and transitions in the next two chapters, although I will not go into detail about each life-stage or transitional point. There is already plenty of literature on the subject. Instead, I raise some general points then explore two stages, with an interest in what time-related issues come up for people as they enter these stages. The first is early adulthood; then, in Chapter 7, I turn to the late-life transition and how that links with the first existential challenge of living in time. As you read, I invite you to keep the following questions in mind:

- At different stages of life what time-related themes emerge?
- How do we or our clients respond to life-transitions? What do they mean to us?
- What do we seek or fear when facing a major transition?
- And, returning to the idea of past, present and future selves, where are we most likely to locate the self-concept?

Jung believed that life-stage transitions are periods of crisis leading to potential growth (Stevens, 1990, pp. 62–3) and, if you recall, my seventh proposition about our existence in time, is that our identity inevitably changes as we move through the life-cycle. Our assumptions and beliefs about who we are and our relationship to others can be called into question as we traverse a major transition, and there will generally be judgements, comparisons, and stories about the change. It will also evoke feelings and beliefs, some positive, some negative. Our thoughts about where we are in the life course will be coloured by our individual circumstances, our observations of family members' experiences at later stages, and by our gender. I am not going to cover gendered relationships to time in any depth here. The subject merits a book of its own. Nor do I feel particularly qualified to do so being an "atypical" female in my personal experience, both of women's cyclical time and the major transition periods, childbirth and menopause. However, my own experiences highlight the need to acknowledge diversity. Most important from the remit of this book is to ask, what might how people navigate different stages in the life-cycle tell us about their relationship to time and how they deal with finitude? And what does it reveal concerning social constructs about time?

Our responses to age and life transitions are also coloured by cultural norms and judgements. This is illustrated if we look back in time or to more traditional cultures today. I often refer to Erikson's "Stages of Man" when reflecting on a client's difficulties and where he or she is in the life course.[1] But Erikson was by no means the first to use a life-stage model. They have guided people's thinking for centuries and are all underpinned by the prevailing ideologies of the period. In the Anglo-Saxon period, for instance, man's life was divided into four: childhood, adolescence, prime and old age, echoing the tetradic grouping of the elements, seasons and humours (Stevens, 1990, pp. 68–71). The model was part of the scientific and philosophical emphasis on cycles and the interconnectedness of human and natural phenomenon. During the Middle Ages it was common to think of three stages: youth – childhood being subsumed under this term, maturity and old age (Ariès, 1962). But in later models the earliest phase of life was increasingly subdivided. For instance, Erikson delineated five stages before the age of 20 followed by early adulthood, middle age and old age (Erikson, 1965). By his day, childhood was viewed with far more significance than in pre-modern times when birth rates were high, life expectancy was low and people were generally less attached to their children, and this is one reason why it had now become common to think of discrete periods during childhood. Another dominant feature in the models prevalent in pre-modern and early industrial times is that they were based on the idea of a life-curve characterised by an ascent, a peak, then an inevitable movement downwards until death. They did not recognise the possibility of continual personal growth.

In traditional societies where, as Giddens pointed out, things stayed more or less the same from generation to generation, another difference was that "on the level of the collectivity, the changed identity was clearly staked out" (1991, p. 33). Transitions between one life-stage and another were governed by institutional processes and formalised rites of passage designed to support people through the change process. Characteristically, a rite of passage consists of rituals symbolising a journey of three phases. The first stage marks life as it was. This is followed by a period of abrupt separation from one's community, a liminal phase during which the participants engage in challenging tasks and rituals. The third stage involves a period of re-entry when they are welcomed back into the community and their change of status, for instance from adolescent to adult, is marked and celebrated (Woodcock, 2017). One example concerns the rituals surrounding the birth of a child. All that remains of older traditions in the Western world is, for a minority of families, the ceremony of baptism. Before that, in medieval England the mother would go to church to be "churched" several weeks after delivery. In other cultures she was expected to remain confined to her room for up to a month whilst she and her baby were supported by other women. Underlying this particular separation were beliefs about impurity, as well as expediency. Not to return immediately to her daily round might improve the chances of the baby's survival in periods of high infant immortality. Civic transition rituals were also common in pre-modern Europe. In urban communities, for example, craftsmen progressed from apprentice, to journeyman and then master craftsman through a carefully defined and ceremonialised process. These ceremonies also bound communities together.

We have lost many of the rituals that used to support people as they started a new phase of life and assumed a new identity or status in the family and community, and those that remain are watered down versions, emptied to a large extent of their original meanings. We can only wonder if our ancestors experienced some of the anxiety and conflicting emotions and disruption to the known Self that we hear about in our work today. And if they did, did their rituals contain them? For any major transition in age, role and place demands some form of inner adjustment. "Every ending", argued Salzberger-Wittenberg, "requires us to come to terms with what we have lost and to begin anew. Most beginnings involve having to let go some aspect of life, and/or the views on life, that we held before" (2013, p. 2).

In today's world some transitions are shared with others and occur relatively quickly and at defined ages. For instance, in education we progress from one class to the next with our peers. Others occur over a long period, like the onset of puberty or the menopause, and although we have expectations about when they might begin, there is so much variation that individuals can feel rather alone with their experience. Another way to think about life-transitions is the extent to which we have choice. To a large extent we have far more freedom of choice than our ancestors about if, when and how to engage in a life transition. We can choose whether to marry, have a child, change job, start a degree, or move home. Where we don't have choice, much as we'd like to deny it, are those situations when we are at the mercy of circumstances such as the vagaries of our biological clock, the onset of illness, the death of a relative. In such cases, the transitions are marked by loss and need to be mourned (Salzberger-Wittenberg, 2013, p. 3). They can also evoke feelings and thoughts about earlier endings. There are more benign transitions, for example, moving to new places and settings, which can challenge the individual, especially if the earliest transitions in his or her life were traumatic and not meditated by supportive others – the transition to nursery school for instance, and then from primary to secondary school and school to university. As Salzberger-Wittenberg pointed out, at any of these developmental milestones someone who has apparently been doing well can suddenly struggle or even break down, her thesis being that transitions in later life can evoke the primitive anxieties of the baby ending life in the womb or being weaned. "The dread evoked by even ordinary endings can be understandable if we realise that they stir up fears of the loss of security, of being abandoned, left to die" (p. 12).

Whilst we can consider life-transitions from the point of view of developmental norms, age-related tasks and challenges, or cultural practices and expectations, as psychotherapists our focus will be on what their place in time means for our clients. What hopes and fears does a new beginning evoke? What do they find hard to leave behind? What does it feel like to be a parent? To reach 30, 40 or 50? To retire? And how might the individual's responses be coloured by his earliest experiences of novelty, changes of routine, the loss of things to which he was attached, and how did others respond to his excitement or distress? In addition to being curious whether a client's attachment story might explain why he or she encounters unexpected problems when going through a transitional phase, what if we also considered whether his or her feelings about one of the existential challenges of living in time night also be in the field? As an example, one man told me that his first bout of depression occurred after the birth of his son in the 1950s. "I thought I'd be over the moon", he said. "Instead I was plagued with guilt. I couldn't stop worry about bringing a child into the world when everyone was talking about a nuclear war." Similar concerns have been expressed by people today: "Is it right to have children if we are heading for ecological disaster? Am I being selfish?"

When commenting on stage models like Erikson's, Jacobs used the image of development being like a tower. "It is stable as long as each brick is placed squarely on the one below and the first has a firm foundation." "If not built squarely the tower has internal structural weaknesses and can collapse under stress back to the level of the original fault" (2011, p. 12). Jacob's metaphor is applicable to a number of models. I think for instance of Stern's Emergent, Core, Subjective and Verbal Selves, each building on the last (1985). The tower metaphor captures how no developmental achievement is a once and for all, "I've got it" capacity. As Jacobs said, we don't just negotiate the core issues of a stage and move on. We can keep encountering them and so there is an artificiality in demarcating issues and confining them to certain ages. For this reason, Jacobs thinks it is more useful to think of developmental themes rather than stages. "Aspects of all of Erikson's stages can be present in one stage" (pp. 15, 20). We can slip in and out of any of Stern's selves according to circumstances, for they are still implicit in the present self, although we may not be aware of them. Likewise, most of the time we might function at the level of Klein's depressive position and, to use a different language, in most situations be able to mentalise. But if tired, hungry, in pain or in some way overwhelmed, we can slip into a paranoid-schizoid state with recourse to splitting and projection and temporarily, mentalising goes offline. Expanding Jacobs' metaphor, let's imagine that over the centuries successive builders added buttresses and joists to prevent the tower falling. These are the protective strategies and relational patterns that we creatively evolved to keep us safe and get our attachment needs met, adding new strategies at different ages to meet the challenges of that time. In the present, under stress, we can go back to the scaffolding of an earlier period. In reality then we don't live in Chronos time, but in our own idiosyncratic Kairos-based experience. Our lived experience is progressive, regressive and recursive. It does not flow simply along the river of time.

Waddell made the important point that "the development of personality is not in any simple way bound to chronology" (1998, p. 198). She also argued that when thinking about maturity "it makes more sense to think in terms of states of mind and not stages of development" (p. 175). This fits with what I said about the dynamic nature of the Self in Chapter 2. It is an aspect of our "normal multi-plicity", our fluidity. A wonderful poem' ostensibly written by an old lady called Kate in which she listed her past selves and their passions from a small child onwards' captures beautifully what I mean (McCormack, 1972). It also captures the tasks and challenges of different ages. Kate's poem was a protest to her nurses who she imagined saw her as a "crabbit old women". She wanted them to see *her*, inside still "a small child of ten with a father and mother"; a young girl of 16 dreaming of a lover; a bride; a 25-year-old with children of her own, and onwards to the time of being a grandmother, a widow facing dark days and then an old woman in touch with nature being cruel with "her jest to make old age look like a fool".

Whether we slip into a more infantile or adolescent or mature, adult self – the child of ten, the bride, the 50-year-old grandmother – these states of mind and, importantly, of body, "constantly shift and oscillate in relation to one another, whatever the age under discussion" (Waddell, 1998, p. 176). And at the threshold from one stage of life into another earlier states of self are likely to emerge.

Facing adulthood

I know from professional and personal experiences how easy it is to shift between adult and younger states of mind, but what is an "adult self"? In Waddell's view "the difference between maturity and immaturity hinges not on the fact of chronological years but on a person's capacity to bear intense emotional states" and to engage with and learn from emotional experience (1998, p. 197). And the foundations for this lie in early childhood when we need others to contain and reflect on such states before we internalise the capacity for ourselves. The task of "growing up" is to accommodate and integrate earlier states, Waddell added, not to get rid of them, and to mourn what has been lost. If we can do this as we move through life, then in the last stage of life it will be easier to find integrity rather than slipping into bitterness and despair. Yet some people, perhaps because of attachment failures and traumatic experiences – the basic faults in their 'tower', find it hard to reflect on their experiences and manage difficult feelings. They try to "avoid or deny the hard bits and clutch onto the right to be happy" (p. 197). When encountering the later life transition and encountering the losses and traumas of older age such people can find themselves troubled by unresolved issues from earlier transition points, such as that from childhood to adolescence or adolescence to adulthood, and may "have recourse to earlier patterns of functioning, ones mobilised in the service of avoiding pain" (Waddell, 1998, pp. 199–200; King, 1980, p. 155).

At different ages what fantasies and expectations do we have about the stages yet to come? For a child, for instance, being "grown up", a father, "old" will have different meanings to those of someone twice or thrice his age. When he was about four, I recall my brother saying that you are not a "proper" adult until you are 50. What could be read into that? And in one of her memoirs Diana Athill described her reluctance to grow up. She related how one day at the age of 10 it dawned on her that in three years she would be 13 and she felt appalled. "To be in my teens, I saw suddenly, would be to leave childhood behind, to be in a world where impossible things could happen". She imagined a time when she could no longer return to the family house as if it were her home; a time when her father's admonition that one day she'd have to earn a living would be something she would have to do. And this frightened her (Athill, 2008, p. 173). As she got closer to the transition point however, her views were very different. Athill had no idea what she wanted to do as a career – and perhaps there is a Peter Pan in all of us who does not want to face the serious aspects of growing up. But she eagerly looked forward to romantic relationships, sex and getting married, and thoughts about both preoccupied her late teens.

The young adult in time

Once someone has made the transition into adulthood what is his or her relationship to time? We could make some generalisations, for instance:

- Young adults are more likely to locate their self-concept in the future.
- Until they have family responsibilities and a solid career, they are likely to organise their time in unstructured ways. This could, for example, be said of someone at university.
- They may not worry much about time. The future can seem infinite. Wrong paths might be taken. Yet there is still a lot of time to try other ones.
- For many young people these days, there will be a period in Higher Education, which for some entails leaving home. To some extent we could consider university as "an event in parentheses" with clearly defined book-ends; or like the second stage in a rite of passage, a separation from the community to engage in "challenging" tasks with peers. It is a time to experiment with one's identity; to move between more adult roles and responsibilities and more adolescent and dependent states of being. It is a period that straddles the fourth and fifth of Erikson's life stages in which the individual grapples between identity versus role confusion and intimacy versus isolation.

However, we will see younger adults in therapy whose relationship to time differs markedly from this hypothesised norm. Sometimes this is because their experiences are out of synch with their peers, sometimes because of wrong time events. With the caveat that at other stages of life people can experience wrong time events and feel out of synch, I want to describe four groups whose anticipated future gets blocked.

Blocked futures

Increasing numbers of young adults become out of synch because they cannot get a job and so it is impossible to envisage acquiring a house of their own. Indeed, even with a relatively good job, many people are still living with their parents into their 30s because they cannot afford to get a foot on the housing ladder. For those who see all their school friends in stable jobs and settling down it can be demoralising. If I stay with the metaphor of a rite of passage, for someone who has embarked on a degree or some form of training and is unable to find a job or a home of his own, the third phase is blocked. Rather than re-entering the community with a different status it is all too easy to slip back into adolescent ways of being. Meanwhile, the unemployed young adult becomes trapped in limbo, an indefinite waiting time, often filled by playing computer games or engaging in substance abuse in the pursuit of what Greenfield described as sensory-laden raw feelings, mind-numbing rather than mind-enhancing. The boundaries between night and day can easily blur, for they have no reason to get rise early and they may fall into a pattern of staying up into the early hours. Their lives lack meaning. Another person whose experience of time is out of synch with her peers is the woman who is struggling to conceive. Anyone in this category will be acutely aware of the passage of time, highly conscious of the monthly cycle, painfully aware of anniversaries of losses, or a birthday that should have happened, and of time passing by, whilst others more fortunate celebrate their children's developmental achievements.

The third group takes us back to a theme introduced in Chapter 2 and which I will say more about in Chapter 11, that chronic illness and disability can also have a radical effect on people's temporal phenomenology. When it strikes people in their 20s and 30s, before they have had a chance to do many of the things they and their families had dreamed of, what impact does this have? Alice was a young woman who was diagnosed with ME, shortly after we first met. She constantly ruminated about her pre-illness self and the plans she had then for her future. She was already moving forwards in her chosen career when ME struck. When she had enough energy, she filled the present with activity, only to be left exhausted and then needing to go to bed. "All my friends go out in the evenings. They do things at the weekend. I keep saying no when they invite me out." Alice's social world shrank. "I feel old", she said, "old before my time". And understandably she was angry. In Lew's case, his difficulties were caused by living with OCD, and his benchmark was his twin. Jim was in his fifth year of medical school and had a plan mapped out to eventually become a consultant. He and his girlfriend were engaged and looking for a house. Lew's compulsions and phobias devoured his time. Anxiety caused him to leave university after only a term, and relationships proved impossible. Lew felt a failure, intensified by beliefs that he should be doing as well as Jim and that it was shameful to be on benefits.

Young refugees also experience a sudden rupture in their sense of an ongoing past-present-future self. Not only have they lost their home, family members and country, but they face the dilemma of moving into early adulthood deprived of former expectations of what their adult lives would become and of what they had worked towards in school and college (Salter, 2017, p. 152). There are other traumas too that shatter the plans and dreams of someone entering adulthood and colour the future in many ways – sexual assault, being in a coercive relationship, experiences whilst serving in the armed forces or an NGO in a war-torn area. And there are "wrong time events".

Wrong time events

A wrong time event is one that takes people out of the expected developmental order, that step-by-step shifting of one's identity and priorities described in Kate's poem: the death of a parent, for instance, when you are a child or teenager, or the loss of a child when you are still young. For the former, it shatters the secure sense of being protected by caring parents and disturbs the ground bass rhythms of their lives. And even when the child is an adult, if both parents die relatively young, it takes away the buffer of a generation between oneself and death. For the latter, it shatters the visions they had of the future with children growing into adulthood and then having their own children. As Rolls said, "death creates a fracture in time – a rent in the fabric of existence" (2010, p. 332). Another wrong time event is when young people are catapulted into being self-reliant and taking an adult role prematurely – young carers, parentified children, an abused child who is pulled into precocious sexuality, or a child soldier. Young refugees too often find themselves in a part teacher, part parent role. Because they acquire English faster than their parents they become translators, often having to decide how much of what is appropriate to share. As Briggs said, in traumatic and highly stressful circumstances it may not even be safe to have an adolescence, meaning being able to experiment with one's identity and ways of relating (1999, p. 31). Nor, for those who have experienced sexual abuse, is it possible to gradually explore one's sexual identity in an organic way. Then later, on starting an intimate relationship or becoming a parent can evoke incredible anxieties. I will say more about the pervasive impact of early traumas in Chapter 9. When someone is expected to take on adult responsibilities long before they should, later in life they sometimes react by refusing to be grown up. I think of a mother who turned to partying and became preoccupied with clothes and how she looked in a vain attempt to be the teenager she never was. She did not realise that she was recreating history for her daughter who had to become the parent – looking after young siblings and trying to care for her mother when she had a hangover.

In all four groups, what impact does this have on the individual's sense of self? No longer anchored by the role of student, how does the unemployed person define himself? For someone with infertility problems, what does this mean in terms of being a woman or a man? Is the experience of Alice and Lew, in repeatedly comparing themselves to others and believing themselves to be failures common? And for the refugee, no longer able to settle into a career but instead take on the role of "man of the family" if his father has been killed, or if he has fled leaving a wife and young child behind, what then happens to his self-esteem? Severed from all the familiar aspects of his life, who is he now? Salter said that in her work with young refugees she often hears the words, "I have lost myself", and argued that the part of self they feel they have lost "may be their close family and the internal and external coherence provided by that relationship" (2017, p. 297). Not only can certain life events interrupt our sense of ongoingness in time. They create a diminished, hated Self

Family and communal expectations

I have mentioned some of the issues for young people as they enter the adult world, but it is important to point out that it is a significant transition point for everyone in the family when a young person leaves home and demands significant psychological adjustments on all sides. For instance, marriage and other forms of commitment to a forever relationship often entail a host of conflicting wishes, dreams, fears and losses for the young couple. But parents can experience equally conflicting feelings: positive ones, perhaps worries and also the awareness of loss. As Salzberger-Wittenberg said, "although no umbilical cord has to be cut as it was at birth it may feel to the parent just like that" (2016, p. 99). If parent and child have been very close, she stressed that the loss will be profound and will need to be mourned. I recall how my own marriage affected my father. It was something that I was surprised by and had not anticipated because by that stage I was not really living at home. Yes, I had been going back during university vacations and although these "coming home" periods were much shorter now that I was a postgraduate, I did not have my own permanent home at that stage. I realise in retrospect that in his mind I had not yet finally left home and I don't know what visions he had for my future. He was certainly very involved in the plans for my wedding. But I suspect that one cause of his depression the following year, whilst it was never named, was that he had not yet found a way to come to terms with "losing his daughter". For other parents, observing their now adult sons and daughters going to university, or on the first step of a career as a lawyer or doctor or teacher, can evoke unresolved issues from their own adolescent–adult transition and stimulate envy, grief, regrets or fond memories. If their child is not following the path they dreamed for him or her, like Alice, Lew, or a young unemployed person, it can lead to frustration and anger, causing rifts between the generations that may never heal.

Holding in mind the family "others" in the background who are also being impacted when a client is going through any life transition is important. It is also important to be aware of communal "others" and cultural expectations. As a colleague pointed out to me, our educational norm is that after 'A' levels comes university or college. It does not allow for a more organic process which suits the maturational process of the individual. Someone who drifts in his 20s or falls into addiction or crime, often returns to education later in life and does extremely well. Pye, who worked as a university counsellor, argued that such "returners" have complex reasons for doing so, some pragmatic, but others unconscious. "Every return", he argued, "has its own story to tell about time". "Each returner is haunted by a sense of lost time, or by an unconscious wish to go back in time and start again", and he observed how issues concerning lost or stolen chances often surface when students experiences difficulties (2017, and personal communication).

Another individual whose adolescent to adult transition can be overshadowed by communal expectations is the overseas student, sent abroad to university with the expectation that he or she will return home to work in the family business. As true of the "millennial" needing to return to live with his parents, for these "returners" it can represent a reversal of the step-by-step developmental order pursued by university friends. As another colleague in the university sector commented, some overseas students, persuaded to take subjects that don't interest them and, like the refugee, cut off from the familiar rhythms of their former life and the peers who could have accompanied them on this rite of passage, speak of feeling adrift and of losing themselves. Some thrive. But there is a risk that some fall behind and become increasingly isolated. Salzberger-Wittenberg pointed out that even for the more secure, mature student the challenges of this transition period are significant. She advocated bearing in mind not only the loss of the familiar external world, but the disturbance to the individual's inner world because of encountering a wealth of knowledge, new ideas, and some very different people. "Taking on board new ideas, whilst perhaps exciting, changes the picture we have of the world, both as it was in the past, and as it is in the present; it may feel as if one's world is turned upside down" (2013, p. 81). There are similarities here with the process of counselling and psychotherapy which also involves encountering new ideas. But this time there is a supportive other alongside to help make sense of the disturbance to the inner world.

Note

1 Again, with prevailing ideologies in mind, a critique of Erikson is that his model fails to consider gender variations.

References

Ariès, P. 1962. *Centuries of Childhood*. London: Penguin.

Athill, D. 2008. *Somewhere Towards the End*. London: Granta.

Briggs, S. 1999. "How Does it Work Here? Do We Just Talk? Therapeutic Work with Young People Who Have Been Sexually Abused" in R. Anderson & A. Dartington (Eds.) *Facing it Out: Clinical Perspectives on Adolescent Disturbance* (pp. 23–36). London: Duckworth.

Erikson, E. 1965. *Childhood and Society*. Harmondsworth: Penguin Books (1st edition, 1950. New York: W. W. Norton & Co.).

Giddens, A. 1991. *Modernity and Self-identity: Self and Society in the Late Modern Age*. Cambridge: Polity Press.

Jacobs, M. 2011. *The Presenting Past*. London: Oxford University Press. (1st edition, 1985. Milton Keynes: Open University Press).

King, P. 1980. "The life cycle as indicated by the nature of the transference in the psychoanalysis of the middle-aged and elderly", *International Journal of Psychoanalysis*, 61, 153–60.

McCormack, P. 1972. "Kate". *Nursing Mirror*. December 1972.

Pye, J. 2017. "Full Circle: 'We had the experience but missed the meaning'". Conference presentation.

Rolls, L. 2010. "Narrating time: Minimising the disruption and discontinuities of children's experience of death", *Illness, Crisis and Loss*, 184, 323–39.

Rovelli, C. 2018. *The Order of Time*. London: Allen Lane.

Salzberger-Wittenberg, I. 2013. *Experiencing Beginnings and Endings*. London: Karnac.

Salter, A. "Therapy with Separated Young People" and "Trauma, Attachment and Development" in J. Boyles (Ed.) 2017. *Psychological Therapies for Survivors of Torture* (pp. 135–55; 288–306). Monmouth: PCCS Books.

Stern, D. N. 1985. *The Interpersonal World of the Infant.* New York: Basic Books.

Stevens, A. 1990. *On Jung.* Harmondsworth: Penguin.

Waddell, M. 1998. *Inside Lives: Psychoanalysis and the Growth of the Personality.* London: Duckworth.

Woodcock, J. 2017. *"Living with someone else's trauma: extreme events, time, liminality and deep subjectivity".* Conference presentation.

7

FACING THE LATE LIFE TRANSITION AND THE FIRST CHALLENGE OF LIVING IN TIME

I could introduce myself properly, but it's not really necessary. You will know me well enough, and soon enough … It suffices to say that at some point in time, I will be standing over you as genially as possible. Your soul will be in my arms …

I will carry you gently away.

(Zusak, 2005, p. 14)

Our collective fears of dying and death

I want to turn now from beginnings to endings and the transition into what Erikson (1965) described as the stage of integrity versus despair. Of all the life-stages, the last merits particular attention. It is the stage when the challenge of existing in finite time can no longer be ignored. We have to acknowledge that lurking figure, enigmatically personified by Marcus Zusak, and face not knowing when he will appear, nor how gently he will carry us away. This is also a stage in life when for other reasons too, people's relationship to time can be markedly different than in earlier phases. Wherever we are personally in the life-course, holding this existential challenge in mind can enhance our understanding of the concerns of those who seek counselling in their later years and also of clients of all ages who might be dealing with elderly relatives or grappling, prematurely, with fears about their own ageing and mortality. And even if we don't work with people of advanced years there are things to be learned from studying their temporal phenomenology that are applicable to other clients. For instance, people who are much younger with terminal conditions or chronic illness often experience similar time-related issues.

What beliefs, fears and concerns arise when we think of entering our last decades? As I said earlier, our thoughts and feelings about where we are in the life-course will be influenced by our individual circumstances and our observations of the experiences of others. Our age will inevitably colour how we view old age and how older people describe themselves will be different from the language used by a child or someone in his early 20s. To children grandparents are "old", yet they could still be in their 40s. Meanwhile, in her last book, written as she approached 100, Athill defined the very old as over 95, and when writing about her decision to move to an "old people's home" she mentioned her initial alarm at "so much oldness" around her (2015, p. 111). The diversity of responses to imagining ourselves at what Athill described as "somewhere near the end" (2008), is also linked with emotional expectancy. This is "based on family history and experience, of particular kinds of losses that will come with ageing. Going bald or grey, being more prone to backache, becoming arthritic, developing cancer, heart problems" and so on. In the same way that we think death happens to others, we imagine we will sail through it. However, "any change that goes beyond what is realistically expected and emotionally prepared for attacks our central belief in ourselves as autonomous beings" (Sinason, 1992, p. 89). It can also be based on our experiences, either personally or professionally, of caring for or visiting older people no longer able to lead independent lives.[1]

Of course we like to imagine that old age is something that happens to others, that our time is endless and, as Atul Gawande pointed out, "we rarely pay more than glancing attention to how we will live when we need help until it's too late to do much about it" (2014, p. 55). Is this from narcissistic vanity or fear? But what is it that we fear when we think of ageing? And how do we defend against our fears? One might assume that if you asked someone they would say dying, and this could be either a fear of the process of dying or of not existing. But Michael Stern argued that "death is certainly a concern, but way before that there is a fear of uselessness and irrelevance, being unneeded, a burden rather than an asset, being obsolete" (2014, p. 155). The Beatles' well-known lyric: "Will you still need me, will you still feed me when I'm 64?" captures two concerns: will others value me as I get older, and if I need support, will people be there? If we think from an attachment perspective, young children quickly pick up that parents seem to like them best when they are good, helpful and being whatever the grown-ups need and want them to be. It also fits with social mentalities thinking (Gilbert, 2005). We want to feel that we have significance; that we fit in with and can be useful to our family, social group or tribe. Both are fundamental to our survival as social animals. There is also an existential aspect. As Shabad pointed out, we do all we can to hide the overwhelming smallness, fragility and insignificance of our individual lives in the face of the majesty of the universe. We cover up our insignificance with the "masks of narcissism" and use other people's meanings to lend ourselves a sense of significance (2001, p. 115).[2] However, losses, disillusionments and reminders of our mortality due to illness and ageing, all threaten the mask and rob us of a steadying sense of meaning and purpose. Being "made redundant", whether this be to lose one's job or place in the local cricket team as younger players come to the fore, or no longer be taken seriously by one's children can hit hard. Witness how many people, whatever their age, become depressed after being made redundant, and for older people, demoralisation quickly slips in when they consider the obstacles to finding another job at their age. If having a status and being the "bread winner" has contributed to someone's sense of worth, then the loss of these roles can erode confidence and lead to demoralisation, emptiness, and withdrawal.[3]

Stern referred to obsolescence as a slow death, gradually draining life's energy (2014, p. 155). Even when someone has chosen to retire, suddenly feeling useless, irrelevant and full of contradictory emotions can take people to the state of despair which Erikson spoke of and which Waddell described as "shallowing out" (1998, pp. 199–200). Statistics confirm how loss of role, purpose and self-esteem contribute to depression and other forms of ill health. But is this a modern phenomenon? Would our forebears have fallen into despair in the last years of their lives? Stern argued that the fear of obsolescence is part and parcel of our current consumer culture which touts the benefits of the new and looks down on anything out of date. Marketing is geared towards convincing us we need new and improved versions of everything from mobile phones to breakfast cereals. We throw away things that are still perfectly functional. Stern also pointed out that "as individuals live longer, the struggle to remain up to date starts earlier and earlier within one's expected life span" (2014, p. 155).[4] From a very different perspective, Allan Chinen, a Jungian and author of a fascinating book on fairy tales in which "elders" are the heroes, also observed how in today's society "most ideals of human life revolve around images of youth – strength and beauty, for instance", and he argued that "without any vision of what succeeds youth and its heroic paradigm, the second half of life seems frightful, a time only of deterioration" (1994, p. 4). Simone de Beauvoir wrote: "in a society centred around youth, the older individual is caught between the spectre of decline and the dream of eternal youth. Despair is usually the victor" (1994, p. 3). Or is it? The overriding message in Chinen's analysis of elder tales is that we have to negotiate certain psychological tasks in the later stages of life, and these are not about growing up but growing psychologically and spiritually. As a group the stories symbolise these developmental tasks and offer a vision of what life can become in the middle and later years. They are concerned with the psychology of maturity – of wisdom, self-knowledge, and transcendence. Erikson and Jung both emphasised this vision and in calling the last stage of life "late maturity" Jung challenges us all to reconsider the myth of inevitable decline exemplified in life-curve models.

Changing perspectives on the elderly

Attitudes to old age have changed considerably over time, from periods when the elderly were for the most part respected and involved in many aspects of family and communal life, to a situation today when many do feel irrelevant and live isolated and lonely lives. How can we explain this? Cozolino argued that "social status is all about adaptation to particular ecosystems" and the leaders in any group, whether animal or human, is determined by "the value of that individual to the survival of the group in a particular environment". For instance, in the case of elephants the alpha is most likely to be the oldest female whose "trump card" is an accumulated knowledge of the locations of water holes and the ins and outs of childrearing. In a troop of gorillas, it will be the largest male, the one best equipped to protect the group from attack. "The successful group is the one with the most effective leadership matched to the survival challenges, be it strength, cunning or forethought" (2016, p. 141).

In pre-modern societies the elderly had "scarcity" value and what anthropologists term "ritual strength" (Pelling & Smith, 1991, p. 3). In predominantly oral traditions culture was passed on through stories and song and it was the role of older men and women to act as teachers, healers and the ones who carried and transmitted the wisdom and history of the community. Older people were also a crucial source of skills knowledge. Those involved in agriculture knew from experience and a trained eye how crops were doing and the best times to carry out certain tasks. Craftsmen passed down their skills through taking apprentices and to their own children. Moreover, and very different to Western society today, elderly people of both sexes were engaged in many aspects of economic life. They worked in the fields and in many craft and trade activities. Only in crafts demanding considerable physical strength would older, frailer people be unable to contribute. Another reason why older people were revered is that they were usually the ones who owned the land, and in towns, the equipment required for a diversity of trades from tanning to weaving, metal work to carpentry and baking to brewing as well as all the things needed to run an inn or alehouse.

By the eighteenth century, attitudes to the elderly were mixed. For instance, the influential position of older people in political and juridical affairs was revered whilst their allegedly scurrilous and ridiculous behaviours were condemned. From the mid-eighteenth century an increasingly negative view prevailed which stressed the degenerative aspects of ageing and failed to appreciate the possibility of ongoing personal development. As one writer commented, "old age is not the age of advancement, of expectation, but that of loss and merely managing to survive" (Von Kondratowitz, 1991, p. 143). Another eighteenth century trend was to distinguish between mature age, usually between 45/50 and 65/70, and beyond that *decrepitae aetas*. This emphasis was partly due to beliefs in the parallelism of physical and mental decline which were only challenged at the beginning of the twentieth century. The concept of *marasmus,* a wasting away, or *marasmus senilis*, the inevitable enfeeblement of advanced years, coloured medical beliefs and practices and the language of decrepitude was ubiquitous (pp. 136–49). It took advances in research in anatomy and forensic medicine from the late-nineteenth century to challenge these wisdoms. People began to distinguish between the effects of illness and of old age. Even more important was the development of the concept of specific illnesses of old age, now a medical discipline in its own right.[5] Despite the changes which came about as biological and medical concepts advanced, a preoccupation with the idea of the final degeneration of the human body dominated thinking and practice for a long time and this impeded treatments with rehabilitation in mind. Moreover, popular opinion lagged behind that of the medical fraternity (pp. 138, 153, 159, 160).

Another cultural trend lies behind the erosion of respect for older citizens. It is part of detraditionalisation, a shift from valuing tradition, the past being seen as a resource and anchor, to privileging innovation and the future. We take linear time and with it the notion of constant change for granted. But until the late-seventeenth century the emphasis was on cycles and continuity. The past was revered (Thomas, 1978, pp. 505–7).[6] Anyone wanting to stress their status would emphasise a noble lineage and anything innovative had to be disguised as a return to the past. As Thomas said, whilst "all societies seek links with their own past", this marked a world in which the fact of change was essentially unrecognised, and from a therapist's perspective I wonder, essentially feared? (p. 507). How different from today when we have clear views about what is fashionable or out of date; where so much is targeted at younger audiences and where originality is feted. It is as if the fears these days are the other way around.

The fear of ageing

Jung thought in terms of a later life crisis as we enter into the stage he called "late maturity" (Stevens, 1990, pp. 62–3). But I think we should consider two transition points in later life: the first from middle age to "late maturity", and the second into a stage not visited by all in which the frail elderly can no longer cope living alone. We could call it the stage of loss and support. When considering Jung's context, I doubt whether he would have encountered many people in the latter stage. During his lifetime life expectancy was shorter than today, his father died at 54 and both grandfathers in their early 70s, and although Jung suffered two heart attacks and ongoing tachycardia he led a highly productive life until his death at 85, highlighting that to be of advanced age does not inevitably entail mental and physical decline. I know of some octogenarians and nonagenarians who lead amazingly active lives and interestingly some of them have been heard to describe people younger than themselves as "old".

What would Jung have said about the stage of loss and support and how we might transcend it? I would argue that it is not just that we fear becoming redundant. We try hard not to think about becoming "decrepit" because we fear losing control over our bodies and returning to a more infantile state, completely dependent on others, stripped of dignity and privacy, someone people won't really want to be with. We also fear losing our minds and with this the anchoring of our memories and the capacity to think and communicate. A poem written by a woman in her late 90s highlights how fundamental memory is to our sense of self and our sense of past, present and future. Implicit in the last words, I feel, is an anguished "no identity! No me!" and the fear that goes with such a loss of one's ongoing self.

> I am afraid, afraid my memories will leave me,
> As he did – alone despite givers.
> But this aloneness is malignant,
> It steals silently into one's mind,

Steathily into all crevices. Without memory
I have no past, no present. No future.

(Settlage, 1996, p. 552)

In such needing-care states once again we may be acutely sensitive to whether we matter or not to others. One 81-year-old complained that she felt increasingly at the mercy of others who "assumed a right to intrude upon her most personal moments and functions without showing the respect of even the smallest recipro-city in their dealings with her". Her experience was of "no-give-and-take to pro-vide evidence that she mattered, that she, as an individual existed". To deal with this she had become increasingly demanding, angrily pushing carers away and projecting her feelings of being unwanted, neglected and distained in order to elicit a response and gain some sense of power. As she explained, any response "pre-vented her from giving up, just rolling over and dying" (Long, 2007, p. 243).

Another reason why we dread the thought of going into some form of care is that we fear the loss of the activities and roles that contribute to our sense of self and give our lives meaning. As one woman told Gawande, what she missed most now that she lived in a home were "her friendships, privacy and a purpose to her days". "I want to be helpful, play a role" (2014, p. 75). Nursing homes are what Goffman described as "total institutions" which are characterised by the fact that all aspects of life are carried out in the same place and in the company of others who are all treated alike. Moreover, "all phases of the day's activities are tightly sched-uled, with one activity leading at a prearranged time into the next" (p. 75). At home, Gawande pointed out, *you* decide how you spend your time, share your space, and manage your possessions (p. 89). If we control our time and can shape our own story life retains its meaning. As soon as others become the guardians of our clock, and especially if the transition into care is sudden, time becomes a confusing place. Its boundaries start to blur. I have often heard elderly people say, "I've no idea what day it is". Without the familiar "occasions" that used to pattern the week, the familiar warp and weft of life, we become disconnected from our natural rhythms and the things that define us. One day becomes like another and we can drop out of the continuity of life. Another poem written by the non-agenarian speaks of the strangeness of time when we are "somewhere near the end", the very shortened horizon, the speeding up of time and its slowing down when little new happens from one day to the next.

Myself shrinks to a continuum,
A thin calendar of days,
Physical mobility becomes constricted and relationships
And activities are curtailed.
The elasticity of time!
Sometimes an hour strikes a minute,
Sometimes an era.

(Settlage, 1996, p. 552)

At this stage in life, do we slip into despair and give up, or reach a position of integrity? Erikson's definition of integrity being "the acceptance of one's own and only life-cycle as something that had to be". It implies an emotional integration, something we know many of our clients struggle with whatever their age, and the capacities for renunciation and wisdom. "Despair" meanwhile, "expresses the feeling that time is now short, too short for the attempt to start another life and to try out alternate roads to integrity" (1965, p. 260). Diana Athill is someone who in my view exemplified Eriksonian integrity and illustrated that it is possible to appreciate and enjoy later life despite the losses and challenges it brings. In her 89th year she wrote:

> It is obvious that life works in terms of species rather than of individuals. The individual just had to be born, to develop to the point at which it can procreate and then to fall away into death to make way for its successors, and humans are no exception whatever they may fancy. We have, however contrived to extend our falling away so much that it is often longer than our development, so that what goes on in it and how to manage it is worth considering.
>
> *(Athill, 2008, p. 10)*

It is indeed worth considering, and I think Waddell would agree given her point that we will be able "to face up to and undergo middle and old age insofar as it has been possible, all along, to embrace the complexity of (our) experiences and to integrate the painful with the pleasurable, rather than to seek to avoid, or to deny the hard bits and to clutch onto the right to be happy" (1998, p. 197). The problem is that some people, perhaps because of attachment failures and traumatic experiences, find it hard to reflect on their experiences and manage difficult feelings. When encountering the later life transition such people can find themselves troubled by issues from earlier transition points and may "have recourse to earlier patterns of functioning, ones mobilised in the service of avoiding pain" when encountering the losses and traumas of later life (Waddell, 1998, pp. 199–200; King, 1980, p. 155).

In Chapter 4, I listed the "dimensions of hope" that enable us to remain hopeful, and keep going when things seem hopeless. In later life, or certainly the second stage, it could be argued that the dimensions that support people in earlier life-stages may not be as viable. But if so, do other things take their place to prevent people from falling into hopelessness and despair and help them face rather than avoid whatever ageing brings? Starting with *mastery and agency:* it is understandable that someone in his late 80s or 90s who is housebound because of arthritis and progressive loss of vision, who has recently lost many old friends and whose family live at a distance, would complain that this dimension no longer applied. Illness, disability and the need to rely on others for basic care can erode our sense of agency and choice and the onset, especially if sudden, can traumatise us. At a stroke we can find ourselves requiring the type of help we needed as young children, but with the added tragedy of knowing something very different. The attitudes of others – family, doctors, care services – plays a part in this. Do we listen? Do we offer choice? Or does anxiety about someone's welfare or lack of time make us forget our shared humanity and relate to the older, less-abled person in "I-it" ways? Such a person might also complain that life no longer holds *meaning or purpose.* Shabad argued that "living for something or someone other than oneself is fundamental to being human" (2001, p. 38). In the middle stages of life, we usually define our lives as meaningful in terms of what we do. But as already argued, later life is marked by a systematic loss of roles and capacities to do the things we used to enjoy and gave meaning to our day. I recall an elderly relative asking anxiously "What should I be doing? Where am I meant to go? Do they need me to help with lunch?" when we visited her in a nursing home. Nancy was confused and bewildered by her changed circumstances. She had always kept busy, even when she became frail and the "to dos" took longer and longer. But they gave her a sense of dignity and kept her going.

Regarding the third dimension a *sense of future possibilities,* as I have described, time can become a confusing place for the very elderly and they can be left feeling that there is no future, just the inevitable "descent towards death". Far from offering vistas to look forward to, for some older folk time feels endless, whilst at the same time they know it is running out. Moreover, in the confusion of crises, sudden transitions, visits by many professionals to check on their welfare, and the loss of their familiar routines, people can struggle to make *meaning of their experiences,* the task of the fourth dimension. Meaning-making is a human characteristic and after loss it is an essential aspect of grieving. Indeed, some would argue that the central task of mourning is "self-reorganisation, transcendence and meaning-reconstruction". As Argano said, from a constructivist perspective the human mind is seen as able to shape and create an adaptive process and to "gather the threads of personal continuity" and rediscover meaning "in the aftermath of loss and despair" (2007, pp. 29–31). It entails trying to make sense of why these things have happened to us as well as looking back on our lives, on all the threads that have contributed to our identity. It also entails the capacity to yield to change, in Argano's view a prerequisite for psychological maturation, and to embrace the "complexity of our experiences" mentioned earlier.

The fifth dimension, *trust in others and the capacity for meaningful relationships,* is perhaps the most important of them all, and especially when we are dealing with something difficult. Meaningful relationships support and sustain us, but here again the losses associated with ageing from the loss of small daily encounters with others whilst out shopping or at work to the loss of key attachment relationships, mean that many older people become isolated and can feel incredibly lonely. The sixth dimension of hope is *having faith in something larger than the self.* Some people become increasingly sceptical about a creator or a possible after-life as they get older. For others, spiritual beliefs become increasingly important and they gain comfort by contemplating a divine purpose and an after-life. Sometimes this divine has a human face, sometimes it is more a sense of a higher creative power. Equally, something from the natural world can bring a measure of solace, a reminder that there are things which endure. As Mr Johnson, a man with Alzheimer's disease, told Sinason, he was frightened but his beloved garden helped. "I can't remember the names of all my favourite plants and maybe one day I won't be able to say 'tree', but I will still see it" (1992, p. 100).

There is a seventh dimension and this is *acceptance*. When the others no longer seem viable, to adopt a philosophical stance of accepting the "it is as it is-ness" of life can support people to shift from bitterness, depression and fear to a place of equanimity and even gratitude. Carstensen's research indicated that, far from being unhappy when their world shrinks, many older people speak of an appreciation of everyday pleasures and relationships.[7] It feels more important than achieving, having and getting (Gawande, 2014, p. 95). And this was equally true of much younger people facing the possibility of an early death or who experienced a near death experience or significant loss. As Gawande emphasised, "a sense of our mortality reorders our desires" (p. 99). It is about our perspective changing according to how finite we sense our time in this world is. "When horizons are measured in decades", Carstensen wrote, and this "might as well be infinity to human beings, you most desire all the stuff at the top of Maslow's pyramid – achievement, creativity, and other attributes of 'self-actualisation'. But as your horizons contract – when you see the future ahead of you as finite and uncertain – your focus shifts to the here and now, to everyday pleasures and the people closest to you" (pp. 94–9).

I have already cited Athill. Another exemplar of Eriksonian wisdom is Oliver Sacks. In his final essays, written when he knew he had less than six months to live, he wrote that even though it can feel like "tearing away part of myself … when people die, they cannot be replaced. They leave holes that cannot be filled, for it is fate – the genetic and neural fate – of every human being to be a unique individual, to find his own path, to live his own life, to die his own death" (Sacks, 2015c, p. 20). This is the place of integrity, of authenticity – to live one's own life in the face of existential challenges. The book ends: "And now, weak, short of breath, my once-firm muscles melted away by cancer, I find my thoughts increasingly, not on the supernatural or spiritual but on what is meant by living a good and worthwhile life – achieving a sense of peace within oneself. I find my thoughts drifting to the Sabbath, the day of rest, the seventh day of the week, and perhaps the seventh day of one's life as well, when one can feel that one's work is done, and one may, in good conscience rest" (p. 45). When we come close to losing our life or lose a loved one, we have a different experience of what really matters to us. As Clive James wrote in a poem entitled *Sentenced to Life*:

> Now, not just old, but ill, with much amiss,
> I see things with a whole new emphasis.
> *(James, 2016, p. 1)*

Transformation and transcendence

As psychotherapists, what can we do to support older clients as they engage in the struggle between integrity and despair? First, we need to be alert to our personal beliefs, fears and concerns at the thought of ageing. I believe we touch on the fears of body/mind failure, like thoughts about our death conveniently ignored for most of the time, if we visit a ward or home for elderly people. We might feel repulsed by the smells or the sight of people with food-stained clothes or misshapen, shrunken bodies, and at the same time be ashamed of our feelings, of the emotion of disgust which is as hard-wired into us as fear. We might also feel trapped by the lack of air in what John Terry (1994) described as "deadly institutions", whilst simultaneously feel guilty that we can leave. Reading about the reactions of people who have worked in such settings reveals a lot about our very human fears and some of the strategies we all use to avoid them. In writing about his work in a long-stay hospital for the frail elderly, for example, Terry realised that his initial emphasis on working with the staff was due to a reluctance to actually engage with people on the wards. Sometimes Terry felt persecuted or attacked when he spoke in the staff/patient groups which were eventually set up, or desperate, demoralised and unable to think, perhaps catching feelings familiar to both these groups, and he was aware of dreading going into the weekly group sessions. But in this way, he colluded with the staff's difficulty in becoming emotionally engaged with their patients. Instead, their primary task became one of "servicing" them in "regimes of routinization and control" (pp. 23, 38, 40–43). Another dynamic noticed by Terry was a collective denial of death as if by not mentioning people who had passed away this harsh fact could remain "not known". At the heart of our counter-transference reactions, he reminds us, are the fears about our own inevitable decline and death and that one day we might be like his patients (pp. 40).

In addition to Terry's examples of how we might defend against our fears of ageing and death, other defences mentioned in the literature include splitting, projection and some of the other hallmarks of Klein's paranoid-schizoid position, namely, recourse to anger, envy, bitterness, suspicion and blame. For example, some people project the ageing part of self onto others, whilst simultaneously envying those younger than them (King, 1980, p. 156). In our case, the others might be our clients. Some people avoid facing the reality of ageing by day-dreaming of sexual relationships with much younger people, and in some cases acting this out, or acting and dressing as if they were much younger. Meanwhile, people who have reached the last stages of life may enviously attack those to whom they turn for help. As Cohen pointed out, in the long run whatever strategies we adopt, the successful adaptation to ageing depends on the ability to mourn and recognise dependency, separateness and death (1982).

Coming back to the question how we, as psychotherapists, can best support our older clients: we need to understand that loss and trauma in later life often evokes a crisis of meaning and identity and a sense of disconnectedness from life, and this crisis is intensified if the individual's memory begins to fail and the familiar anchoring of the known is no longer reliably in place. We need to be as flexible as we can and, what seems most important, to offer certain relational qualities and attributes so that the older client feels able to embrace and integrate the complexity of his experiences. In order to do this, I have certain therapeutic tasks in mind. First is the task of telling one's story, something I suspect we are all drawn to do as we get older. But in this context, it also entails a shared process of sense-making, including exploring unresolved issues and in the process, finding meaning once more. Second is the task of facing and grieving the painful reality of life's finitude and the failures of body and mind. This may involve working through former losses and traumas. Last but not least, is to find a way to transform and transcend the challenges of later life through symbolic and creative processes. There are a number of things a secure therapeutic relationship can provide to support an engagement in these tasks. They include:

Opportunities to reconnect with others. Although I am focussing on individual therapy this could also be within a therapeutic group (Terry, 1994; Stockley, 1992). Spending time with someone who is interested in you as a person, who listens to your stories and concerns, who will also speak of her own life or talk about something in the news, a book, the changing weather, animals – and more than that who conveys a shared humanity, is hugely important for anyone who feels isolated and unvalued. It is a committed, humanitarian gift of our time.

Being treated with dignity and respect as a unique individual. In the last words of her poem this, I believe, is what Kate was crying out for:

> So open your eyes nurses, open and see,
> Not a crabbit old woman, look closer – see ME.

To experience being confirmed and accepted via mirroring and holding. Much has been written about the importance of mirroring in early childhood, but Long pointed out that this experience is needed throughout life for optimal functioning and he described significant changes in how the dying patients he saw in a nursing home interacted when he reflected back their experiences (2007, p. 237).

To feel that you matter to and can impact another person. Long described this in terms of mutuality, that there are times when our clients need to know what *we* feel in order to feel connected (p. 244). Another therapist who worked with people who were dying described this as "affect sharing" – to know that we have understood someone deeply enough to feel what they are feeling. When someone is dying, he stressed that the mutual sharing of affect state can assuage loneliness and convert this tragic process into one that is considerably more comfortable and humane. As one woman said "when I knew that you could feel how it felt for me, then I knew things had really happened … I don't feel as alone as I used to" (Herzog, 2007, pp. 247–55).

To have someone who can organise and hold your memories. For frailer elderly people the last thing we can offer as psychotherapists is a containing function as well as helping them to find words for their emotional experiences and courageously naming what others often skirt around. This was a crucial strand in Sinason's work with Mr Johnson (1992).

Even if we feel that there is so little we can do to alleviate an elderly client's suffering, our willingness to sit alongside them is enough. It is what Orange eloquently spoke of as a willingness to look into the face of the suffering stranger with empty hands (2011, pp. 63, 69, 70). And I believe that when people feel connected, which does not always demand the presence of an engaged other for an experience of deep connection can be found through art or the natural world, they can discover that old age does not have to be merely survived. It can indeed be a period of growth as Jung believed, and Settlage, an analyst, illustrated in a moving account of his work with the lady whose poems I quoted earlier. Settlage's client, who was 94 when she first entered therapy and in her eleventh decade when she sought help again, found a way to represent and transcend her experiences of bereavement, the limiting effects of old age and a shrinking world through writing poetry. As he said, "her much diminished access to the external world brought about increased engagement with the always available inner world" (1996, p. 551). And through the medium of her poems she found a way to represent and come to terms with her experiences. The last poem from Settlage's client that I am going to cite hints at this transformative process:

> It is at the mouth of rivers
> That we learn, as fresh water
> Enters the salt, so wisdom
> Enters man.
> We learn by flowing
> Static water breeds no sage,
> Breeds only lassitude
> That shackles man." (p. 561)

Although the creative process may be undertaken alone, my sense is that implicitly it is with an audience in mind and that sharing this in therapy, having a witness to one's story, someone who can indeed be impacted and feel with you, is a fundamental part of the transformative process. This is illustrated in a paper by White and Flax. In their work with elderly patients they observed the role art and creativity can take in rendering ageing and death something thinkable and bearable. Through symbolisation, they wrote, "we can find solace … thereby attending to the soul's needs" and "creativity, with its life-affirming qualities, can bring to bear the beauty of the ephemeral and the 'in-between', the living on of meaning through objects, ideas and symbolic space" (2014, p. 164). One very withdrawn lady became lively and present again when they began to talk about death through the medium of poetry's symbolic space, both client and therapist bringing different poems to their meetings. Another woman with inoperable cancer who believed that you either had to be stoical or collapse discovered a third possibility through sharing poems, that of welcoming and embracing the emotions that "knocked on the door of her mind". Her avoidance of psychic pain gave way to being able to contemplate and grieve not just her own death but those of her husband and her parents (pp. 168–70). White and Flax summed up their discussion with a point that is crucial given the way society has made death "invisible", namely that whilst poetry and art facilitated the therapeutic process "it is relatedness that saves and consoles. The intimacy and grasp between two connected souls renders these symbolic forms so powerful. In turn it is creativity with its life-affirming, generative potential, that allows the relatedness to take hold. Creativity within the human connection awakens the spirit and allows for its perseverance in the face of bodily failure" (p. 170).

The last transition of all – facing our mortality

I have discussed the fears we have about getting older, about the loss of physical and mental capacities and independence, and about feeling unneeded. But what emotional responses come up when we contemplate our mortality? And what defences do we adopt to deal with them? To answer the first questions let me return to history. In the classic work, *The Hour of our Death*, Philippe Ariès provided a detailed account of the transition from the "Tame Death" of the early Middle Ages to the invisible or "Dirty Death" of the current day and the horror this evokes. Each major shift in the practices and rituals surrounding the dying and the dead was informed by the significance of a death to the individual, his family and the community as a whole, and by changing ideas concerning the afterlife. In the era of the "Tame Death", a period when epidemics could devastate the population, "death was not a personal drama but an ordeal for the community, which was responsible for maintaining the continuity of the race". To deal with the savagery of nature death had to be ritualised, "imprisoned in ceremony, transformed into spectacle" (Ariés, 1971, pp. 603–4). Along with these deathbed rites was the belief that after life we enter a period of repose before the true end, the glorious resurrection and the "life of the world to come".

As we move towards the seventeenth century practices changed with the growing cult of individualism. There was now a stress on the separation between the body and an immortal soul which was released by death. In effect, our forebears were clinging to the belief that their existence as unique individuals would continue into the next world and they did all they could to ensure this by investing in good works and masses to be said on their behalf. Another feature marking this period was the concealment of the body in shrouds, coffins and catafalques. What had once been calmly accepted was now hidden in order not to upset or frighten the survivors. Ariès saw this as a reversal from a once-tamed death to something savage and therefore needing to be made remote. The concealment of the body continued during the seventeenth and eighteenth centuries. Nineteenth-century Romanticism and the shift from community to the nuclear family led to further significant changes in Western attitudes to death. The fear of death of the self gave way to a fear of the loss of those closest to us. To deal with this the afterlife became a place of reunion with loved ones. Whereas whole communities shared rituals around the deathbed in the preceding centuries, now this became a deeply personal family occasion, supposedly marked by a beautiful and perfect union between the deceased and those left behind.

During the last 200 years the medicalisation of ageing and death has been particularly influential and as forms of social cohesion have steadily broken down the medical profession has stepped in. Ariès commented that the intimacy of the final exchanges between the dying and their families in the Romantic era was poisoned, "first by the ugliness of disease, and later by the transfer to the hospital". The Romantics beautified death. Whilst "they preserved its immemorial association with illness, pain, and agony; these things aroused pity rather than distaste. The trouble began with distaste: Before people thought of abolishing physical illness, they ceased to tolerate its sight, sounds, and smells" (p. 613). Ariès was writing in the 1970s. If he knew the lengths we go to today to disguise wrinkles and greying locks as well as to prolong life at all costs, he would see just how phobic we have become of our inevitably changing and ageing bodies. But our current strategies are simply part of mankind's attempts to tame, conceal and deny our animal nature. Likewise, our attempts to do as much as we did when younger and to prolong life are just another version of our ancestors' attempts to extend life with the different concepts of an after-life in which we attain some perfect, non-suffering state.

Interestingly our strategies to avoid death all hold elements of basic survival strategies. We try to fight it for instance, in determinedly trying to stay active or, if diagnosed with a terminal condition, pushing for yet another treatment despite knowing that there is only a small chance of it working. We turn to flight. We avoid thinking of our death; we ignore warning signs. Alternatively, we slip into submission, a state of giving up while sliding into depression and despair. Whilst all have their uses, what we most need to help us navigate our last years is to be able to connect with others. As Bowlby stressed, "intimate attachments to other human beings are the hub around which a person's life revolves, not only when he is an infant or toddler, but throughout his adolescence and his years of maturity, and on into old age" (Bowlby, 1980, p. 442).

Freud observed that "at bottom no one believes in his own death, or to put the same thing in another way, that in the unconscious every one of us is convinced of his own immortality" (Freud, 1915, p. 289), and this denial is evident at individual, family, systemic and societal levels. For example, in the family we all expect Mum and Dad to be just the same as they were before, until there is a crisis. As Shabad pointed out "we really do proceed in our relationships as if there were no death" (2001, p. 20). We adopt a "slumbering unconsciousness" rather than face the fact that in risking love we risk losing our loved ones, and if the potential absence of a significant other is denied, he believes our relationships become stale. We take for granted that people will be around for ever and so fail to appreciate them or make time to visit them. How often have people regretted not calling a friend when they learned of their death or that they had moved? But if they were really there forever, putting off that phone call for another day is understandable. For some people, however, the opposite is true. They have what Shabad called pressurised hyperconsciousness about potential loss (p. 20). As an example, one woman I worked with was deeply anxious about losing her husband and wracked with obsessive fears that he might die whilst travelling to and from work or that if he exerted himself at the gym or in the garden he might suddenly have a fatal heart attack. She phoned him each day to make sure he had arrived safely at the office; could not rest when she knew he was travelling home and tried to stop him doing heavy labour. Not only did this get in the way of fully living her day, but it was detrimental to their relationship. Another client was preoccupied with fears about losing me and any small hint that I might be unwell or tired lead to checking if I was OK. For her, a cough or some other indication that I was not 100 per cent fit was a warning of my possible death. It made me appreciate just how debilitating her fear of losing her mother when she was young must have been.

Another way we ignore finitude is by trying to buy or make time. Shabad saw this as a way of shielding ourselves from the cost of fully appreciating time's limits and the quality of each moment and each relationship. We take things for granted and when we "cannot distil a certain quality of intensity from our experiences … we attempt to make up for it in quantity; that is we attempt to extend our time unconsciously, as if we were imploring the powers that be to compensate us for what was missed". But "when we grab on desperately to a series of moments … we may not pay sufficient heed to any one particular moment". In this way the defence becomes self-perpetuating and "by focusing too much on quantity of time … we can miss the particular ways that death informs a life" (2001, p. 19). We never fully live.

I was struck how endemic our avoidance of facing the finitude of life is in our culture when reading Gawande's brave and honest account of how he and fellow doctors might fail to confront the realities of decline and mortality. In relating Mr Lazaroff's story, Gawande acknowledged that although they "had no difficulty in explaining the specific dangers of various treatment options (they) never really touched on the reality of his disease". "We could never bring ourselves to discuss the larger truth about his condition or the ultimate limits of our capabilities, let alone what might matter most to him as he neared the end of his life. If he was pursuing a delusion so were we" (2014, pp. 1–10). The name 'Lazaroff', sounding so like the biblical Lazarus, made me think: our challenge is to face the fact that doctors cannot raise people from the dead, and with the same humility nor can we as psychological aid workers provide perfect "cures" for everyone we see. We too are called to confront our limitations and be honest about what can be achieved.

Facing the second challenge that we are insignificant in the context of vast, "deep time"

It is interesting that both the first and second challenges of living in time call us to face our fear of insignificance, the first to others, the second in the context of a universe that is unimaginably vast and old. For a long time, I questioned whether the vastness of time and space really did challenge people. If we think about this at all it is more with fascination and amazement than anxiety. The hugeness of the numbers is hard to grasp. They have little meaning when our lived experience is bound up in much smaller quantities. And initially, what I would have talked about was the fleetingness of our individual lives. But it is as if the scales have fallen off our eyes. It is no longer possible, as we do with the knowledge of our death, to hide beneath a slumbering unconsciousness. We are having to confront the reality that within this century life on earth could be destroyed unless we act radically now. And we are not saying that the planet would vanish. No, it is *homo sapiens* that would become extinct: another species like the dinosaurs that came and went, "a poor player who strutted and fretted his life on the stage, and then is heard no more", to misquote *Macbeth* (5.5.17–28). If it was just the individual that died, part of the natural order, we could cling to the comforting thought of everlasting life through symbolic immortality, that even when we die something of us is passed on. But what if there are no monuments to mark our existence or heirs to succeed us? What if there are no narcissistic illusions to hang onto? In turning to face the second existential challenge of living in time we are confronted with the primitive terror of annihilation, that death really means the end of time. Implicitly or explicitly these are themes we are hearing more about in our consulting rooms and there is a calling for us, as psychotherapists, to bring all our accumulated skills and wisdoms to sit beside our clients, our fellow human beings, in this. Returning to Tillich's concept of the "courage to be", the question to ask is "can I find courage not only to bear knowing their past and hold hope alive when the present feels unendurable, but also to face with them the 'deep but silent grief'" (Bednarek, 2018, p. 11) that comes from the loss of our attachment to the natural world and our shared fears for the future? This, I believe, is what we *can* do with our knowledge and skills.

Notes

1 Another factor influencing definitions and perceptions of the elderly is the age structure of a society, and this has changed significantly over the last century. As illustrated in a range of documents, historically the classification of old age has been given to people in any of the decades after 40 (Pelling & Smith, 1991, p. 7). For instance, in traditional fairy tales people were described as "old" if they were over 40 and 50 and anyone over 60 was seen as "miraculously old" (Chinen, 1994, p. 2).
2 Shabad's view is that using other people's meanings occurs during adolescence when as part of navigating a path away from childhood dependence we "unconsciously borrow a sense of significance from the standards and values of peers" (2014, p. 117). But I believe that identifying with others and adopting their meanings begins much earlier.
3 Whilst men and women share some of the issues to be faced when roles are lost, it is important to be aware of gender differences. For instance, the loss of reproductive capacity at menopause is made more complex because this hormonal change does not coincide with the onset of physical ageing and for some women may begin relatively early in life.

4 Another factor contributing to the fear of being unneeded and a burden is that we are living longer these days. In 1851, England was home to well over a million people aged 60 and over and at least half a million were over 70 (6 per cent and 3 per cent of the total population respectively). Those aged 65 and over formed 5 per cent of the population in the UK in 1901, 11 per cent in 1951 and 17.8 per cent in 2015 (Pelling & Smith, 1991, pp. 196, 166; Office of National Statistics, 2017). In particular an increasingly large proportion are living until their late 80s and 90s, with average life expectancy in the UK today being 80.
5 The first textbooks on geriatrics were published in the early twentieth century.
6 During the seventeenth century historians began to subdivide the past into defined periods such as ancient, medieval and modern and terms like epoch, synchronise, anachronistic and out of date first appeared (Thomas, 1978, pp. 50–59).
7 Athill (2008, 2015) and Sacks (2015c) include some wonderful examples of this.

References

Argano, A. 2007. "Transforming Mourning: A New Psychoanalytic Perspective" in B. Willock, L. Bohm & R. Curtis (Eds.) *On Death and Endings: Psychoanalysts' Reflections on Finality, Transformations and New Beginning* (pp. 21–41). New York: Routledge.
Ariès, P. 1971. *The Hour of Our Death*. London: Penguin.
Athill, D. 2008. *Somewhere Towards the End*. London: Granta.
Athill, D. 2015. *Alive, Alive Oh!* London: Granta.
Bednarek, S. 2018. "How wide is the field? Gestalt therapy, capitalism and the natural world", *British Gestalt Journal*, 27(2): 8–17.
Bowlby, J. 1980. *Attachment and Loss, Vol. 3: Loss, Sadness and Depression*. New York: Basic Books.
Chinen, A. 1994. *In the Ever After: Fairy Tales and the Second Half of Life*. Wilmette, IL: Chiron Publications.
Cohen, N. 1982. "On loneliness and the ageing process", *International Journal of Psychoanalysis*, 63: 149–56.
Cozolino, L. 2016. *Why Psychotherapy Works*. New York: W. W. Norton & Co.
Erikson, E. 1965. *Childhood and Society*. Harmondsworth: Penguin Books (1st edition, 1950. New York: W. W. Norton & Co.).
Freud, S. 1915. "Thoughts for the Times on War and Death", trans. E. C. Mayne (1925), *C.P.* 4, 288–317.
Gawande, A. 2015. *Being Mortal: Illness, Medicine and What Matters in the End*. London: Profile Books.
Gilbert, P. 2005. *Compassion: Conceptualisations, Research and Use in Psychotherapy*. London: Routledge.
Herzog, B. 2007. "Love and Death: Affect Sharing in the Treatment of the Dying" in B. Willock, L. Bohm & R. Curtis (Eds.) *On Death and Endings: Psychoanalysts' Reflections on Finality, Transformations and New Beginnings* (pp. 247–56). New York: Routledge.
James, C. 2016. *Sentenced to Life*. London: Picador.
King, P. 1980. "The life cycle as indicated by the nature of the transference in the psychoanalysis of the middle-aged and elderly", *International Journal of Psychoanalysis*, 61, 153–60.
Long, S. 2007. "A relational perspective on working with dying patients in a nursing home setting" in B. Willock, L. Bohm & R. Curtis (Eds.) *On Death and Endings: Psychoanalysts' Reflections on Finality, Transformations and New Beginnings* (pp. 237–46). New York: Routledge.

Orange, D. 2011. *The Suffering Stranger: Hermeneutics for Everyday Clinical Practice*. New York: Routledge.

Pelling, M. 1991. "Old Age, Poverty, and Disability in Early Modern Norwich: Work, Remarriage, and Other Expedients" in M. Pelling & R. Smith (Eds.) *Life, Death and the Elderly: Historical Perspectives* (pp. 74–101). London: Routledge.

Pelling, M. & Smith, R. (Eds.) 1991. *Life, Death and the Elderly: Historical Perspectives*. London: Routledge.

Sacks, O. 2015c. *Gratitude*. London: Picador.

Settlage, N. 1996. "Transcending old age: Creativity, development and psychoanalysis in the life of a centenarian", *International Journal of Psychoanalysis*, 77, 549–64.

Shabad, P. 2001. *Despair and the Return of Hope: Echoes of Mourning in Psychotherapy*. Lanham, MD: Jason Aronson.

Sinason, V. 1992. *Mental Handicap and the Human Condition. New Approaches from the Tavistock*. London: Free Association Books.

Stern, M. 2014. "The Challenge of Obsolescence" in B. Willock, R. Coleman & L. Bohm (Eds.) *Understanding and Coping with Failure: Psychoanalytic Perspectives* (pp. 155–63). New York: Routledge.

Stevens, A. 1990. *On Jung*. London: Penguin.

Stockley, S. 1992. "Older Lives, Older Dances: Dance Movement Therapy with Older People" in H. Payne (Ed.) *Dance Movement Therapy: Theory and Practice* (pp. 81–101). London: Routledge.

Terry, J. 1994. "Working with staff and patients in a hospital for the elderly", *Psychodynamic Counselling*, 1(1), 21–45.

Thomas, K. 1978. *Religion and the Decline of Magic*. London: Penguin.

Von Kondratowitz, H.-J. 1991. "The Medicalization of Old Age: Continuity and Change in Germany from the Late Eighteenth to the Early Twentieth Century" in M. Pelling & R. Smith (Eds.) *Life, Death and the Elderly: Historical Perspectives* (pp. 134–64). London: Routledge.

Waddell, M. 1998. *Inside Lives: Psychoanalysis and the Growth of the Personality*. London: Duckworth.

White, G. & Flax, J. 2004. "Failure of the Body: Perseverance of the Spirit" in B. Willock, R. Coleman & L. Bohm (Eds.) *Understanding and Coping with Failure: Psychoanalytic Perspectives* (pp. 164–71). New York: Routledge.

Willock, B., Bohm, L. and Curtis, R. (Eds.) 2007. *On Death and Endings: Psychoanalysts' Reflections on Finality, Transformations and New Beginnings*. New York: Routledge.

Zusak, M. 2005. *The Book Thief*. London: Transworld Publishers.

8

TELLING STORIES AND INTERLOCKING TIME-ZONES

> We live in stories the way fish live in water, breathing them in and out, buoyed up by them, taking from them our sustenance, but rarely conscious of this element in which we all exist. We are born into stories; they nurture and guide us through life.
>
> *(Taylor in Roberts, 1999, p. 10)*

Introduction

The stories we breathe in include the family myths and legends we have absorbed since birth as well as stories belonging to our community – stories that inspire, encourage, teach, transmit values and sometimes, warn. They also include stories told about us and the ones we tell ourselves – narratives that shape our identity in both affirming and limiting ways. But why is it that human beings have always told stories? How do they sustain and guide us? And why is story-making an essential part of psychotherapy? In this chapter I intend to look at the functions and attributes of story-telling and in particular how they play a part in shaping us as "selves-in-time". I shall then focus more specifically on the place of narrative in psychotherapy and how it is related to the change process. But first, let me share two more quotations which connect story-telling with the themes of time, identity and meaning:

> Without a story one had no class or family; without a story of one's own, no individual life; without a story of stories, no life giving continuity with the beginning and therefore no future.

Van der Post's words (Roberts, 1999, p. 12), highlight three of the essential functions of stories. They are inherently integrative and as such are fundamental to our sense of ongoingness and identity. They connect people within groups and across time. They also help provide meaning – whether at the level of making sense of an event or helping us to find meaning in existence (a "story of stories"). The next quotation from Oliver Sacks also speaks about the connection between narrative and identity:

> We have, each of us, a life-story, an inner narrative – whose continuity, whose sense is our lives. It might be said that each of us constructs and lives a 'narrative', and that this narrative is us, our identity.
>
> *(Sacks, 2015a, p. 117)*

As argued in Chapter 2, our identity is shored up by a sense of ongoingness over time and by having a verbal, autobiographical self, capable of constructing a narrative of our life. It is not just that our identity is shaped by our past experiences. It depends on being able to remember earlier states and on having a continuous inner narrative that helps us to connect and reflect on our shifting self-states in the present and to remember earlier states-of-being and locate them in time and space. In Sacks' words, "To be ourselves we must *have* ourselves – possess, if needs be repossess, our life stories. We must 'recollect' ourselves, recollect the inner drama, the narrative of ourselves. A man *needs* such a narrative, a continuous inner narrative, to maintain his identity, his self" (1995, p. 117). The words possess and recollect in this context are evocative. To possess one's story suggests being able to own oneself and say, "This is me! Here I stand"; and to recollect, it could be argued, is not just about recall, but about gathering in, re-membering and connecting.

How do we acquire the capacities to possess or know ourselves, something that is fluid and not fixed and which some people lack, and to recollect and integrate different aspects of our life-story? In *The Diary of a Baby*, Daniel Stern described the great leap in development that occurs around the age of three when a child begins to tell himself the story of things that happen to him. He chatters to himself whilst playing, conversing with what Meares suggests is "a quasi-illusory person who is a condensation of himself and his mother" in a language qualitatively different from that used for social communication (1998, pp. 879, 880). It is less grammatical, condensed, makes leaps, and uses associations. This chattering, explained Meares, is "an embryonic narrative of self" which becomes what we think of as the "stream of consciousness", the language of inner life, when children progress to inner dialoguing at around the age of five (1998, p. 881). In order to tell ourselves stories in this way the acquisition of language and being able to use symbols is crucial. But stories are not just about naming things or listing events. As Stern argued, "they involve seeing and interpreting the world of human activities in terms of story plots" (1998, p. 131). The other key element of stories is that they are located in time and space – a context which helps to interpret the plot, and they generally have "a dramatic line, with beginning, middle, and end". To put this another way, the young child "starts to see human activities, his own now included, in terms of psychological explanations embedded in the structure of a narrative" (p. 132). This newly emerging skill requires an experience of "self", to possess ourselves or, to use Tulving's term, to have autonoetic consciousness. It also demands the capacity to mentalise, meaning to see ourselves and others as actors or intentional beings with desires and motives – and both are founded on our earliest relational experiences.

Stern embedded his own narrative about Joey, the "author" of the diary, in a universal context, explaining that story making is common to all cultures as well as an expected developmental landmark for all children. He continued: "the human mind seems naturally to seek explanations for what happens to us and around us ... to select meaningful details out of the disarray of our extremely diverse lived experience" (1998, p. 133). So stories are a way of organising our world, a process of sense-making, which is inherent to all forms of psychological therapy. And once we have acquired the capacity for narrative "the story plot becomes for the rest of our lives the basic unit for understanding the human events that affect us". Stern's imagined diary entries for four-year-old Joey brought together memories from both the near and the far past, as well as imaginary or pretend elements – the stuff of autobiographical memory that I mentioned in Chapter 2. They are rich in associations. The story is also adjusted according to the listener. In creating this story Joey "is creating a new reality" so that he has two realities to live with – as lived subjective experience and as narrated in a story (pp. 134, 135). This highlights the fact that subjectively we live within different time spheres. Events in the present, recent and distant past, as Stern pointed out, all activate one another and flow together. This is the introspective state Meares described as "roaming around in the mind through scenes brought up at will in memory and imagination" (2012, p. 53). I would add here that alongside whichever time-zone is in the foreground, we will be having a lived embodied experience. In other words, whatever we are remembering, imagining and narrating will evoke emotions and a range of body responses, including sensations, impulses to move, and changes in arousal level.

We take for granted the complex process of creating stories of our experiences in which we connect different periods, reflect on our motives and reactions, and adjust the story for our listeners, both real and imagined. But let us take a step back to consider the intersubjective foundations of those capacities. Here I turn to Donnel Stern whose theory of narrative was important in giving shape to some of my own emerging ideas (2010). Stern emphasised that "we are called into being by the recognition of others" and described the interactive process whereby we begin to tell and live stories. Through mentalising and reflecting back feelings and desires when we are babies, our caregivers help organise our "relatively inchoate world in terms of narrative, and self-states begin to cohere in and around these earliest stories" (p. 110). We learn we're hungry because someone feeds us when we have a certain uncomfortable feeling inside. "So we then have a story that goes with that feeling: 'I am hungry'". We learn we're sad because someone comforts us or that we're angry when she says, "Oh! You're so cross aren't you!" Then we have stories that go with two other nasty feelings: "I'm sad" or "I'm angry". One of the important things about these everyday acts of recognition – we could call them micro-stories – is that "we have an experience of continued existence in someone else's mind and that someone cares about what we experience and how we feel" (p. 111). It is fundamental to our sense of ongoingness. Indeed, as Nachmani said, "being in existence is the precursor to identity" (2005, p. 322).

As we develop, we internalise the process of recognising and formulating our experiences. We tell ourselves the story and act as our own witness, the process so evocatively illustrated through the imagined mouth of Joey. As Laub observed, "one comes to know one's story only by telling it to oneself, to one's internal 'thou'" (2005, pp. 314, 315). "We construct what we know about ourselves by identifying with the other and 'listening' through his ears to the story we are telling", argued Stern, and to be able to listen to our own thoughts we need parents "who left us able to believe, in at least some states, that there exists others, especially certain imaginary others, who are continuous presences interested in knowing our experience" (2010, pp. 112, 113). Stern used the term "partners in thought" for these imaginary witnesses. But what if there was no one there initially to act as a live partner in thought? What if we were not recognised and attuned to? If we repeatedly felt frightened and alone? If we absorbed a projected story of our caregiver's distress or depression or trauma? Not only can this inhibit the formation of autobiographical competency, for as Stern said, "without a witness, even an imaginary witness, events fail to fall into the meaningful pattern of episode that is narrative, or we merely enact our stories blindly, unable to think about them or know what they feel like" (p. 111) – but those projected stories become the ones we subsequently live by. They shape our internal working models and personality organisation.

Later experiences can also compromise the capacity to form and reflect on stories. As Laub argued, massive psychological trauma is a deadly assault on this imaginary internal witness or, to use the language of object relations, empathic "good object" (2005, p. 315). It undermines the processes of association, symbolisation and narrative formulation that ordinarily proceed in a routine way as we mull over and make sense of the events of our day. It leaves us with "no one to turn to, even inside oneself" (p. 315). Story-telling, curiosity, self-reflection, and meaning-making break down, and with it the ability to assimilate events into the ongoing tapestry of our lives (Stern, 2010, p. 126). Another way of putting it is that "the me-you psychological glue" which enabled us to develop benign, imaginary partners in thought ceases to exist (Nachmani, 2005, p. 329).

The functions of story-telling

I want to home in now on the functions and attributes of narrative. As I said earlier, stories integrate, and most importantly, they help to integrate our experiences across time. They shape and maintain our identity. They provide a vehicle for meaning-making and have a containing function. Lastly, they bind together groups and communities. I will consider each of these in turn.

Narrative as an integrative process

Narrative integrates different areas of the brain. In order to tell a good story, meaning one in which a series of events are grounded in the passage of time and there is some emotional experience to give it meaning, "the linear linguistic processing of the left hemisphere must be integrated with the centres in the right hemisphere that process sensory and emotional information" (Cozolino, 2016, p. 239). There is also an integration between higher cortical structures and the limbic region of the brain and therefore between explicit, verbal memories and implicit somatic-affective memories. When narrating, we organise and structure our memories, embedding them within the contexts of time and space, and temporal integration is important from an evolutionary perspective. As Levine pointed out, it is a survival-based imperative to search our memory banks for prior information that might provide relevant strategies to enhance current survival, and stories help us to navigate the future by shaping and interpreting our memories and infusing them with either a positive or negative tone (2015, p. 131). All narratives oscillate in time (Rolls, 2010). They move backwards and forwards, stretching time out from now to the distant past or the distant future, focussing in detail on small periods of time or connecting events at different times with similar themes. They involve sequences with beginnings, middles and ends. They provide a sense of causality: "This happened because of that". They are prospective: "If I do this, then this will happen". And like our memories, because they have the potential to change as new information, understanding and experience is integrated with what went before, personal or communal narratives never have a final version.

Narrative and self-identity

Stories help to shape our identity and maintain our sense of self. The integration of emotions, thoughts and images during the narrative process supports our sense of a coherent, cohesive self that holds all the disparate bits of experience together. In connecting past, present and future, stories also contribute to our sense of ongoingness. As Cozolino said, "having a conscious narrative of our experience helps us to remember where we have come from, where we are, and where we are going. In other words, our stories ground us in the present, within the flow of our histories, and provide a direction for the future. This linear blueprint helps us to avoid feeling lost in an eternal present while reducing the anxiety caused by uncertainty" (2016, p. 237). Is it any wonder that we often hang on to self-limiting stories if their familiarity softens such anxiety?

Being stuck in an eternal present is the experience of many survivors of trauma, especially early relational trauma when there was no partner in thought who would listen and help them make sense of their experiences. Rather than having a coherent, chronological narrative of what happened, survivors often have large gaps in memory and are troubled by intrusive fragments of sensory data (emotion and body memory) which feel as if they are happening in the present. The memories have effectively been frozen in time – until later in life a new experience of safety, perhaps within a therapeutic relationship, enables the story to slowly be pieced together and made relationable. People with certain neurological conditions can also be stuck in an eternal present. Oliver Sacks wrote some masterful accounts of such people. For instance, he described how one man with Korsakov's syndrome, a condition marked by the loss of memory of very recent events, was "isolated within a single moment of being, with a moat or a lacuna of forgetting around him". He was a man "without a past (or future), stuck in a constantly changing, meaningless moment" (2015a, p. 31). "What sort of life", asked Sacks, "what sort of world, what sort of a self, can be preserved in a man who has lost the greater part of his memory and with this his past and his moorings in time?" (p. 25). His philosophical question highlights how crucial our past and, more than that, our autobiographical capacity is for our sense of self. It is a terrifying prospect to imagine being stuck in a completely disconnected, timeless world, to be "nothing but a bundle or collection of different sensations, which succeed each other with an inconceivable rapidity, and are in a perpetual flux and movement" (p. 32).

Stories also tell us who we are, or who we are perceived to be. Our parents tell stories about us from very early in our life. Indeed, sometimes before we are born each parent already has an imagined narrative of who we will become, and these "parental constructions" start to shape our identity or public self (Stern, 1998, p. 7). In overt and subtle ways "we are told who we are, what is important to us, and what we are capable of" (Cozolino, 2016, p. 237). As we listen to anecdotes of what we and others have done or not done we get the message about socially preferred versions of self and ones that are less acceptable. Then we repeat those stories to ourselves and construct new ones based on how we think we are compared to others. Some narratives foster self-esteem and confidence in our potential. They can be a spurt to growth. Equally, a positive forecast can sometimes become a millstone round our necks – something we feel compelled to live up to whatever the cost. Other narratives are deeply limiting – for instance, if we are related to as if we were "such and such" whilst other aspects of us are denied or ignored (Bromberg, 2011, p. 57). They can lead to a sense of not being OK, not belonging and not having the wherewithal to succeed. In other words, they stifle our author's voice and become self-fulfilling prophecies.

For a moment, notice your reactions to the following remarks. What if this had been said about you?

> "She looks just like my sister – the bitch!"
> "He's like Granddad – always level-headed. He never said no to a challenge, and I think he's going to be just the same".
> "She's the clever one. She'll go far – university, a good job, nice house. But her brother's a different kettle of fish" (said with a weary sigh).

In such remarks and the family stories surrounding them, lurk unresolved, unspoken issues from the past. As Stern pointed out, they are created out of our parents' past and present and reflect "deep wishes, fears, and aspirations" (1998, p. 7). Perhaps the mother who hated her sister had never been able to work through the hurt she felt when the latter humiliated her when they were young. The parent who stressed the grandfather's strengths may not have been able to fully grieve his death, whilst the man who privileged academic success might have been trying vicariously to meet his own unfulfilled wish to go to university and to project how his parents had belittled him onto his son. As well as disconfirming who we truly are, the stories told by others can also impose attributes or roles upon us that belong to other members of the family. As MacIntyre argued, we are never fully the author of the narrative that we live out. "We enter upon a stage we did not design and find ourselves part of an action that was not of our making. Each of us being the main character in his own drama plus playing subordinate roles in the dramas of others" (Philips, 1999, p. 38).

The reason why it can prove so hard to throw away limiting, defined-by-others stories is that for every human being, as Bromberg emphasised, "the preservation of self-continuity has the highest evolutionary priority". To some extent therefore, everyone will "continue to preserve the procedurally learned attachment patterns upon which his core self rests in order to be recognizable as 'himself' in all circumstances and during all phases of life" (2011, p. 58). Put another way, we have an attachment-organised core identity and even if it is self-limiting, its familiarity, along with the thematic continuities of our personal stories, helps contain the fear of the unexpected.

Containment and meaning-making

The third function of narrative is to make meaning of life's happenstances – indeed many of the earliest known stories address the question why there is life at all. As Daniel Stern said, we seek explanations for what happens to us and around us. We like to figure out "why?" and turn to narrative to create coherence and meaning out of the unpredictability of our lives (Grossmark, 2018, p. 125). In this sense, story-telling has an organising, containing function. Meaning-making involves psychological explanations which we weave into our stories. We look for motives behind what we, or others, said and did. We have stories that go with different feelings and states of self. We account for things not going to plan by explaining them in terms of personal inadequacy or blaming others. Sometimes our meaning-making draws on a "story of stories", for instance arguing that there is a higher purpose to what we are going through or that fate or wrathful gods lie behind misfortune and disaster, as in Tillich's Ages of Fate and Judgement.[1] And as I argued in Chapter 4, part of our struggle today in the Age of Meaningless is that we lack overarching structures of meaning which can bring comfort when facing adversity.

Putting things into words and into a meaningful context is inherently containing, reminiscent of how an attuned caregiver digests what is chaotic and unmetabolised and gives it back to the infant in manageable form. Part of our ongoing attempts to maintain a cohesive, continuous self and to manage change is to tell ourselves stories about who we think we are, how we came to be and how we might be in the future, and problems arise when we cannot form such meaningful narratives. This would not be possible had we not seen ourselves reflected back by attuned others or heard them making meaning of things. Nor would it be possible without memories on which to draw.

Another containing aspect of stories is that they are framed by conventional demarcation signs that indicate a beginning – when one is entering the "tale world" – and an ending (Gergen, 2005). And even if we don't begin with a more formulaic "once upon a time", or "if you're sitting comfortably, then I'll begin", the same is true of a therapy session. As in an adventure, telling a story occurs in parenthetical time. Another parallel is that, as in an adventure, we don't know what is going to happen in either a fictitious or a clinical narrative. Things could work out well – a "happy ending", or a tragic one.

Stories connect us

The last function to consider is the potential of narrative to connect people across time and space. Denise Inge wrote about our need to pass on our stories, values and hopes, and "to weave our memories into those of another, taking our past into the future and leaving with the next generation the memories we hold". She argued that "memory inheritance is a kind of signature of existence" and that "to leave no memory or to have none at all is in a way … to not be quite real" (2014, p. 128). This takes me back to my proposition that to have a sense of ongoingness we need to feel connected to past and future generations, and sharing and passing on stories supports this. But memory inheritance does more than that. As Roberts argued, "our shared stories are the fabric of relationships and the basis for community" (1999, p. 11). When one family member asks, "do you remember that holiday …?", and another replies with a linking memory, a moment of bonding has occurred. Such co-created stories connect families. They also hold together large and diverse groups of people, which for social animals has an evolutionary advantage (Meares, 1998, p. 883). To use Roberts' descriptive image, they provide a "shelter of shared meaning", something that offers containment, comfort and solace and helps people get through difficult times and make sense of and come to terms with disasters and losses (1999, p. 12).

Communal narratives often emphasise the maintenance of traditional value systems, for instance by evoking figures from the community's mythology, or continuity between the courage shown by people who died in the past and the resilience and resourcefulness of their survivors. In Guatemala, for example, women widowed as a result of the massacre of indigenous communities during *La Violencia* (1978–1985) linked contemporary widows with characters from Mayan history and the Bible. Judith Zur noted that through creating shared narratives these women, left with grief and guilt at not being able to protect their menfolk, managed to "present themselves in a different light and re-position themselves within memory and history" (1999, p. 55). Testimonies from another community studied by oral historians – the Mississippi Delta – linked more recent struggles for civil and political rights with the efforts of people to protect their families and achieve some independence from white control during the era of segregation and violent lynchings in the first half of the twentieth century. Lacy Rogers argued that these acts of testimony restored agency to the surviving family and community. But the narratives were two-sided for they acted as a warning to future generations about remaining vigilant about white supremacism (1999, pp. 115–17). Communal narratives can also romanticise the past in ways that offer comfort and a means of facing an uncertain present and future. Field described how the former residents of a Cape Town community torn apart by apartheid laws between 1958 and 1963, spoke of Windermere in glowing terms as place of peace and togetherness and glossed over the fact that life could be harsh and violent even then (1999, p. 70). These "emotionally sustaining myths" supported a sense of self and identity in the present, a "community-in-memory", and affirmed social ties amongst black people (1999, p. 61). Yet Field argued that they were shaped by an unfulfilled desire for peace and stability in the present (p. 76). By contrast, the narratives of Field's coloured[2] interviewees focussed more on the harsh conditions of the present. They tried not to discuss the past and did not acknowledge the social and emotional impact of their memories.

When violence is done to people's memories

The "narrative strategies" adopted by these communities – emphasising continuity, courage and sacrifice, turning to nostalgia and romanticising, or denial – are also used by individuals, couples or families in order to connect and to help them manage the trials and uncertainties of the present. There are other ways too that the co-creation and transmission of stories bind groups both large and small. But returning to what Inge said about "memory inheritance", her argument also begs questions about the types of stories that are passed on. What is remembered? And what forgotten? What can be spoken and what has to be silenced, or if mentioned, is swiftly denied or swept under the carpet? As Zur pointed out "remembering and forgetting is a cultural process", and memories are shaped by the cultural past and by norms and processes of the group in the present, be it a family, or communal or national group (1999, p. 53). It should be added that this applies both to the memories of shared events – the horrors of war, the attack on the Twin Towers, the London bombings, a devastating flood, or the memories of a personal loss, terrible illness, or interpersonal trauma.

Zur's case study, and others in the same book, offers some powerful examples of cultural forgetting. In Guatemala, remembering the atrocities of *La Violencia* was forbidden. Official histories suppressed alternative and oppositional voices and the dead were repeatedly vilified as enemies of the state. Zur described it as a deliberate violence to people's memories which weakened their sense of identity and deprived them of a sense of efficacy (1999, p. 48). In Argentina, after defeat in the Malvinas

War of 1982, the "official past" blamed the military High Command and portrayed the ex-combatants as passive victims. These "victims", who had left home surrounded by support and patriotic fervour, were quickly forgotten and effectively ordered to forget, for they had to sign forms agreeing not to discuss the war when demobbed. However, they do not see themselves as victims and, because the real truth remains unknown, feel progressively alienated from those closest to them and the community at large (Lorenz, 1999, pp. 97, 98). The Argentinian veterans are not alone in returning home from war to find that people do not want to hear their experiences. Books written by or about former prisoners of war testify to this. And as Lorenz argued, for people whose story cannot find a voice this disconnection in memory can itself be a form of trauma (p. 96).

In his study of a community closer to home with a long history of communal splits and atrocities, Dawson wrote about institutional amnesia and the practice of "state-organised forgetting" of the causes and consequences of Ireland's very troubled past. He pointed out that although the 1993 Downing Street Declaration was intended to bring about reconciliation, the rhetoric of drawing a line under the past and moving on amounted to a denial of the psychic and political realities of the communities of Northern Ireland. "To consign dreadful deeds firmly to the distant past", Dawson argued, ignores the psychic scars of those who have lost people close to them and the fact that violent conflict remains fresh in living memory (1999, p. 183). Dawson also noted that public commemorations, for instance after Bloody Sunday, whilst sometimes healing, can recognise the traumas of "our" community, and forget those of the Other (pp. 189, 191, 192).

Reading these accounts made me think of more subtle forms of violence to people's memories – in families, for instance, when a child who starts to talk about something shameful is hushed; when sad and difficult events are never spoken about again; when recourse to minimisation, humour or blame is the response when someone mentions an interaction that hurt them. How many families have their "skeletons in the closet"? Their "ghosts in the nursery?" This includes the unmentioned relatives or events that are never mentioned for fear of shame and disgrace on the family – the illegitimate child who was sent away; the "mad" relative put in an institution. I have in mind too the abuse of a child swept under the carpet; the husband's affairs conveniently forgotten; the mother's or father's drinking that everyone knows about but never mentions or challenges; and black eyes after a night of shouting and banging downstairs which Mum passes off as being clumsy and bumping into a door.

Violence is done to the memories of children who, when they tell of abuse, are disbelieved or warned never to speak of it again. They are left confused about their reality when what they saw, heard or experienced is denied. What is true? Did they imagine it? There are smaller moments too when our story is not socially recognised and allowed to become a shared reality. We have probably all been told "it wasn't that bad" or "you're imagining things". Such dismissals constitute what Bromberg called "traumas of disconfirmation" (2001, p. 57). In all cases, whether it is a nation, sub-group or family that does the forgetting, there is a wish to draw a line under the past because it holds inconvenient truths. People want to go back to the soothing rhythms of daily life and regain a sense of order and ordinariness. But it isn't so easy. Scars remain and so do splits. The past cannot be integrated into the present and future without a process of shared remembering, and splits remain in the individual psyche when people have had to silence and compartmentalise what they know. Healing demands social recognition. As Dawson said, those who do attempt to remember "are struggling to shape the traumatic event into narrative form, to integrate it into their world of meaning, to fashion words that are in some sense adequate to the dislocation and the horror". They are also seeking validation of that "pain, disturbance, dislocation, and horror, from others". When the personal suffering and mourning of survivors is publicly recognised and affirmed it can be given dignity and meaning (1999, p. 189). When such recognition is denied, the trauma becomes entrenched (p. 191).

In Chapter 10 I discuss the process of forgetting after traumatic events in more detail and explore how unknown and unwritten stories can emerge in psychotherapy. I will also give specific examples of individuals who were called to find recognition for their suffering. But to end this section, let me share some examples of public acts of commemoration which I found moving to read about. Following a visit to the Killing Fields in Cambodia, Evelyn Rappoport described seeing an enormous glass cylinder full of skulls – a totemic marker of all those massacred by the Khmer Rouge (2017, p. 174). This memorial was "composed of tangible remains of skeletal fragments of lives previously lived, symbolically linked each to the other, as well as to the collective, to the clan of human being". It was a "living memorial of a lost generation erased from the annals of history". Rappoport concluded that although in all genocides people are stripped of anything indicative of individuality and become "enumerated objects", in the skull totem the remnants remain recognizable as human heads – a powerful, reminder of "the individualities and complexities of humanity" to live on in the memories of survivors and all those who come to pay tribute (pp. 172, 176, 181).

Another inspiring example is the Clothesline project which began in Pennsylvania in 1991 and since then has spread worldwide (Rose, 1999). Led by women's movements, survivors of domestic abuse, sexual abuse and rape were invited to design T-shirts representing their suffering on the front and their recovery on the back. The shirts were then exhibited on washing lines. By 1995, 250 clotheslines representing 35,000 women had been assembled across America. Having interviewed women involved in the project, Rose commented on the layers of meaning in their visual testimonies, reflecting how survivors' narratives continue to develop over time. She also made the crucial point that, "by breaking through the silence, survivors are constructing oppositional narratives that defy the taboo against talking about incest and torture" (pp. 163, 164).

Like the cylinder of skulls, like Holocaust memorials, like the An Crann project in Northern Ireland (Dawson, 1999, p. 186), and like the stories our clients slowly tell and re-tell in psychotherapy, the oppositional narrative is about creating a new experience, and this, as argued later, is a key element in story breaking. Such examples of opposition and social recognition are antidotes to evil. Indeed,

> only when we recognize, acknowledge and share the events of the past, when the unspeakable is communicated, can we remember, locate, and place the 'unforgotten' into the historical landscape of generations. Without recognition and acknowledgement, denial will continue to propel history to the collapsing of past, present, and future into a timeless vortex of a living death. Without an antidote, on both an individual and collective level, the wounds of history will continue to bleed as scar tissue is ripped open again and again whilst history goes unheeded.
>
> *(Rappoport, 2017, pp. 184–5)*

Story-telling in psychotherapy

> Narration, the telling of one's story, is proof of life.
> A person's signature is his or her story.
>
> *(Nachmani, 2005, p. 329)*

The stories people arrive with

People come to therapy with stories of pain, loss, conflict and confusion; stories that are fractured, incomplete and incoherent, charting difficulties for which they lack an explanatory narrative; stories that are enacted or "told" through the body. In some cases, our clients' stories are brief and factual; in others elaborate, even confabulated. There are stories that deeply move or concern us, that hook us in, and others that we find hard to listen to. There are stories that have been silenced by others or evoke too much shame and fear to repeat. Tales of successes, failures, wishes and dreams; of relationships, illnesses, losses and accidents. Those who seek our help also bring stories of other treatments – past therapies or involvements in the health service – the narrative of "nothing helps" or "no one cares" or "she was great, but she left". Sometimes people come to therapy because their story – the signature of their identity – has fallen apart. This can happen for instance, when a couple grows apart, perhaps after one partner changes course, and the old narrative of a shared life with common values and aims no longer seems to fit. It can happen in later life if dementia breaks the connection between past and present and a constricting "illness narrative" starts to shape the sufferer's identity (Bruce, 1999, p. 197). For the partners of people with dementia their story also falls apart as they suddenly find themselves in a caring role, "parenting" someone who has become childlike, the shared vision of how their lives would be once they retired now in tatters (p. 189). We also encounter people facing other unexpected, challenging life events which unhinge old stories and the expectations that went with them.

Narrative and attachment style

On first meeting a client we can learn a lot about him from his narrative style and the dominant themes in the tales he tells (Siegel, 2010, pp. 176–85; Holmes, 1999, p. 54). The story is likely to be coherent and reflective with someone who has a secure attachment style. He is able to give a thoughtful account of his past, acknowledging the goods and the bad, and backing up points with examples. Very different are the narratives of people who are insecurely attached. Someone with an avoidant-dismissive style is likely to claim few memories of childhood or say it was fine and that his parents were great, without being able to provide substantiating evidence. It is a left-brain story lacking emotional tone and much reflection. The narrative of an insecure-preoccupied client is likely to ramble, to keep slipping into the present when asked about the past and to be full of emotion. Even less coherent is an unresolved-disorganised narrative. As Siegel pointed out, "if past trauma and loss is not resolved our internal narrative will break down. If we try to tell our story to others, we may be overcome by feelings and images that have not found a place in the large narrative of our lives" (2010, p. 182). In particular, there will be fractures in the flow of the story whenever it gets too close to the traumatic events themselves – and this applies even if the events are held in explicit memory.

Meares identified two types of incoherent, unresolved narrative: chronicles and scripts. When someone is securely attached their narrative has a freedom in sequencing and generally incorporates emotional and philosophical reflections. But a chronicle, defined in the *Concise Oxford Dictionary* as "a continuous register of events in order of time", lacks these qualities. According to Meares, clinical chronicles are characteristically catalogues of problems with the family, work, or the body. "Nothing comes from the interior world. The individual's experience is outer oriented, the language is linear, and there is relative poverty of metaphoric usage" (1998, p. 884). There is a sense of deadness, of stagnation. "Both partners are bored but also afflicted with a vague sense of unease" (p. 886).

I am struck by the link between the word chronicle and chronic, the latter being defined as "lasting and lingering". "Chronicity", argued Roberts, "arises in part by telling dead or static stories" (1999, p. 6). Such narratives don't go anywhere. Nothing new emerges, and so they, or their themes, keep being repeated in slightly different guises. Jonathan comes to mind here. He would usually launch into complaints as soon as he sat down. In response I would try to say something empathic, whilst aware of a sinking feeling and thoughts such as, "what am I meant to do with this? What can I offer that will change things?" I tried to keep my mind alive to listen out for bigger themes that might engage us in thinking collaboratively about links with the past. But Jonathan seemed disinterested in my suggestions and would quickly jump back to the present or the next problem in his catalogue. Sometimes I grappled with boredom. Sometimes, perhaps with some sympathy for the latest victim of Jonathan's anger, I asked questions such as "why do you imagine he or she might have said that, not been in touch, got annoyed?"

and so on. But for a long time, Jonathan seemed unwilling or unable to mentalise himself or others. He wanted his frustration and hurt to be known and tended to – like the young child who can't be settled until you have given the grazed knees lots of attention, and the story of how he came off his bike is given the gravitas the situation demands. Perhaps the most important theme in Jonathan's narratives, now I think back, was the lack of playful creativity, and this told the real story, of a lack of aliveness in his earliest relationships. For the chronicle, argued Meares, is a manifestation of damage, the result of a mismatch between the infant's experience and maternal perception, and such mismatching "triggers the child's experience towards the outer world, leaving the inner zone stunted, depleted, and, at times, painfully vacant" (1998, p. 886). From all Jonathan said about his childhood this fits. His mother had been present in a practical way, but not emotionally or play-fully. I cannot imagine this rather grey, depressed woman, struggling to raise four children on her own, having much space in her mind to reflect on her son's inner world, and in an attuned way to mirror him. Nor can I imagine moments between them of mutual pleasure, of dyadic dancing, of play. Jonathan was a child whose experiences had not been recognised and unconsciously he craved that now.

Whereas chronicles are disconnected from inner experience and told in a rela-tionship of disconnection – with people like Jonathan I can sometimes feel that my presence as a unique being is irrelevant – scripts, according to Meares, have trau-matic origins and reflect a broken sense of self. They are triggered by situations that echo the original trauma and are experienced not as memories, but as present realities. In other words, as he pointed out, time is relatively absent and the action takes place in the present. Traumatic scripts[3] show less sequencing than chronicles, less voluntary control, and less complexity. They are also repetitive and are governed by fixed beliefs about the self and expectations about how others will behave (p. 887).[4] We could say that in script mode people are embedded in their experiences, constrained by these habitual patterns of thinking, feeling and doing and unable to envisage alternative perspectives (Wallin, 2007, pp. 135–6). More-over, they may not have words for the original experiences. They are dissociated but can be communicated through the body and in enactive ways.

Much then can be learned from the non-verbal dimension of our co-created relationship. As Grossmark pointed out, although "we are accustomed to speak of 'narrative' or 'the telling of the story' as a product of language and interpretation in psychoanalysis … a story is told in the events, interactions, affects, and states that emerge in the analytic couple" (2016, p. 50). Wallin said something similar: "That which we cannot verbalise, we tend to enact with others, to evoke in others, and/ or to embody". In this way we communicate what we "know but have not thought – and, therefore cannot talk about" (2007, pp. 121, 122). As therapists we need, therefore, to look out for muscular patterns, subtle movements, expressive gestures, incongruous facial expressions and changes in arousal level. We also need to become curious about what is evoked in our own bodies – the movements we make or feel impelled to make, the postures we adopt, visceral stirrings – and about what is enacted between us.

Story making and story breaking

So what can help people to free themselves from limiting, constrictive or dead stories? To find words for and make sense of narratives that are confusing, incomplete or embodied? To support the integrative functions of story-telling discussed earlier? Jeremy Holmes asserted that, "psychological health (closely linked to secure attachment) depends on a dialectic between story making and story breaking, between the capacity to form a narrative, and to disperse it in the light of new experience" (1999, p. 59). I find the idea of story making and breaking compelling – a concept that is simple, even obvious at one level, but at another hard to pin down. To explore what we do in psychotherapy that supports people in making and breaking stories about the past, I began to look at what different theorists and therapeutic traditions have to say about narrative process, and, in a microscopic way, at what goes on in my own work. My "formulation" has come down to the following:

Firstly, that there are two aspects to story making. One is actually finding a story – contextualising and integrating remembered situations into a more coherent, chronological pattern; perhaps discovering things about significant others that enable us to fill in puzzling gaps; and encountering and piecing together fragments of implicit memory, however they have come to be represented, and giving words to them so that the "unthought known" can finally be "possessed" and assimilated into our life-story (Bollas, 1987). Bollas described the narrative process in psychotherapy as "a kind of layering of narratives" as we go over our past, often returning many times to the same period and in the process recalling more details about what happened and about our responses (1995, p. 115). Through reflecting on what emerges new meanings are created and transformed into "a tapestry holding them in a new place" (p. 143).

Finding meaning is the second aspect of story making, and in the same way that the frame of a tapestry holds a multitude of coloured threads and patterns, sense-making is inherently containing. Through repeated re-tellings we can find meaning in known and half-known stories as we discover more details, more nuances and what that situation means to us in the present, and those details include more than facts. As Siegel pointed out, "making sense goes way beyond having a logical understanding of past events – a coherent story involves all our senses, head to toe" (2010, p. 178). Processing unresolved memories therefore entails accessing and being with the emotions, sensations, impulses, thoughts and beliefs that go with the details of what happened. Meaning-making is also much more than answering the question "why?" We could see that as the first level – for instance, someone grappling with a question that has preoccupied her since childhood: "Why was I abused, but none of my sisters? What was it about me?", or another person, who could never understand why his mother walked out leaving him and his brothers, all under ten, with their taciturn father. Or a woman who always had a sense that she had lost something important, reinforced by odd things her mother used to say on her birthday, but had not been able to piece things together until discovering that her twin had died in the womb. The second level is when we start to make sense of our own patterns of thinking, feeling and behaving in the light of our history and significant relationships.

Let me give two examples. The first is a simple, fairly ordinary example of sense-making. Something might have upset me during the day but only later, as I recount what happened to a friend and feel the prickle of tears in my eyes, do I realise that I felt hurt by what someone had said. It had reminded me of an experience in the past, and that explained why I reacted sharply to someone else later on. In other words, in the process I began to mentalise myself. My second example illustrates how accessing movement impulses helped one client develop a more nuanced, detailed story of witnessing domestic violence as a young child and make sense of why she kept experiencing pain in the joints of her hands. Whilst explaining how her mother always said she was imagining things whenever she mentioned the shouting at night, I noticed that she was flexing and extending her fingers as if they were stiff. Through exploring these movements Zoe realised that what they wanted to do was to grip her ears tightly. "I don't want to hear. I don't want to see anything. I don't want to know." The memory of how she had tried to cope with overwhelming fear was stored in her body.

Turning to story breaking – there are a number of ways we could conceptualise this. Bollas viewed the narrative process of "reviving the past in different ways" as one of transforming the past into history (1995, p. 115). Holmes conceptualised something similar – that nodal or prototypical memories become reworked through being unpacked then reassembled, taking on a new perspective. As new details come to light people begin to realise that there are many versions of the same story and their "range of admissible experience broadens" (1999, p. 61). What Holmes seems to be describing is a process of mentalising self and others in order to develop what I have described elsewhere as an "alternative perspectives mind" (Wright, 2016, p. 164). It is a process in which the therapist acts as an "assistant autobiographer" – witnessing, holding the narrative boundary and helping the client to shape the story into a more coherent pattern through the use of enquiry, mirroring and reflecting back (Holmes, 1999, pp. 58, 64).

But story breaking is not simply about telling and refashioning a tale in different ways then reflecting on what emerges. To view it like this fails to do justice to the depth and complexity of the narrative process. What needs emphasising is that the transformation of the past into history, and along with this a loosening up of the principles around which we organise our present-day experiences, comes through interweaving new, alive experiences in the present with the stale, repetitive and limiting narratives from long ago. These new experiences can be intersubjective, intrapsychic or embodied. Let me turn to Donnel Stern whose writing, along with that of other relational analysts, has informed my thinking about the intersubjective and the intrapsychic domains. In a subsequent chapter, I will cover the place of the body in creating new narratives. Stern's version of story making and breaking (and he does not use these terms), is of acquiring narrative freedom – "a new freedom to feel, relate, see, and say differently than before" – and I would add, increasing freedom of self-definition (2010, pp. 116–18). His thesis is that "the destabilization of old narratives and the emergence of new ones are the outcomes of unpredictable relational events", and that the new story is not itself "the engine of change, but the mark change leaves behind" (p. 128). That change comes about through the ongoing relatedness between therapist and client, a relatedness which includes rifts and enactments, moments when both encounter dissociated aspects of self, when the therapist feels challenged, and the client is convinced that she will act according to the old, rigid story, but ultimately does not. Stern concluded that enactments "provoke a change in each participant's perceptions (*and stories*) of the other and himself. Insight into the changed state of affairs comes later". But "therapeutic action lies in becoming a different person, usually in a small way, in the here and now" (p. 124). We could put it another way – that our present experience of past events is altered, old scripts are modified, and fresh stories can be envisaged for the future.

Robert Grossmark is another relational analyst who regards encounters with dissociated states as central to the change process. He argued that in mutual enactment or "enactive co-narration" we find "the emergence and arising of narratives that hitherto had no form or representation and therefore could not have been told in language" (2018, p. 127). Grossmark's use of the term "enactive" is informed by Loewald's distinction between "enactive" and "representational" remembering. The latter is verbal – we are back in the territory of factual and episodic memory. The former belongs to the realm of implicit memory and, in Loewald's words, "shares the timelessness and lack of differentiation of the unconscious and of primary process", such that "instead of having a past (the patient) *is* his past and does not distinguish himself as a rememberer from the content of his memory" (2018, p. 130). Essentially, he is a "self-out-of-time".

Although I can testify to the potency of rifts and ruptures that momentarily destabilise the therapeutic relationship, something not emphasised in the literature by Stern and Grossmark, is that stories can also be broken and our relationship with self and others altered when something occurs that is developmentally required. It could be being heard for the first time – and I will talk later about the healing potential of being witnessed and validated; being accepted unconditionally; being believed in and encouraged, or being supported to stay with and express overwhelming feelings. The changes in the people mentioned in this book would not have come about had we not been able to weather some storms, or if our relationship had not offered something missing during childhood.

Coming to the intrapsychic domain, story breaking also occurs when people become aware of the stories and beliefs of other parts of self; when they start to understand the "survival logic" of their ways of being; and when their different narratives are integrated into a whole. Stern argued that the freedom to inhabit multiple self-states simultaneously and tell many self-stories at once is "what gives to the stories that express the ways we know ourselves and others the plasticity to change with circumstances". His contention is that "one way to define states of self is as narratives: Each state is an ever-changing story. Or rather … because self-states are not simply experiences or memories, but aspects of identity, each state is an aspect of self defined by the stories that can be told from within it" (2010, p. 122). The narratives of our various "selves", each expressing different ways of locating ourselves in the world, can be thought of as different temporal experiences. In a moment, how we feel and act is suddenly influenced by the echoes of earlier times – rather like being pulled back through the years by a powerful magnet. The time/state dislocation can be subtle, a snagging that momentarily derails us. Alternatively, and this is more likely if traumatic events haunt us, we are catapulted into a completely different state of mind and body – a dissociated, "not-me" state. When unhinged in this way it is impossible to tell ourselves many stories at once – to be able, for instance, to say after a moment of reflection – "ah, that's that old feeling of shame I get when someone criticises me. No wonder I feel little and want to hide … and I'm aware of feeling angry too and wanting to retaliate".

As Stern said, "not-me cannot be told" and remains "insistently, stubbornly, defensively unformulated, not yet shaped or storied at all, isolated, existing in dissociation and thereby rendered mute" (2010, p. 122). "Not-me", if we think of our identity, is a "self-out-of-time". Change occurs when these procedurally encoded states, expressed, using Meares' terminology, as scripts, can be recognised, felt and assimilated into the known narrative of our lives. The transition from dissociated states to a more integrated place in which the memories held by those parts of self can be woven into the tapestry of our lives is an important aspect of psychotherapy with people who have experienced early trauma and are frequently hijacked by younger parts of self, all with different versions of the same event and different strategies for managing life. For example, when Terry's abusive mother became seriously ill, he was plagued with anxiety about what to do. He did not want to have anything more to do with her. But he felt incredibly guilty about his "selfish" thoughts and his former decision to hold firm boundaries around contacts crumbled in the face of a child part of himself that had grown up believing he had to protect his mother and who felt terribly afraid whenever she was unwell. This "caretaker" part always hoped that one day she would tell him she loved him. Another part of the self was furious, because his mother had never protected him and also angry with himself when he gave in to her entreaties for help.[5] As Terry began to articulate and reflect on these contradictory self-stories, and this was towards the end of a long therapeutic journey, he found it easier to recognise when he had been hijacked, to pause for breath before reacting and to stick to his boundaries.

With Grossmark's concept of enactive co-narration and my point about the need to mentalise ourselves as well as our clients in mind, I recall occasions when – and this is often near the beginning of a therapy – I catch myself doing something slightly uncharacteristic – perhaps calling the person by another name, or something goes on between us around timings. At an ordinary level we could see this as part of settling into a new routine and perhaps of some ambivalence on the client's or my part to fully engage. But these hiccups and uncharacteristic responses often prove informative. Several interesting happenstances occurred in the early days of work with Rose. For example, she had been coming for about a month when I got a call five minutes into session time saying she was terribly lost. A local road was closed and the diversion signs had petered out. I offered what advice I could and she eventually arrived 30 minutes late and terribly flustered. Whilst waiting I contemplated why I had not sent Rose a message about the road closure. It had crossed my mind when I learned about it the day before. Then I completely forgot – or did I? I recalled thinking, "there will be signs. She's organised, she'll find the way", then thought no more about it. Yet I do try to warn clients if I know of nearby road closures, so there was something uncharacteristic about this – something tinged I confess with inhospitality. What was being enacted?

At one level Rose was a competent, efficient and respected professional woman – a go-to person for help. So, trusting that she would find her way was not unreasonable. However, what had been emerging in our initial meetings was the story of a woman who was terrified of not coping. She worried that if she let up for a moment everything would fall into chaos. She had told me the previous week she was just hanging on, waiting for something to break. It had happened before – some years back at the same time of year. There was something about autumn that unnerved her. "It feels like something bad's going to happen, but I don't know what. I'm getting edgy, looking out for making a terrible mistake, waiting for bad news. I'm not sleeping well, irritable with everyone. There's so much to do and I feel exhausted." Stress accumulation? Or something deeper? Noticing my assumption that Rose would cope, I suddenly realised what might be being co-enacted and why this time of year was significant. It marked being left on her own to cope with frighteningly new situations. When she was seven, for instance, her adoptive father died suddenly. Far too young, Rose was propelled into being a young carer, told by her grandparents to be big now and look after her mother and brothers, and when she did cry, she was told "not to upset Mummy", an emotionally frail, histrionic woman. When she tried to talk about her father, her mother collapsed into tears and Rose ended up comforting her. There was no one to help her make sense of her shock and distress about her father's death. Almost a year later, as autumn approached, another shock: Rose was told she was going to boarding school because her mother couldn't manage looking after the house and three children. "She was a big girl now. It was time to look after herself." And that was that – "as if someone had pronounced a life sentence. I had to manage". Like many other boarding school survivors, Rose quickly learned that managing meant putting on a brave face and not showing emotions. But it was a brittle coping. Lacking the foundations we all need of parents who manage our feelings for us before we internalise the capacity for emotional regulation, and who support us over time to become increasingly independent, Rose became a pseudo-adult whilst often feeling little and lonely inside.

Grossmark said that "more than simply an other to receive the already formulated narrative, we seek the Other with whom we can make the narrative, to be the co-narrator", and within the therapeutic relationship our task is to unobtrusively companion our clients in the unfolding enactive co-narration (2018, pp. 128,

132). In living through something together what starts as a "no-thing" can be transformed to "a potential and then to a something, a narrative" – a representational remembering (p. 127). Even within that session with Rose, and of course the unfolding process took place over a long period, I noticed small shifts into more coherent story-telling. For instance, she tearfully admitted that she wasn't sure how long she could keep pretending to be strong and capable. She felt so lonely, never able to tell anyone how she felt. I responded saying, "I guess the seven-year-old you felt like that too – everyone expecting you to be strong, not letting you be sad or scared, or even cross. That must have felt very lonely". Rose nodded, it was, and for a while what had begun as a halting, hard-to-find-words account of the two years after her father died, became more organised, linear, reflective – until something took Rose back to the present – I think talking about arriving at her new school, seeing the trees starting to turn colour and feeling terribly homesick – and she returned again, her voice agitated, to her fear of breaking down. But after pausing to help Rose regulate her breathing, she was able to describe in a more coherent way her moments of panic. "It's like losing the adult me", she said. "I feel more like a child than 40-something". She might be driving her children to school and momentarily aware that she was working incredibly hard to appear calm and competent. Would this small piece of narrative about shifting self-states – a stepping back from and reflecting on being hijacked – have been possible had the session not begun as it did? I suspect not.

The last example I want to share is of a story breaking process that involved a client making sense of long-standing beliefs and survival strategies. One of the limiting stories Theresa lived by concerned her creative and academic ability. She enjoyed learning and now she had retired wanted to learn to play the violin, having a lifelong love of music. But time after time her plans to practice or get going with other creative projects were thwarted. We often explored the limiting beliefs behind this such as "I'll never be good enough". We also experimented with different ways Theresa could organise her day in order to make time for things she really wanted to do. "But I still feel so blocked", she complained. "I tell myself I haven't got time. There are too many other things to do. Or a voice pops up saying I'm not good enough or it won't be good enough, so why bother."

Eventually we stumbled across the meaning behind such a limiting story, or rather we found two stories that explained Theresa's recurrent struggles. One began in her early teens when her mother went back to work and she was expected to take over lots of household jobs. Theresa remembered how angry her mother would be if things weren't done by the time she got home. "I really wanted to get on with my homework and do well. But I usually had to cobble something together at the last minute. Everyone kept saying 'you could do better than this!'" The other story predated this but endured throughout her childhood. It was the memory of her brothers' cruel taunts if she got good marks. They called her a "goody-goody" if they caught her working. They teased her mercilessly when she practised her flute, making screeching sounds to drown her out and telling her how awful she was. "So I ended up believing I was really no good and gave up. It was easier that way." I reflected that an old story was at work of a Cinderella child who was under so much pressure. She had to do all the chores, and all that homework, and if she didn't woe betide her. Her mother got cross. Her teachers were impatient. Her brothers teased her if she worked hard. As I outlined the "plot" Theresa became visibly anxious. Then when I said, "but that story is over. Now you can choose how you organise your time", she sighed, then smiled as if something had struck her. "I've got it! Now I understand why I don't do as well as I could. I began to deliberately mess up so there was nothing they could attack. I acted stupid and after a while the teachers stopped going on about how bright I was and could do better. So maybe the reason why I find it hard to sit down and get on with something is because I'm repeating how it used to be." I remarked on the cleverness of Theresa's survival strategies back then and observed how sad she suddenly looked. She agreed and tears began to well up. After giving space for her sadness we discussed how she could break the old stories now by determinedly doing things differently and reminding herself that her life also included positive stories, stories of determination and achievement once she had left home. And slowly this began to make a difference.

Although I am citing material from one session, it should not be thought that story making and breaking is a quick process. As Feldman pointed out, sometimes we have to remain immersed for long periods in powerful, not yet symbolised experience, to become fluent in a "spectral language". To prematurely articulate such processes can push people into intellectualising and repeating well-worn scripts. It can also rupture the alliance because they feel missed (2016, p. 73). Yes, there are certainly critical moments as occurred with Theresa when something unprocessed from the past – and note that her survival brain, and with this a more traumatised part of self, was activated when she mentioned her brothers – was made sense of and became integrated into narrative memory. But this was part of ongoing work weaving back and forwards in time and stitching in the emotional and physiological responses that accompanied her memories. The ongoing process also entailed dialoguing with different parts of self in order to access deeper layers of meaning and regulating Theresa whenever she stepped out of the window of tolerance and lost touch with the present moment. What is important to emphasise is that new narratives are formed as part of an ongoing process within the matrix of a safe, holding relationship – a new, alive, experience. Psychotherapy and its different traditions provide a variety of ways to tell, re-tell, refine and alter our stories. But it is how we *are* with our clients, not what we do or say that makes the difference.

Conclusions

To sum things up and return to the key functions of story-telling outlined at the start: If our clients can share their story whilst staying in the window of tolerance – meaning they can think about the past, but still have one foot in the present and be aware of and able to articulate their feelings about things that have happened – this supports the integration of vertical and horizontal regions in the brain. It also helps to integrate past, present and future as "interlocking modes of experience" (Bromberg, 2001, p. 290). For instance, in the present relational sharing and constructing of narratives we can explain the past (why I am as I am), and mediate the future. Through constructing meaningful narratives – weaving what has been forgotten or silenced into the tapestry of what is known, and telling and re-telling events with increasing, sensory-rich elaboration over time, we develop a more solid, integrated sense of self. For people who feel empty or fragmented inside with little sense of personal ongoingness, it is possible to find themselves. Some people come to realise that they are more than the versions of self they used to live by, versions inherited from others or shaped by negative beliefs about their worth. Others use story-telling as part of a process of reinventing themselves, perhaps as part of a life-stage crisis.

Meaning-making is also a critical, and inherently containing, element of the therapeutic process, and has been since the dawn of psychoanalysis when Freud recognised that "we construct meaning and direction out of our memories in order to suffer less and live more fully in the present" (Harris, Kalb & Klebanoff, 2016, p. 123). I have cited a number of authors who emphasise that meaning needs to be found and that this occurs as an intrinsic part of the therapeutic relationship. As Grossmark said, "meaning is an event". "It does not exist that it can be interpreted, but rather comes into being through enactment itself, through dialogue and intersubjective engagement" (2018, p. 176). Too often, perhaps when excited by an idea or anxiously caught in trying to change something, I can offer my thoughts on the meaning. But the real changes that ultimately transform the past into history come when people make their own discoveries. From a relational perspective this occurs when something that has been dissociated and hence empty of meaning is actually lived through in a co-created enactment. Whilst I agree about the transformative potential of "enactive co-narration", I want to stress several points. Firstly, that with some people, or at certain points in the therapy, to actually speak about what might be going on between us is too dysregulating. We have to hold that and work on our own responses. Secondly, it is not just what goes on between therapist and client that supports meaning-making, but also what can emerge when people get in touch with split off parts of self and start to dialogue with those selves. Thirdly, as the brief example about Zoe's hand illustrates, new meanings can also emerge through the body and creative processes.

The fourth function of narrative, binding groups and communities, is particularly applicable to family and group therapy, the communal sharing enabling people to feel acknowledged and to realise that they are not alone. In individual work, to be heard and validated also helps to reconnect people who feel isolated and alienated, and this is particularly true if their stories evoke shame or had to be kept secret. The transformative potential of being witnessed in such contexts cannot be underestimated and will be discussed further in Chapter 10. I have also noticed how when people start to contemplate the lives of their parents and grandparents and to appreciate how their history shaped them, or to think of the history of their community and their place within it, there is a growth in compassion for themselves and others.

My journey exploring the function of narrative in our lives and within psychotherapy has taken me again and again to my core themes – time, identity and meaning. Given that our identity is inextricably linked with our existence in time, the ability to construct meaningful narratives and weave things into the tapestry of our lives contributes to our sense of personal ongoingness and anchors us in time. We can find ourselves anew when we start to fashion coherent narratives which connect and make sense of things already known and give words to what has hitherto only been experienced in the register of emotion, sensation and enactment. In the next two chapters I will examine how loss and trauma create ruptures in time and the particular ways that story making and "doing meaning" help heal those ruptures.

Notes

1 And even though we might ridicule superstition, at times we still attempt to explain natural events and especially disasters in terms of fatalistic stories: "I must be cursed"; "I walked under that ladder"; "It was jinxed from the start"; "It's my lucky day" and so on.
2 Field used this term explaining that 'black' is used to refer to people defined as African, coloured and Asian under apartheid laws. Those he termed 'black' spoke Xhosa, those termed 'coloured' spoke Afrikaans or English.
3 Because the word script is used in slightly different ways in other theoretical traditions, I would prefer to use the term traumatic scripts here.
4 Meares speculated that narrative depends on autobiographical chronicles, on episodic scripts or semantic memory (1998, p. 887).
5 It could be argued that "caretaker"/attach parts keep orienting to the future in a vain attempt to remake the past. "One day, he/she/they will …". They are waiting patiently for what was sorely needed in childhood to be provided by someone in the future. Angry, fight parts are both past and present oriented in their vehement protests – "I'm angry that she never …" or "that you …". Flight parts are seeking to numb themselves into a timeless state where thoughts and feelings about the past are obliterated. Meanwhile the parts of self that freeze are stuck in the nightmare of an eternal past.

References

Bollas, C. 1987. *The Shadow of the Object: Psychoanalysis of the Unthought Known*. New York: Columbia University Press.
Bollas, C. 1995. *Cracking Up*. London: Routledge.
Bromberg, P. 2001. *Standing in the Spaces: Essays on Clinical Process, Trauma, and Dissociation*. Hillsdale, NJ: Analytic Press.
Bromberg, P. 2011. *The Shadow of the Tsunami and the Growth of the Relational Mind*. New York: Routledge.
Bruce, E. 1999. "Holding on to the Story: Older People, Narrative, and Dementia" in G. Roberts & J. Holmes (Eds.) *Healing Stories: Narrative in Psychiatry and Psychotherapy* (pp. 181–205). Oxford: Oxford University Press.
Cozolino, L. 2016. *Why Psychotherapy Works*. New York: W. W. Norton & Co.
Dawson, G. 1999. "Trauma, Memory, Politics: The Irish Troubles" in K. Lacy Rogers & S. Leydesdorff (Eds.) *Trauma and Life Stories: International Perspectives* (pp. 180–204). London: Routledge.

Feldman, M. 2016. "Travel Fever: Transgenerational Trauma and Witnessing in Analyst and Analysand" in A. Harris, M. Kalb & S. Klebanoff (Eds). *Ghosts in the Consulting Room: Echoes of Trauma in Psychoanalysis* (pp. 52–75). New York: Routledge.

Field, S. 1999. "Interviewing in a Culture of Violence: Moving Memories from Windermere to the Cape Flats" in K. Lacy Rogers & S. Leydesdorff (Eds.) *Trauma and Life Stories: International Perspectives* (pp. 60–79). London: Routledge.

Gergen, K. 2005. "Narrative, Moral Identity and Historical Consciousness: A Social Constructionist Account" in J. Straub (Ed.) *Narrative, Identity and Historical Consciousness* (pp. 99–119). New York: Berghahn Books.

Grossmark, R. 2018. *The Unobtrusive Relational Analyst.* New York: Routledge.

Harris, A., Kalb, M. & Klebanoff, S. (Eds.) 2016. *Ghosts in the Consulting Room: Echoes of Trauma in Psychoanalysis.* New York: Routledge.

Holmes, J. 1999. "Defensive and Creative Uses of Narrative in Psychotherapy: An Attachment Perspective" in G. Roberts & J. Holmes (Eds.) *Healing Stories: Narrative in Psychiatry and Psychotherapy* (pp. 49–66). Oxford: Oxford University Press.

Inge, D. 2014. *A Tour of Bones: Facing Fear and Looking for Life.* London: Bloomsbury.

Lacy Rogers, K. & Leydesdorff, S. (Eds.) 1999. *Trauma and Life Stories: International Perspectives.* London: Routledge.

Lacy Rogers, K. 1999. "Lynching Stories: Family and Community Memory in the Mississippi Delta" in K. Lacy Rogers & S. Leydesdorff (Eds) *Trauma and Life Stories: International Perspectives* (pp. 113–30). London: Routledge.

Laub, D. 2005. "Traumatic shutdown of narrative and symbolization: A death instinct derivative?", *Contemporary Psychoanalysis*, 41(2), 307–26.

Levine, P. 2015. *Trauma and Memory: Brain and Body in a Search for the Living Past.* Berkeley, CA: North Atlantic Books.

Lorenz, F. 1999. "The Unending War: Social Myth, Individual Memory and the Malvinas" in K. Lacy Rogers & S. Leydesdorff (Eds.) *Trauma and Life Stories: International Perspectives* (pp. 95–112). London: Routledge.

Meares, R. 1998. "The self in conversation: On narratives, chronicles and scripts", *Psychoanalytic Dialogues*, 8(6), 875–91.

Meares, R. 2012. *A Dissociation Model of Borderline Personality Disorder.* New York: W. W. Norton & Co.

Nachmani, G. 2005. "Proof of life: A discussion of Dori Laub's traumatic shutdown of narrative and symbolization", *Contemporary Psychoanalysis*, 41(2), 327–40.

Philips, J. 1999. "The Psychodynamic Narrative" in G. Roberts & J. Holmes (Eds.) *Healing Stories: Narrative in Psychiatry and Psychotherapy* (pp. 27–48). Oxford: Oxford University Press.

Rappoport, E. 2017. "Tower of Skulls. A Totemic Memorial to the Cambodian Genocide" in S. Grand & J. Salberg (Eds.) *Trans-generational Trauma and the Other* (pp. 172–86). London: Routledge.

Roberts, G. 1999. "Introduction: A Story of Stories" in G. Roberts & J. Holmes (Eds.) *Healing Stories: Narrative in Psychiatry and Psychotherapy* (pp. 3–26). Oxford: Oxford University Press.

Rolls, L. 2010. "Narrating time: Minimising the disruption and discontinuities of children's experience of death", *Illness, Crisis and Loss*, 184, 323–39.

Rose, S. 1999. "Naming and Claiming: The Integration of Traumatic Experience and the Reconstruction of Self in Survivors' Stories of Sexual Abuse" in K. Lacy Rogers & S. Leydesdorff (Eds.) *Trauma and Life Stories: International Perspectives* (pp. 160–79). London: Routledge.

Sacks, O. 1995. *An Anthropologist on Mars.* London: Picador.

Sacks, O. 2015a. *The Man who Mistook his Wife for a Hat*. London: Picador Classics (1st edition, 1985. London: Duckworth).

Siegel, D. 2010. *Mindsight*. London: Oneworld Publications.

Stern, D. B. 2010. *Partners in Thought: Working with Unformulated Experience, Dissociation and Enactment*. New York: Routledge.

Stern, D. N. 1985. *The Interpersonal World of the Infant*. New York: Basic Books.

Stern, D. N. 1998. *The Diary of a Baby*. New York: Basic Books.

Wallin, D. 2007. *Attachment in Psychotherapy*. New York: Guilford Press.

Zur, J. 1999. "Remembering and Forgetting: Guatemala War Widows' Forbidden Memories" in K. Lacy Rogers & S. Leydesdorff (Eds.) *Trauma and Life Stories: International Perspectives* (pp. 45–59). London: Routledge.

PART III

Ruptured time

9

WHEN THE PAST HAUNTS THE PRESENT

The impact of trauma on our relationship to time

> Memory is sacred ground. But it's haunted too. It's the place where my rage and guilt and grief go circling like hungry birds scavenging old bones.
>
> (Eger, 2017, p. 21)

In this chapter I intend to think about the different ways trauma can influence our relationship to time. Let me start with a wonderful definition of madness from Louis Sass: "the end-point in a trajectory consciousness follows when it separates from the body and the passions, and from the social and practical worlds, and turns in upon itself" (McGilchrist, 2009, p. 393). This is decontextualisation par excellence – a splitting off of both internal and external connections, and without a grounding in context it is impossible to make sense of our world and hence, know how to navigate it. In the Introduction I mentioned that traumatic experiences fragment and decontextualise, and I believe that decontextualisation is a core issue in all the trauma-related disorders and perhaps also psychotic illnesses. Both relate to experiences that cannot be assimilated into our assumptive world. They do not make sense. During and after traumatic events there is a failure of integration when aspects of experience are severed from their context. Memories, feelings, body sensations may all become fragmented and dissociated. And unable to locate these inner experiences within narrative memory as definite events with a before, during and after, survivors often fear that they are going mad or making things up. Yet they are compelled to react to them.

In Chapter 2, I argued how important it is for our sense of self to be embedded in time, to have a sense of going-on-being and an awareness of a connectedness to both the past and the future. However, trauma threatens our sense of identity and distorts our perception of time. A traumatic event has some of the properties of an adventure, except that it is terrifying rather than exciting. There is no surety of return to the familiar continuity of life. At first people cling to what Frankl called the "delusion of reprieve" (2004, p. 23). One survivor of Auschwitz described how at first she comforted herself with the thought that it was only temporary, despite everything people told her each day. "Soon I'll be home, well, things will be back to normal" (Eger, 2017, p. 58). People view the situation as an interruption in time and are convinced that they will resume their usual affairs and pre-crisis identity if they just wait, endure, and don't think about or fight what they are experiencing. Then despair creeps in when whatever has happened seems to be permanent and getting worse.

Time is distorted at the moment of a traumatic event and, for many people, in its aftermath. For example, in describing a near death experience we hear people speak of time stopping or speeding up or envisaging their whole life passing before them. After severe trauma many survivors become unable to differentiate past and present. As Allen pointed out when discussing PTSD, "exposure to traumatic events can result in an illness that is continually retraumatising". People with PTSD "cannot live in the present because they are continually haunted by the past" (2001, p. 103). It is as if they have been sentenced to repeatedly relive that past, like birds endlessly scavenging old bones, making it impossible to live in the present. Of course, in the aftermath of trauma people can be affected in a variety of ways. Some experience a relatively short period of dysregulation when the world and its temporal order are thrown upside down. But for others, time is lost and distorted on a regular basis in a number of ways: they may lose their anchoring in time completely, as in the case with dissociation. They can be repeatedly haunted by the intrusion of the past into the present. They can be sensitive to time-related triggers, and they can find it hard to envisage a positive future in which things are different from the past so the normal fluidity between past, present and future as mutually interacting and influencing modes of time breaks down (Bromberg, 2001, p. 290). "Their psychological reality", as Mollica said, "is both full and empty, full of the past and empty of new ideas and experiences" (Roberts, 1999, p. 20).

Trauma and memory

Let me digress a moment to recap the discussion in Chapter 3 about the areas of the brain affected by traumatic experiences and the differences between traumatic and other memories because this can help us understand the decontextualisation and distortion of time during and after trauma.

- Memories take different forms and those we are conscious of form only a subset of a bigger, complex memory system.
- Unlike ordinary memories, traumatic memories are never fully processed and integrated. They are encoded as implicit memories and can be triggered by features in the present which echo the past and emerge as vivid visual, auditory, olfactory and somatic fragments that lack context.
- Critical to this process is the amygdala, which retains the imprint of traumatic and very early experiences, and the hippocampus. Ordinarily, the amygdala

and the hippocampus are meant to work together. But under intense stress the latter can go offline leaving us at the mercy of amygdala-driven responses (e.g. fight, flight or freeze). Le Doux called this the fast circuit compared with the slower circuit in which the hippocampus scans incoming sensory data for relevance, compares different memories, and passes information to the higher cortex for executive planning.

- When something echoes a traumatic memory that takes someone out of the window of tolerance, it can activate other, long-forgotten memories of previous trauma, and create a "domino effect". The example of Deborah in Chapter 3 illustrates this and it is what kept happening to Theresa, Mark and Lily mentioned later.
- People can become increasingly conditioned by procedural memory. Over time the neural circuits containing traumatic memories become more sensitive to further exposure to matching or similar stimuli. This is known as kindling.
- An additional problem is that the amygdala can pair any stimulus with anxiety and fear.

Flashbacks and body memories

Flashbacks are one example of the influence of the silent, unprocessed past – those moments when something from the past intrudes into the present in visual, auditory, olfactory or kinaesthetic ways. When Van der Kolk first saw someone having a flashback, he realised that however horrendous the traumatic event that triggered it, it had a beginning, a middle and an end, but the flashbacks could be made more severe by never knowing when they would strike, nor when they would stop (2014, p. 16). Being repeatedly subjected to intrusive images or sounds or painful body sensations that come out of the blue and make no sense, can either freeze you or make you feel like doing something out of character and is incredibly frightening. Until people learn that these are body or emotion memories they often fear that they are going mad, and even if they can tell themselves it is not happening in the present, the physiological responses to a flashback are very real and can persist for a long time.

One of my clients had flashbacks that took the form of intensely disturbing body enactments for which she had no narrative memory. They made little sense to Laura and she was frightened because although she usually maintained some level of awareness, they made her feel completely out of control. She lost the capacity to speak. She felt intense pain. Sometimes her body shook. Sometimes her limbs contorted or struck out as if she was trying to escape from something. Only after much courageous work in therapy did a narrative with a temporal context slowly emerge, and instead of being ashamed of having a body that did these seemingly bizarre things, Laura came to appreciate that it had been endlessly repeating what she must have felt and done when she was tortured as a child. Another trauma survivor was haunted by visual flashbacks after an unexpected encounter with the man who sexually assaulted and degraded him in his late teens. Because of their content, Mark felt deeply ashamed. He became scared of people looking at him in case they saw how perverted he believed himself to be and, because seeing men of a particular build evoked flashbacks, he began to avoid going out. Once Mark lost the anchoring of a regular routine, he was left with too much time in which to ruminate and, as often happens, the flashbacks occurred with increasing regularity. No wonder he felt increasingly hopeless and suicidal.

Time-related triggers

Anyone working with traumatised clients will also be familiar with time-related triggers. These can occur at certain times of day, for example, at night or on the hour of return from school or during particular periods of time such as weekends, holidays, or on anniversaries. The following examples illustrate situations which trigger many trauma survivors: There was Theresa, who habitually knocked herself out with a cocktail of drugs and alcohol in the afternoon. Even if she had a good morning there was something about the latter part of the day she found very frightening and she could not imagine getting through the evening without numbing herself. There was the teacher who always became depressed and anxious over the long summer vacation and to the immense frustration of his wife, refused to go away for family holidays. Another woman called Lily could not bear weekends and it was interesting to observe that the chronic pain that had troubled her for years was always much worse at the end of the week.

As a child Theresa had been mercilessly taunted and abused by her older brothers when she came home from school and she recalled dreading walking into the house. Matt, the teacher, used to be sent to his grandparents' farm for the school holidays where his grandfather abused him from the age of seven, and Lily's mother went out to work at weekends, leaving her alone with her alcoholic and frighteningly violent stepfather. I also have in mind survivors of ritual abuse for whom certain calendar dates are very triggering because they evoke implicit memories of the horrific things that occurred on those occasions. Such people can experience mounting anxiety before the date, often not understanding why, and are more at risk then of dissociation, vanishing for several days while experiencing suicidal impulses.

With people like Theresa, Matt and Lily we can help them in practical ways – using mindfulness, for instance, to stay in the present, teaching strategies to regulate emotions and inviting them to think how they can make evenings or weekends or summers as different as possible from those terrifying times of childhood. But it is the painstaking work of regulating people during sessions, helping them to appreciate what triggers them and, in safe ways, to process the memories of what happened that ultimately enable them to enjoy the gift of living each day as they choose. I will say more about this in the following chapter.

Dissociation and "incomprehensible time"

Boon and her colleagues pointed out that time loss is a hallmark of Dissociative Identity Disorder (Boon, Steele & van der Hart, 2011, p. 16). "It is as though parts of you do not live in time and even have trouble understanding the concept of time. Time can seem too fast or too slow, gaps of lost time make it hard to keep track of the day; time may not be experienced at all, and time sense may differ among various dissociative parts" (p. 115). All these problems lead to confusion and difficulties in establishing a structure and routine to the day, something we all need to anchor us. There are some detailed examples of time loss in the remarkable book by Florence Schreiber about Sybil – a woman who endured horrific abuse at the hands of a schizophrenic mother and was one of the first people recognised as having dissociated parts of self. Schreiber wrote about the reality of Sybil's repeated experience of something happening that had no beginning. "She asked herself in panic 'will there never be an end that also has a beginning? Will there never be continuity bridging the awful void between now and some other time, a time in the future, a time in the past?'" (Schreiber, 1974, p. 101). Time loss completely disoriented Sybil. For example, when describing her feelings when she had regained her "adult" self after a long period of time loss, "The word 'now' was tantalising, elusive since there was no knowing how much time had passed since she had been waiting in the elevator" (Schreiber, 1974, p. 21). Imagine for a moment that you had no recollection of the past. You keep waking up and don't recognise things around you. You are utterly disoriented. How frightening that would be. It makes me think how important it is to help our traumatised clients to be more mindfully in the present. Without this they remain at the mercy of overwhelming feelings, living lives that are constricted by the need to avoid danger at all costs.

To understand the adaptive logic of dissociation we need to keep in mind that each of us has multiple and varied selves able to respond to the different circumstances in which we find ourselves. When faced with situations that are overwhelming or people close to us are suddenly and incomprehensibly inconsistent and incongruent – situations that cannot quickly be assimilated into our assumptive world – dissociation is a strategy to protect us from self-fragmentation and preserve that illusion of a unitary self mentioned in Chapter 2. It shields us from the irresolvable dilemma of having to respond simultaneously to conflicting realities. It stops us going crazy, and this, according to Bromberg, occurs by "hypnoidally unlinking the incompatible states of consciousness and allowing access to them only as discontinuities and unrelated mental experiences" (2001, p. 260). These incompatible states become part of what Davoigne called the "cut-out unconscious", a not-knowing what you know (Davoigne, 2014). Let me give an example how "cutting out" helped one child deal with irreconcilable emotions and realities. Alice's dilemma was how to relate to a father who was sometimes loving and ordinary, but at other times frightened and hurt her. How could she be raped by him then pretend to enjoy the picnic which had been the excuse for going out together? Perhaps significantly, he always made her tidy up the picnic things, whilst the real mess and injury was split off and never thought about. But without the capacity to shut out or compartmentalise certain memories, thoughts and feelings it would have been impossible for Alice to act as normal with the rest of the family and go to school as if nothing was wrong. The reality of her father's brutality had to be held by other segregated parts of self. And this was clearly true of Sybil and of many children subject to ongoing sexual and physical abuse by a close relative.

A doctor diagnosed with DID in her 40s used a wonderful metaphor to describe dissociation. She wrote:

> In a dysfunctional and traumatic home environment an outward appearance of normality must be maintained in order to avoid aggravating the abuser. Imagine a lake, the quiet surface representing daily life and consciousness. When overwhelming painful traumas occur threatening to disturb the surface, dissociation separates and contains the memories and emotions, as if in a bubble or balloon which is then weighted down out of sight on the bed of the lake, far away from consciousness. Daily life goes on, the secrets of abuser and abused protected.

However, the woman came to appreciate that the strategy also brought problems. "By adulthood I had twelve such 'balloons' on my lakebed, each still chock-full of unbearable pain and horror, some of them revisiting the surface when circumstances required, some of them later bursting up unannounced and catching the adult me off guard" (Sachs & Goulton, 2008, p. 50). In other words, although they are out of sight, dissociative memories and emotions do not vanish. As Cozolino pointed out, we can have memories that we don't consciously remember "but never forget" (2016, p. 5). They constitute the phenomenologically silent past which even if not available in words, can nonetheless haunt us. Another problem with dissociation is that it can become generalised to anything echoing the original trauma and then as time goes on, used in an addictive way to avoid emotional discomfort.

Returning to Sybil, she felt ashamed of repeatedly dissociating and could not bring herself to talk about it. After a time lapse she learned, like people I have worked with, to pretend to be fine and to knowing what they had been doing despite having missed something. Claiming to have a bad memory or inventing stories about what they had been doing are other 'faking-it' strategies. But it is through talking about time loss and their fears about this that our clients can be helped. It makes the experience relationable, something that has a name and an understandable protective logic behind it. Then later, if the client is sufficiently stable, it might be possible to start finding words for the contents of their hidden away "balloons".

The impossibility of now and of tomorrow

Daniel Stern remarked that the "present moment can be held hostage by either the past or the future", his meaning here being that not only can the past haunt the present, but the imagined future reorganises the present so much and so quickly that it now becomes ephemeral (2004, p. 27). Living fully in the present is incredibly difficult when plagued by intrusive memories and many survivors find it hard to conceive a future with things to work towards and look forward to. They remain stuck in an endless fear-filled present and hold fixed beliefs, or what Brothers calls "trauma-related certainties", that the future will be an inevitable repeat of the terrible past (2014). People will always reject them. Everyone they become close to will fall sick, die or move. They will be criticised or humiliated. They will inevitably fail and therefore it isn't worth trying anything new. The list is long, but there are common strands which speak of abandonment, rejection, scorn, being hurt and a lack of the qualities we know to be essential ingredients of good parenting and the creation of secure attachments – attunement, mirroring, encouragement, safe boundary setting and mentalising. And of course, these "trauma-related certainties" play out in the therapeutic relationship so that we get pulled into time-zones and roles that initially make no sense.

The frozen past

The passage of time does not necessarily mean becoming less anxious, hyper-alert, easily startled and pulled into automatic survival responses. The examples given so far make this clear. Instead, trauma survivors can become more and more triggered by things in the present, and this compromises gathering and integrating new information, a massive problem when it includes details that could tell people they are here now in the present and that things have changed. It means that traumatic memories remain frozen in time rather than being assimilated and integrated into the ongoing story of their lives. How traumatic memories are processed also has implications for identity. With large gaps in autobiographical memory it is hard to retain a sense of an integrated, ongoing self (Wright, 2016, p. 66). Many survivors of early trauma have told me that they find it hard to remember anything about their childhood, sometimes expressing sadness that other people have such memories, and happy ones at that, whereas they don't. The fact that unresolved and unintegrated memories can lead to contradictory somatic impulses and inner conflicts between different "parts" of self also contributes to a lack of personal coherence.[1]

When a traumatic memory is evoked survivors feel as if they are *in* the memory and respond accordingly. They find it hard to distinguish past from present and what is internal from what is external. The frozen past lives on in fragmentary images, sounds, smells and body sensations that disturb and dysregulate them, and because they don't make sense in the present context can make them feel they are going mad. It lives on in phobias, fixed beliefs and automatic behaviours once designed to be protective but in the present often causing problems. It emerges in physical symptoms, the body recounting the story for which there are no words, and interpersonal enactments. As Bromberg eloquently put it, "the mind retains the fear as a dread of what can happen or is happening rather than as a memory of what has happened. The result is that the person, by continually enacting the affective memory, creates a world of miniature versions of the original situation and lives in that world as a reality that is substantiated through his ongoing relation-ships". "Waiting for evils that never arise is a serious problem for a traumatised adult ... by constantly mobilising for disaster the person is already prepared for it" (Bromberg, 2001, p. 260).

Psychotherapists use a variety of terms for these replica versions – internal working models, transference, RIGS[2] and schema to name a few, and now with the "relational turn" embraced by both psychodynamic and humanistic therapists we think more about enactments in a transference/countertransference field. I like Totton's term for this, "embodied relational engrams", because it captures the fact that the frozen past emerges in somatic and interactive ways. It is something that lives on *between* people, and so unfreezing demands something new relationally. As Totton explained, our bodies learn patterns of relating from infancy and we develop a range of embodied relational patterns, our "blueprints to determine new encounters". These patterns tell of the "possession of our bodies by early ghosts", ghostlike patterns of relating as "engrams" (Totton, 2016). Totton's term is appropriate given recent research demonstrating that memories are stored at a cellular level and that a contextual fear memory can be replayed when only a collection of a few hundred cells are stimulated.[3]

Of course, we cannot directly perceive these cellular memory traces. But if we observe carefully, we often discover that distressing memories are engraved on the body in visible ways. As Ogden and Fisher emphasised, "we remember the past not only in word, images, and stories, but also through chronic traits of tension, movement and posture." The body "speaks the nonverbal language of visceral sensations, posture, tightening or relaxing, movements, gestures, facial expression, changes in levels of autonomic arousal, heartbeat, breath, even physical symptoms" (Ogden and Fisher, 2015, p. 99). They also point out that, "our bodies remember and act from what has worked in the past rather than what might be adaptive to our current situation and relationships" and often what were once the best responses available when threatened with attack, rejection, dismissal or scorn, continue long after conditions have changed (p. 101). Thus, even though the mind might say "It's safe now", "I'm an adult not that child anymore" or "I've got friends who really care about me", the body does not know this. When we are under pressure, feeling emotionally overwhelmed, going through a difficult transi-tion phase or triggered by reminders of the past we fall back on old survival stra-tegies. These blueprints, created long ago, are our defaults and can be rapidly set in motion before we have a chance to think.

Our bodies also hold what did not get processed, completed or discharged at earlier points in life when we were overwhelmed. This can lead to repeated recy-cling of emotion and sensation or to behaviours that now bring unintended consequences. As Ogden, Minton and Pain pointed out, "it is as if time stopped at the moment of threat, and the body is continuing to re-enact the sequence of events" (2006, p. 248). This is the "unfinished past", a past which, as I discuss later, can be completed by helping people to perform actions that would have overcome their sense of helplessness during the traumatic experience and to express the emotions associated with the memory (p. 248). As an example of somatic recycling – ongoing tension in the arms may indicate an incomplete fight response, a self-protective impulse that could not emerge for fear of enraging the attacker even more; whilst chronically restless legs are often indicative of the impulse to run, understandable when in danger but for a child or someone who is trapped, impossible to execute.[4]

Given the incredible language of the body, as therapists, part of our role is to observe and be curious about what we see happening physically and feel in our own bodies as our clients talk about the past or a current problem. We can be alert to signs of tension and small movements which may be indicative of what was needed but impossible to execute when under threat; to posture and habitual gestures that speak of learned ways of relating to others; or to the physical manifestations of unexpressed emotion. We can also invite our clients to be curious about what they themselves notice physically and to contemplate what might want to happen or what, if words were available, their bodies might be trying to say. Some unexpected and important answers often emerge. But what can release our traumatised clients from the physical, emotional and interpersonal legacy of the past? What might reduce the tendency for critical areas of the brain to shut down? And, given the differences between ordinary and traumatic memories, how do we help people deal with intrusions from the past and reconnect with the present? I will address these questions in the next chapter.

Unknown histories

> We are histories of ourselves. Narratives.
> If all this disappeared, would I still exist?
>
> *(Rovelli, 2018, p. 154)*

I have considered the implications on our sense of self of a lack of verbal memory, but what does it mean to carry the unworded memories of others? As practitioners we can feel at our most confused, disoriented and disturbed when we are faced with unknown histories – a "silent past" that belongs not merely to the client, but to other people in his or her family. I have in mind birth-related traumas and intergenerational trauma. The former include traumas and losses affecting the mother in the period before or after the birth,[5] traumatic births and periods spent in an incubator if the baby is premature. We know that the mother's state of mind and emotional status has an impact on her unborn child and that unresolved traumas and losses can interfere with bonding, a process which occurs both pre-conceptually and throughout the pregnancy (Weinstein, 2016, pp. 7, 20). However, it is not only the mother's experiences that impact the developing foetus. Its development can also be adversely affected by stress experienced by her own mother during her gestation. Thus, postnatal patterns build upon earlier prenatal and birth experiences and the experiences of the mother and her mother (p. 76). I believe that birth-related traumas also include situations when the mother-to-be has very mixed feelings about giving birth. To some extent it is normal to have misgivings about coping, letting go of former freedoms and the impact on other relationships. But in more extreme circumstances maternal ambivalence interferes with infant/ mother bonding and can constellate an attachment trauma. The woman's ambivalence might be because of the loss of another child – miscarriages during earlier pregnancies, an infant death, a sibling who died when still young – those "ghosts in the nursery" which still haunt her. A woman can also have very mixed feelings about her soon to be live baby if its twin dies in the womb. As one woman said, "my womb felt like a tomb", but while other people focused on the live baby, there was no time or permission for her to mourn the lost of its foetal twin (BBC Radio 4, 2016).

I have worked with a number of people who knew or had an instinctive, bodily sense that they had lost a twin in the womb. Several had long-standing relational problems – for instance they struggled with an existential sense of being alone even when with others or always sought more intense friendships than their friends could offer. For others, the theme of people suddenly disappearing, a fear which evoked considerable anxiety, was a core issue. But they could not locate their fears in any known events. Something was embodied and played out in the present.

If the mother's ambivalence is extreme, for example if she conceived because of rape or is in a relationship with a violent man, or was herself so deprived of love and care that a vulnerable baby evokes feelings of envy and hatred, this can result in an infanticidal attachment pattern (Sachs, 2008, pp. 127–39). Infanticidal caregivers may fantasise about killing the unborn child or take real actions to promote this. Later, because attachment behaviours are designed to ensure proximity to and engagement with the caregiver, a child with this attachment style can perversely feel safe and comforted when being hurt. She may also mimic the parent in some way, for instance, in later life resorting to chronic self-harm and suicidal impulses. She may experience a feeling of "nameless dread", but being detached from its name and cause, the dread is expressed in ways that make no sense. This is an extreme example of an "unknown history", but one that leaves a deep imprint on the living child and then the adult.

The ghosts of others

The other category of trauma that is divorced from context is when extreme experiences are transmitted from one generation to the next. Apprey pointed out that to be born is "to have a history before one's own history" (2017, p. 32). I am struck by the difference between saying, to be born is "to *have* a history" and "for there to *be* a history". The former speaks of a much greater, more pervasive influence of the past on present and future, something that has already caught us in its grip. Davoigne used the phrase the "stoppage of time" in cases of intergenerational trauma. "You have no limit", she said, "no limit between the future and the past. Everything is present" (2014). Imagine what it would be like, as Doris Brothers suggested, "if there never was a 'before' the trauma, because you were born into it – and never an 'after' if you then keep experiencing traumas all your life" (2014). For a moment, hold that in your mind and notice your responses. For me, it brings a feeling of coldness, something bleak, frightening – even nightmarish – and hopeless, and many traumatised people are familiar with this terrifying state.

We are all embedded in the stories of our parents and ancestors before them. Our lives are layered within the trauma narratives of our community and culture however hard we try to forget them. It is salutary to think that "we don't just get a patient. We get someone who is the last part of a chain of family heritage" (Mucci, 2014). Although it can be illuminating to enquire what our clients know about their parents' and their grandparents' lives, they may be unaware of past traumas. The world repeatedly dissociates from the horrors of its past and present. There are layers and layers of secrecy about the horrific, whether this is within the home or occurs between groups or races, and this secrecy has an impact on subsequent generations. Collective forgetting adds to the wounds of trauma. What we are talking about are disavowed, unacknowledged histories. In some cases, members of the second and certainly third generations are unaware of what their relatives endured, or if they know anything, it is scant. There may exist an unwritten rule not to talk about it and the problem with the "unsayable" is that "that which cannot be heard or expressed by another cannot be integrated" (Mucci, 2014). In the language I have been using it remains decontextualised. But somehow the survivors know it in their bones. The imprint of these past stories can emerge through dreams, the body and psychotic symptoms, and can lead to ways of behaving, relating and believing that are protective but make little sense in the present context.

We could conceptualise two forms of intergenerational transmission: of attachment dynamics and patterns, and of unmetabolised, unworded trauma. The two are often intertwined. We know that attachment dynamics can be passed down in the non-verbal dyadic dance between parents and babies; in the projection of emotional states; through things said – family rules, biases and myths, and also epigenetically. There is a lot written on this subject. What I find particularly interesting is how children "catch" what their parents or grandparents could not tolerate – the things they did not want to know or see; the emotions they split off, the unformulated and unmentalised. When descendants start to live out what their forebears could not contain there is a collapsing of time and blending of generations. For example, a child can become a vehicle for projections that represent the parent's own early infant-parent relationship. In discussing infant-parent psychotherapy, Hopkins provided several good examples (Horne & Lanyado, 2015). First, Sukie, who was experienced as imprisoning like her mother's violent father and whom Mrs S. initially rejected as "a monster and exceptionally clingy", and Kiran who Hopkins speculated was effectively grieving on behalf of his mother in his persistent crying and whining all day. There was also Daniel who evoked in his mother her own unmet infantile need for devoted maternal care, whilst his father seemed to expect to be dominated by his son as he had been by his father. Unaware who Daniel represented, the couple responded to his every need and were rapidly becoming exhausted. In each case, once the parents began to realise that their difficulties were related to the past and to express feelings about their own childhood, rapid changes occurred in the parent-child relationship.

In my own work, I think of Chris who had suffered because of and absorbed a generational pattern of not talking about emotions. Not only was he quick to move from feeling to thinking. But he was also prone to becoming distressed or angry if he felt that people had cut off contact with him. I was familiar with Chris turning up in an angry mood because his girlfriend was not returning his texts or complaining about his boss if he had sent him a report that he had taken time over and there was no immediate response. Over time we discovered that Chris's experience of being repeatedly pushed away or dismissed if he was distressed as a child was part of a pattern of people being cut off from attachment figures in various ways. There were ancestors who had been orphaned, disowned by their father, told to cut off their relationship with a sibling, or sent to boarding school at a young age. Putting together all these pieces in the jigsaw of his family history after long conversations with an aunt who had retired to the UK, helped Chris to understand why being alone with difficult feelings could feel intolerable and why he could be so reactive even now to perceived rejections.

When extreme, overwhelming events are passed down how do these unknown stories emerge? I have worked with people who take on a "mission", usually from very young, of trying to heal the family – the sibling of a "wild" or "crazy" or very ill child whose caring role evolves later into a career in a healthcare setting. Others enact the story of a wrong time or traumatic death by repeated attempts at suicide, or, less overtly, engaging in risky pursuits. As we explored her story Bree, who I have mentioned several times, began to appreciate how her occasional suicide attempts were both an expression of despair, but were also bringing into the present the suicide of her grandfather's brother, and of a maternal aunt's repeated attempts to kill herself. In the way that self-harm can often have multiple meanings, I suspect that Bree was also concretising her felt sense that she had not been wanted and that her mother may even have tried to abort her. In other words, it is an example of infanticidal attachment (Sachs, 2008, pp. 127–39). The stories of others can also be expressed through the body. Woodcock described a woman whose father had been a prisoner of war at Changi prison in Singapore. He never spoke of his war experiences so she did not know of his imprisonment. However, she had repeated nightmares of imprisonment and torture, all set in a place with an uncanny likeness to Changi. "She had literally dreamed her father's repressed experience" throughout her life (Woodcock, 2017). Another woman Woodcock worked with, an Iranian, had witnessed her brother being killed during a political demonstration. She suffered from recurrent depression and paralysis of her left arm. During therapy it became apparent that her brother had been shielding her during the demonstration and the bullet that shot him would have shattered her arm had he not done so. As they processed her memories and her intense grief gained expression, movement slowly returned to the woman's arm.

What implications does blending with earlier generations have on one's sense of self? And when people find words for unknown histories, how does this impact their identity? Jennifer Teege was someone whose sense of self was profoundly affected when she found out about her family's hidden past (2015). At the age of 38 she chanced upon a book about her birth mother who was the daughter of Amon Göth the brutal concentration camp commandant depicted in the film *Schindler's List*. Teege had no idea of her lineage. In describing the moment when she found the book, she said it "cut her life in two, into a before and an after. A before when she lived without the knowledge of her family's past, and an after, living with that knowledge" (p. 7). This is a good description of the shattering nature of traumatic events. They create a chasm between the innocent place of before and life as it has to be lived from now on. Teege's discovery led to her questioning everything that had been central to her life including all her relation-ships. She wrote: "I feel like I have been travelling under a false name, like I have betrayed everyone, when really it is I who was betrayed. I was the one who was cheated – out of my history, my childhood, my identity. I no longer know to whom I belong, my adoptive family or the Göth family" (p. 9).

Teege eventually found healing after a journey which included therapy, tracing her family history and through visits to Auschwitz and Kraków-Plaszów, the camp Göth had ruled. Her story exemplifies the point made by Aleyne that "no trauma can be healed until it is recognised. Until it is honoured the pain continues to be there. The intergenerational wound is still open not just because of the pain, but because of the world's forgetfulness" (2014). Like others she emphasised the importance of reconstructing the unremembered, unspoken past in order to heal wounds that still festered, to mourn and to master helplessness. It is also essential in order to help second and third generation survivors find and connect with their own identity, something impossible when unresolved traumas lead to a con-fusion of self-states. As Jacobs-Wallfisch said, for these people it is as if they have incorporated a part of their ancestors which does not belong to them, yet is part of them.

Implications for practice

"If the past is not given meaning then losses … cannot be mourned" and this is true of our individual and our ancestral pasts (Silverman, 2017, p. 209). One of the tenets I hold is helping people to achieve "presentification", the embodied and intellectual knowledge that the trauma is over. It is in the past. I also believe that establishing a chronology in which the survivor can identify a before – perhaps, although not always the case, with some memories of good attachments – a beginning, terrible middle and then eventually an end – is important for many reasons. But most important is knowing that change comes from new relational and embodied experiences in the present.[6] In psychotherapy such healing "now moments" often occur because we are able to survive being pulled into enact-ments, living a part from the past and managing to do something different.

The unknown past can emerge in the consulting room via the transference/countertransference field and through body process, dreams and images and symbolic exploration.[7] We become hostage to the past when we are pulled to enact roles from the client's story. For instance, when working with the survivor of childhood abuse, we might "become" the helpless child or the perpetrator or the person who did not believe her. As Davies and Frawley emphasised, only by assuming roles from the client's story can we "begin to truly appreciate at a visceral level the terror, paralysis, hopelessness and impotent rage lived by the patient when she was a child" (1994, pp. 167, 175). Drawing out their point, I think it is not only that we enact the past, but through somatic countertransference – a sudden pain, or momentary paralysis, or disturbing sensation or impulse to move – that we come to know it. To understand the person with us and hence, so that she can know herself, we have to be colonised by her experience. It helps us to "give the client back herself".

Rovelli was right in saying that we are "histories of ourselves", but only partially so, for we are also the "histories of others". And if we cannot access all these multi-layered histories we lack confirmation that we exist. We cannot be "selves-in-time". I am only a "me" in relation to others. What they show me of myself helps me to define myself. I am also defined by the traces left by the past. It is important, therefore, to be aware that there are often more ghosts in the room than those that haunt our clients. Developing Mucci's point, it is not just that they are the last part of a chain of family heritage. Everyone brings the story of their ancestors to a relationship including therapists, and we also need to wrestle with the traumas that have been passed down to us before we can fully engage with the unknown ghosts of our clients and their untold stories. But if we have the courage to get to know these haunting figures and to help our clients do the same then they can slowly find ways to live in the present and envisage more positive futures – or to put this another way, time need stay stopped no longer.

Notes

1   For instance, at the same moment the individual can feel an impulse to run and to freeze.
2   RIGS: Representations of interactions that have become generalised (Daniel Stern).
3   From the scientist's perspective engrams are memory traces held by the connection of discrete groups of brain cells and marked by chemical and electrical changes in how those cells communicate with each other (Finkel, 2017, pp. 73–5; Levine, 2015, pp. 171, 138). Engrams are created in the hippocampus. However, they are not stored there, but instead compressed and transferred to the cortex. Using optogenetic techniques scientists have now discovered that this uploading process begins immediately, much faster than originally assumed. A copy of the memory is made in the prefrontal cortex at the time and is gradually cemented there as a result of input from both the hippocampus and the amygdala. The imprint in the hippocampus then fades (Finkel 2017, pp. 72–5).
4   We are born with a range of hard-wired survival strategies – tendencies towards action that mobilise us when under threat, the most common being the mobilising defences: attach (call for help), fight, flight, and the immobilising strategies of freeze/shut down and submit. As Ogden, Minton and Pain have pointed out, "failed mobilizing defensive responses can perpetuate action-tendencies, delay resolution of the trauma, and fuel distressing trauma-related symptoms" (2006, p. 248).

5 Whilst there is a lot written about the mother's experiences of losses or traumas whilst carrying a child or shortly after the birth and its potential adverse effect on the relationship with her new baby, I am curious whether the child will also be affected if the father experiences something similar.

6 Experiences which differ from what happened in the past or is anticipated in the future lead to changes in the brain and therefore in our automatic responses.

7 Examples of approaches that facilitate the emergence of past histories through symbolic work include Constellations, psychodrama, and an exercise I use now and then which I call the "four generations exercise". In the exercise, which has similarities with a Constellation, I invite the client to take four cushions to represent her great grandmother, grandmother, mother and herself and to stand by each in turn and feel into that person's experience. For each I ask what the daughter learned from this woman about emotions, relationships and mothering. Some time is spent on each question. Then I ask: "what would you like to give back to her that does not belong to you?" and lastly, "What do you wish her?" Then standing by the cushion representing the self, I ask: "Knowing how … what do you wish for yourself? What gifts have your experiences given you? What has constrained you that you might like to get rid of?"

References

"Aahbee". 2008. "The keeper of the secrets" in A. Sachs, & G. Galton (Eds.) *Forensic Aspects of Dissociative Identity Disorder* (pp. 50–61). London: Karnac.

Aleyne, A. 2014. *Intergenerational Trauma*. Confer Online Module.

Allen, J. 2001. *Traumatic Relationships and Serious Mental Disorders*. Chichester: John Wiley.

Apprey, M. 2017. "Representing, theorizing and reconfiguring the concept of transgenerational haunting in order to facilitate healing" in S. Grand & J. Salzberg (Eds.) *Trans-generational Trauma and the Other* (pp. 16–37). New York: Routledge.

Boon, S., Steele, K. & van der Hart, O. 2011. *Coping with Trauma-related Dissociation*. New York: W. W. Norton & Co.

Bromberg, P. 2001. *Standing in the Spaces: Essays on Clinical Process, Trauma and Dissociation*. Hillsdale, NJ: Analytic Press.

Brothers, D. 2014. *Intergenerational Trauma*. Confer Online Module.

Cozolino, L. 2016. *Why Psychotherapy Works*. New York: W. W. Norton & Co.

Davies, J. & Frawley, M. 1994. *Treating the Adult Survivor of Childhood Sexual Abuse*. New York: Basic Books.

Davoigne, F. 2014. *Intergenerational Trauma*. Confer Online Module.

Eger, E. 2017. *The Choice*. London: Penguin.

Finkel, E. 2017. "Lighting up memory lane", *Cosmos*, 75, 72–5.

Frankl, V. 2004. *Man's Search for Meaning*. London: Rider. (1st edition, 1959. London: Random House).

Harris, A., Kalb, M. & Klebanoff, S. (Eds.) 2016. *Ghosts in the Consulting Room: Echoes of Trauma in Psychoanalysis*. New York: Routledge.

Horne, A. & Lanyado, M. (Eds.). 2015. *An Independent Mind: Collected Papers of Juliet Hopkins*. London: Routledge.

Jacobs-Wallfisch, M. 2014. *Intergenerational Trauma*. Confer Online Module.

Levine, P. 2015. *Trauma and Memory: Brain and Body in a Search for the Living Past*. Berkeley, CA: North Atlantic Books.

McGilchrist, I. 2009. *The Master and his Emissary: The Divided Brain and the Making of the Western World*. New Haven: Yale University Press.

Mucci, C. 2014. *Intergenerational Trauma*. Confer Online Module.

Ogden, P., Minton, K. & Pain, C. 2006. *Trauma and the Body: A Sensorimotor Approach to Psychotherapy*. London: W. W. Norton & Co.

Ogden, P. & Fisher, J. 2015. *Sensorimotor Psychotherapy: Interventions for Trauma and Attachment*. London: W. W. Norton & Co.

Roberts, G. 1999. "Introduction: A Story of Stories" in G. Roberts & J. Holmes (Eds.) *Healing Stories: Narrative in Psychiatry and Psychotherapy* (pp. 3–26). Oxford: Oxford University Press.

Rovelli, C. 2018. *The Order of Time*. London: Allen Lane.

Sachs, A. 2008. "Infanticidal Attachment: The Link between Dissociative Identity Disorder and Crime", in A. Sachs & G. Galton (Eds.) *Forensic Aspects of Dissociative Identity Disorder* (pp. 127–39). London: Karnac.

Schreiber, F. 1974. *Sybil*. London: Penguin.

Silverman, S. 2017. "The Colonised Mind: Gender, Trauma and Mentalization" in S. Grand & J. Salzberg (Eds.) *Trans-generational Trauma and the Other* (pp. 204–26). New York: Routledge.

Stern, D. N. 2004. *The Present Moment in Psychotherapy and Everyday Life*. New York: W. W. Norton & Co.

Teege, J. & Sellmair, N. 2015. *My Grandfather Would have Shot Me: A Black Woman Discovers her Family's Nazi Past*. London: Hodder and Stoughton.

Totton, N. 2016. *Working in an Embodied and Relational Style*. Confer Online Module.

Van der Kolk, B. 2014. *The Body Keeps the Score*. London: Penguin.

Weinstein, A. 2016. *Prenatal Development and Parents' Lived Experiences*. New York: W. W. Norton & Co.

Woodcock, J. 2017. "Living with someone else's trauma: extreme events, time, liminality and deep subjectivity". Conference presentation.

Wright, S. 2016. *Dancing between Hope and Despair: Trauma, Attachment and the Therapeutic Relationship*. London: Palgrave.

10

SHARING THE UNTOLD STORY

Always? Sometimes? Never?

I remember everything. Memory fills my body as much as blood and bones.

(Toibin, 2013, p. 4)

"Begin at the beginning and end at the end", said the Red Queen.
"But which beginning?", asked Alice. "Do I start with my beginning? Or the beginnings of parents? Or grandparents? Or …? Or …? And I'm not sure if it has ended. Will it ever end?

(Wright, 2019)

In Chapter 8 I discussed our human need to tell stories, how they provide a holding, containing function and contribute to our sense of identity. But what about after severe trauma? How can what has been ruptured be integrated, healed and, using Woodcock's words, bought back to life and time? (Woodcock, 2017). How can what is stored in blood and bones be given words? To promote healing is it necessary to talk about the traumatic events and fill in the gaps when someone lacks autobiographical memory? And, given the differences between ordinary and traumatic memories, how do we help our traumatised clients deal with intrusions from the past and reconnect with the present?

We could argue that forming a narrative of what happened offers the same benefits as putting any experiences into words and reflecting on them: For instance, it helps to integrate our experiences. At a neurological level it connects the cortex and the more primitive, sub-cortical areas of the brain as well as the right and left hemispheres. Establishing a coherent, chronological narrative also integrates extreme experiences into the flow of our life. "It helps people to develop an increased capacity for a life that includes language, a past, a present and a future as mutually interacting modes of time" rather than one in which the linear experience of time has collapsed and the individual responds to the present and the future as if they will inevitably reproduce the past (Bromberg, 2001, p. 290; 2006, p. 5). Moreover, as Levine pointed out, "the capacity to move between implicit and explicit memory" is important "in integrating traumatic experiences and in generally learning about who we were, who we are, and who we are becoming" (2015, p. 30). He also said, and the relational element I have highlighted is fundamental: "The linking and processing of raw emotions, nuanced feelings, fact, and communication with *chosen others* is essential in moving from trauma – with a future barely different from the past – to an open future built upon new experiences, information and possibilities" (p. 17). In sharing the story with a chosen other there is also an opportunity to make sense of events that at the time lead to confusion and incredulity. This reduces the grip of beliefs about being the cause of the terrible things that happened, weak for not fighting back, and shameful and unlovable. Story making and story breaking, as discussed earlier, open up alternative perspectives. Stories cut across the taboo of secrecy and provide a new experience of no longer facing horror alone. For some people, establishing and sharing a verbal narrative is therefore an important aspect of recovering after trauma. However, and this is crucial to keep in mind, after severe trauma there is a risk that talking about what happened can be retraumatising. It can shut down those areas of the brain that go offline at the time of trauma and leave people highly dysregulated. Instead of remembering and being able to reflect on the past, they start to relive it. Working on the past with trauma survivors therefore demands a significantly different approach to how we work with other people.

Many trauma specialists emphasise the need to address the effects of the traumatic past in the present, *not* its events, and these effects include persistent autonomic dysregulation, intense anxiety, depression, chronic illnesses, difficulties being with people, shame, self-hatred, addictive and self-harming tendencies, dissociation and compartmentalisation into rigidly segregated parts of self (Fisher, 2017, p. 21). According to Van der Kolk, our aim should be

> to find a way in which people can acknowledge the reality of what happened without having to re-experience the trauma all over again. For this to occur, merely uncovering memories is not enough: they need to be modified and transformed, i.e. placed in their proper context and reconstructed into neutral or meaningful narratives. Thus, in therapy, memory paradoxically becomes an act of creation, rather than the static recording of events.
>
> *(Van der Kolk, McFarlane & Weisaeth, 2007, p. 19).*

Van der Kolk also argued that for real change and for people to live fully and securely, "the body needs to learn that the danger has passed" and those brain structures that deserted them when they were overwhelmed by trauma need to come back online (2014, pp. 21, 73). When they have gained stability, control and perspective therapy can be ended, for he sees no intrinsic value in dredging up past traumas if someone's current life provides gratification and the present is not constantly invaded by intrusions from the past (2007, p. 428).

Changing how people relate to their memories

The idea of memory as an act of creation is inspiring. Indeed, I wonder if in all re-telling, whether going over the story in our head or sharing it with someone else, there is an element of seeking a solution, or certainly answers. It is about unfin-ished business. The fact that memory can be modified and transformed is also inspiring. Of course, we know that nothing will ever change what actually hap-pened. That must be faced and grieved. But recent developments in psychotherapy backed up by evidence from neuroscience highlight that there are ways of talking about and processing traumatic memories that update them and hence alter our *present experience of the past*. This surely is the most important goal to aim for. "Such processing", wrote Allen, "does not create a new memory but rather creates the possibility of *remembering* differently by virtue of establishing new associations with the traumatic memory" (2001, p. 330). The new associations might include feeling calm and safe; being supported, comforted, believed and not judged; or physically of mastery and empowerment – relational and embodied experiences which reduce the likelihood of our clients being so distressed and overwhelmed when something reminds them of the past. The establishment of new associations as a result of something physical or with another person or even imagined accords with what we know about the malleability of memory. As discussed in Chapter 3, whenever we narrate and reflect on a memory, it is modified.

When considering how to support people to establish a different relationship to both their implicit and explicit memories, some therapists place more emphasis on the body, on stabilising and resourcing people, developing missing survival strate-gies and completing actions that were truncated at the time of the trauma. Others focus on what occurs within the therapeutic relationship, what emerges through enactments, and on the missing experiences people seek with us and others. From an integrative perspective I believe in embracing both and being able to move flexibly between the two, knowing that at certain times one may be more figural than the other. We can view them as two strands in one thread, a relational-embodied position. I also believe we need to understand the neurobiology of trauma and how its legacy is experienced through the body *and* relationally, as well as being well grounded in attachment theory and alert to what goes on in the transference-countertransference field.

What constitutes a neurobiologically informed approach? Most important is the fact that the therapist endeavours to focus on present time and on what happens now, and especially in the body, when people remember their past (Fisher, 2017, p. 47). Fisher emphasised that the therapist no longer has to be focussed preferentially on becoming a witness to the client's narrative regardless of its effects on his or her stability. It is possible to acknowledge the past, that as a child our client lived in a world that was never safe or that his parents neglected him and that was wrong, without exploring it in detail. More important is to create a "neurobiologically regulating environment that enables the client's nervous system to experience greater safety and therefore an expanded capacity for tolerating both past and present experience" (p. 48).

Our priority should be on creating safety from day one and carefully pacing work on the trauma. To ensure that our clients have one foot in the present as well as one in the past[1] at any sign of dysregulation we need to pause them, orient them to their surroundings, remind them about what is different now and teach them strategies for managing whatever emotions and sensations emerge as they remember their experiences. We can explain that what they feel so intensely now might be body or emotion memory and help them to recognise what triggers them and the different ways they are pulled into old survival strategies. If we suspect that what is going on is more about the past than the present, for example, the client seems primed for fight, flight or collapse; is speaking or acting in a way that suggests he has switched into a younger part of self,[2] or is responding as if we were someone from the past, it can be helpful to ask questions that evoke curiosity. For example: "How is that part of you trying to help right now"? "How did running or shutting down help when you were young?" Such questions evoke mentalising. They implicitly link past and present, and the answers often reveal how our clients found adaptive ways to stay safe and get their attachment needs met. Over time, as we collaboratively explore the legacy of the past, the survivors of extreme trauma can achieve what Van der Hart, Nijenhuis and Steele called "presentification" (2006, pp. 157–61) – when events are placed into their proper context as "a historical event (or series of events) that occurred at a particular time in a particular place", events that were shocking and painful but are over (Van der Kolk, McFarland and Weisaeth, 2007, p. 419).

The embodied narrative of the past

For body-oriented psychotherapists, there is an understanding that for transformation we need to shift our attention from the verbal to the embodied narrative of the past and make use of bottom-up as well as top-down processing. The rational brain cannot talk the emotional survival brain out of its own reality and insights and cognitive changes alone are not enough. Trauma treatment needs to "engage the whole organism, body, mind and brain" (Van der Kolk, 2014, p. 53). My own approach is informed by the way Sensorimotor Psychotherapy addresses this and Ron Kurtz's wisdom that "every client is an experience that wants to happen not a problem to be solved" (1990, p. 139). There are three key elements to a sensorimotor approach: teaching people to use self-regulating strategies when triggered; developing a greater range of mobilising self-protective defences; and completing what the body needed to do at the time of the trauma but could not because the individual was not big or strong enough, or it was too risky (Ogden, Minton & Pain 2006).

When people feel overwhelmed, sensorimotor informed therapists encourage them to attend solely to body sensations and movements and set aside emotions, thoughts and content. As a result, they learn to tolerate and be curious about what happens rather than feeling anxious about it and reacting without thought. Another intervention is to suggest experiments designed to discover missing somatic resources such as defensive movements like clenching the fists, pushing with the arms, standing and moving the legs or orienting with eyes and head. These "experiments" are guided by the content of what is being discussed, what we see in our client's body or feel in our own; what we experience in the relational field such as small clues about an attachment need or through our embodied or active imagination (McGown, 2013). We try to follow and support what is already emerging – the signs of a fledgling action such as the hands lifting a little or leaning in a particular way or twitching feet (Ogden, Minton and Pain, 2006, p. 260). As people try out the emerging movements and sounds in different ways, they often express relief or excitement. We can see it in their faces. They have discovered something new.

Another aspect of sensorimotor processing is to discover and "sequence" defensive actions that were truncated at the time of the trauma – the things that instinctively wanted to happen such as to run, duck, push away, hit, kick, scream for help or shout "no" or the shaking and trembling of a discharge process (Ogden, Minton and Pain, 2006, pp. 258–9). Levine explained: "In terms of traumatic memories … the key in creating a positive update of the memory lies in experientially incorporating effective, survival-based motoric responses that were overwhelmed in the original situation and that led to the failure of self-protection at the time" (2015, p. 144). This may be by supporting, in a way I liken to midwifery, the gradual unfolding of involuntary defensive impulses and orienting movements in response to engaging with a small piece of traumatic memory. Simply following the emerging spontaneous sensations, movements and impulses until the arousal has subsided helps to restore a sense of distance and control (Ogden, Minton and Pain, 2006, p. 258). The completion of unresolved (i.e. thwarted) procedural memories of defence through embodied interoceptive awareness can also restore "vital self-protective impulses, here-and-now orientation, coherence, and a confident sense (and expression of) flow" (Levine, 2015, p. 146). As impulses transform into action, people often discover that contrary to their beliefs, they had not simply given up when attacked. Their bodies were primed for action. But it had not been possible or safe to see this through. What they discover challenges self-critical beliefs. In completing what was thwarted, they experience what Janet called an "act of triumph". They find their voices and feel more empowered. Instead of "continuing the action, or rather the attempt at action which began when the thing happened" and exhausting themselves in "everlasting recommencements", which means being stuck in the past, they move into actions characteristic of "the stage of triumph" (Ogden, Minton and Pain, 2006, p. 86). Then, as this new experience becomes integrated, which demands practicing the actions in different ways and visualising using them in a current situation, our traumatised clients' survival-related stress systems begin to quieten down and their window of tolerance expands (p. 103).

Let me give an example: Whilst trying to understand why a male colleague intimidated and undermined him, Matt recalled how scared he was of his violent, abusive grandfather. As he described his grandfather Matt's voice shrank to a whisper and he began to tremble. He looked like a young boy, his eyes staring wide and his body shrinking back. Knowing that in childhood he needed a strong but kind adult to support him, I invited Matt to imagine that the teacher who had consistently supported and encourage him during his troubled years at secondary school and who inspired him to become a teacher, was sitting with him. Matt agreed and shut his eyes. I asked him to notice what he felt like now. "Safer", he said with a smile, and then to our mutual surprise his right leg suddenly moved involuntarily. His foot lifted and he kicked out. "Notice", I said, "see what your leg wants to do". His leg kept kicking and Matt laughed. "It's weird. But it feels kind of strong." I invited Matt to observe how that felt, then asked what his leg might be trying to say. "I can!" Matt exclaimed with delight. "I can kick. I can run. If anyone threatens me now I could kick them or run away!".

The process of integration started with teaching Matt's left leg to kick because he said it felt stuck, then standing to feel what it was like supported by two powerful legs. Once again Matt was excited. He could feel his feet, a significant change as he usually felt and looked very ungrounded. "Maybe it will be easier now to stand your ground", I suggested. Matt explored moving from foot to foot then lifting and flexing his arms saying that they felt strong too, "as if I could punch someone". "Who would you like to punch?" I asked playfully. Matt named his colleague. "Not that I would", he added. "But perhaps I need to say something if he keeps putting me down." Because his spine collapsed as he considered this, I invited him to stand and imagine me beside him and his teacher behind him, then to feel his feet supported by the ground. "Now simply imagine the kicking movements", I suggested. Then I asked if his colleague spoke inappropriately again what Matt would say to him with a body that felt strong and supported. "I'd tell him to shut up or I'll make a complaint", Matt said emphatically, and he smiled confidently. "I'm not that child anymore who couldn't possibly challenge his grandfather!"

Whatever approach we adopt, I believe it is the quality of relationship we offer – our ability to create a secure base within which people feel safe and connected and our capacity to act as a "partner in thought" as discussed in Chapter 8, or what Allen called "a willing and nurturant adult conversational partner", that contributes most to healing (Stern, 2010, pp. 113, 115; Allen, 2001, p. 342). As Allen pointed out, "we should not separate the story teller from the listener, or the story from the relationship in which it is created – or not created" (p. 342). Traumatic experiences, whether due to human cruelty or natural disasters, are embedded in social contexts, and the extent to which we can turn to others for support and validation, both during and after the event, has a major bearing on how resilient or troubled we are afterwards. Having a supportive witness helps to make the experience relationable, and this is especially true if it left the survivor feeling utterly debased, dehumanised and separated from all that is human, caring and hopeful. As Kinston and Cohen stated, "it is only when survivors remember with someone, when a narrative is created in the presence of a 'passionate listener', that the connection between an 'I' and a 'you' is remade" (Laub, 2005, p. 322).

To be a passionate listener entails more than being good at listening and offering the core conditions. It demands being willing to know and name the unspeakable and to join our clients in defying the taboo of secrecy. It demands being open and present, rather than leaping in to change things, and to believe and validate rather than judging them. The passionate listener must also be prepared to be impacted, not just by what we hear, but by what we observe going on somatically, what we sense in our own bodies and by emerging imagery. Sometimes, for instance, with Laura what I observed happening physically, led to an implicit sense of what might have been done to her as a child. I felt as if I was with that child and "knew" before she could tell me in words. Images and phrases came into my mind unbidden – a form of implicit relational knowing perhaps (Renn, 2012, pp. 119–20) – as well as impulses to protect her in some way. I had to be willing to entertain knowing that such things can and do happen to children and that they happened to Laura. As partners in thought we can help people to slowly give words to and make sense of events that were horrific and inexplicable and, in Roberts' words, offer "a means of containing wild, threatening, and unpredictable experiences, and re-establishing some kind of order and relationship" (1999, pp. 12–13). From the terrifying aloneness of the original experience and the isolation of not being able to speak, the connection between self and others is slowly and painfully remade. And so too, argued Laub, is the connection between an 'I' and an internal 'you', his thesis being that extreme trauma destroys that empathic "good object" discussed earlier, to whom in an ongoing way we tell our stories internally (Laub, 2005, 315–16).

When telling the story is healing

When debating with colleagues whether creating and sharing a narrative is necessary in order to move on after severe trauma, we agreed that in certain circumstances it can indeed be life-supporting and life-enhancing. Our list included when the idea of talking evokes considerable shame; when others have imposed a rule of secrecy; and when people are troubled and alarmed by what they experience somatically – the inarticulate language of the body. They also include cases of extreme trauma such as ritual abuse, genocide and torture.

Taking shame first: many victims of abuse don't tell anyone what happened because they are ashamed. They live with guilty secrets that colour how they view themselves, hold them back when opportunities arise and get in the way of relationships. Rachel was someone who was crippled with shame. Between the ages of 8 and 16 she had been sexually assaulted and mercilessly taunted afterwards by her elder brothers. She hated her body and anything that reminded her that she was a woman and, imagining they could see her shame, she could not bear anyone looking at her. When I first met her Rachel would become massively dysregulated if anything reminded her of her childhood and she dealt with this by dissociating and drinking heavily. For a long time, my priority was to develop a self-regulating toolkit as well as to teach her how the brain and body respond after trauma. The latter was important because Rachel was also ashamed that, in her view, she had not done anything to stop her brothers, and that in the present she could not cope. She experienced what Lynd called a "double shame" – shame about the original episode, and because seemingly small things in the present could have such an impact (Bromberg, 2011, p. 23). In her mind, her reactions made her as useless and pathetic as her brothers kept telling her.

As Rachel's window of tolerance expanded, she slowly risked telling me more and more details about her childhood (for several years I had only the sketchiest knowledge of her history). But the stranglehold of fear and shame only really loosened when she began to remember some of the things she *had* done to protect herself, not perhaps the more dramatic actions we tend to associate with fight and flight, but clever, subtle ways of surviving. They included volunteering to help her parents if her brothers were around, joining as many after school groups as she could, and learning how to creep in and out of the house without being heard. She realised that she had learned to be as unnoticeable as possible. "It wasn't that I was boring like they said." The final transformative piece, Rachel's "act of triumph", was when she recalled some of the amazing things that her hated body had done despite having a mild but painful physical disability. She had run several marathons, completed a long coastal path walk, abseiled and learned to sail. "They never did anything like that!", she exclaimed with pride. "And the more I think about it I see that my life is much more fulfilling now than theirs. Both of them have made a mess of things." When I asked how it felt to appreciate all this, Rachel laughed, "It makes me realise that after all they haven't won!" I agreed!

The second category involves an explicit or implicit "rule" of secrecy. In some cases, the perpetrators used threats and violence to instil a lasting fear of talking. Many survivors of child abuse, when they do at last feel safe enough to speak, tell of dire threats if they ever dared tell anyone, and of course children will believe this. This is compounded when there was, and regrettably often still is, secrecy in the family and wider culture – a collective dissociation that adds to the wounds of trauma. The world repeatedly dissociates from the horrors of its past and present. There are layers and layers of secrecy about the horrific, whether this is within the home or occurs between groups or races, and this secrecy has an impact on both the survivors and in some cases on subsequent generations. Primo Levi called it the "ever-repeated scene of the unlistened to story", and when talking about her meetings with former prisoners of war, Helen Bamber, a pioneering figure in the early days of Amnesty International and Freedom from Torture, spoke of "a shared resistance to the sweeping away of the whole terrible experience as though it didn't really matter, as though it doesn't have any bearing on what's going on now" (Belton, 1988, pp. 24, 16).[3] But of course it does. The same is equally true for the victims of childhood abuse, domestic violence and torture. As Bamber recognised, "people who have been shattered by violence need to feel acknowledged". "If the particularity of their experience is abolished, they feel traduced" (1988, p. 24). Bamber was not a trained therapist, but her view is echoed by many therapists who work with the survivors of trauma. For instance, Aleyne said, "no trauma can be healed until it is recognised. Until it is honoured the pain continues to be there. The intergenerational wound is still open not just because of the pain, but because of the world's forgetfulness" (2014).

To give an example of a client who knew all too well that "ever-repeated scene of the unlistened to story": Gail was furious about her family's pattern of sweeping things under the carpet. Even after courageously telling her parents about years of abuse by her grandfather she complained that, "they act like it never happened. If I remind them, they say, but that was a long time ago or surely you're over that now!" Gail was also furious about society's seeming inaction to stop child abuse and would have agreed with Bamber's point that people act "as though it doesn't have any bearing on what's going on now". "They've no idea what people like me struggle with every day", she protested. "They just don't want to know!"

The victims of torture also carry unspeakable and unlistened to stories. Elaine Scarry wrote that "in torture the prisoner [becomes] a colossal body with no voice and the torturer a colossal voice ... with no body". Commenting on this, Belton said, "whatever story they had has been degraded; if they had information to give, it becomes a sign of guilt and shame; if they had none, their pain is often incomprehensible to themselves. In a small way, as Scarry points out, the ability to speak reverses the torturers narrative, which, like pornography knows only one dull, repetitive kind of ending". The work of people like Bamber and therapists today who work with refugees and asylum seekers, highlights how important it is to help the tortured find their voices, connect with the changed person they have become, and bear witness to their stories (Belton, 1988, p. 397; Boyles, 2017, p. 28; Lamb, 2017, p. 59). McKinnon cited one refugee who said, "you helped me to remember my past when I could not. You helped me to focus on things here when I could not. You helped me with my past and future. There have been things that happened that, if it was not for you, I would not have come back from". The man also mentioned the importance of being treated with dignity and respect, of being received as a human being, of going very slowly and listening and understanding before trying to help (2017, pp. 36–54). Salutary reminders for us all.

The last situation when reconstructing the unremembered, unspoken past contributes to healing its legacy, is when someone has no verbal memory of trauma but is repeatedly troubled by body memories, often characterised by intense pain, bizarre flashbacks and chronic, medically unexplained symptoms. This is often the case when the trauma was dissociated but is still stored in the body; when it occurred in the womb, during birth or in infancy before the advent of language, or when it concerns events transmitted transgenerationally that deeply impact later generations despite not being part of their lived experience. In each case there is no known narrative and therefore no way of explaining why the person feels, acts and experiences things in the way he or she does.

Let me return to Laura, the client mentioned earlier. She had no verbal memory of trauma until her 50s. For years her experiences of torture and abuse by a group of people when she was very young had been completely split off but were dramatically expressed through the body. Sometimes she experienced paralysis in her

legs or arms. At other times Laura was troubled by intensely painful body sensations and involuntary movements. As therapy progressed, she came to understand
that these frightening somatic experiences were telling the story of what had happened to her as a child. They were a somatic enactment of things beyond her
capacity to comprehend or symbolise at the time. As language slowly emerged
Laura also got in touch with hidden parts of self that held different versions of what
had happened to her. She came to appreciate that the use of dissociative splitting
had not only protected her from emotional overwhelm at the time and enabled her
to get on with life, but because a "rule of secrecy" had been drummed into her
with terrible threats reinforced by examples, it had been imperative to not know
what she knew. That "language" could only be held by her body.

Amongst the different self-states we slowly encountered was a "child" who was
terrified about talking to anyone because of those repeated threats. Breaking the
old rules was frightening. But the more Laura risked telling me what she was
remembering, the freer she felt. Significant to the theme of bearing witness to the
histories of torture and abuse, as she approached the end of therapy Laura noticed
that her route to healing entailed a repeated pattern: First, she needed to face
something awful herself and dialogue with the child parts that were involved. Then
she shared this with me, a narrative that was often interrupted when her body or a
younger self decided to speak, and we reflected on what was emerging. It was an
ongoing process of trying to make sense of things, put the fragmented pieces of
Laura's jigsaw together and find words for our mutual horror in the face of human
evil. Later Laura shared a little of what she was now remembering with a trusted
friend. Only then, she realised, did she really feel that the event belonged to the
past, and with that came a deep sense of peace. She had defied the old rules. She
had cut through intense shame and found people who were genuinely willing to
listen and bear witness to atrocity.

Creating new maps because of new experiences

The examples of Laura, Rachel and Matt illustrate how as memories are encountered
and processed we learn about what Kurtz called the "map maker", the self who built
a particular world view and self-image as a result of his or her experiences in childhood, and discover the "survival logic" of adopting certain beliefs and strategies
(1990, p. 133). Whereas body psychotherapists are especially interested in what is
revealed through posture, gesture and movement patterns about how people learned
to survive and organise their experiences in the past, intersubjective and relational
therapists focus more on implicit relational patterns. What they share is that they are
both experience-near and emphasise process and context rather than content. For
example, the relational analyst Paul Renn wrote that "from a contemporary perspective, memory is important not as an account of history, but as a means of communicating the nature of internal representations of self-other relationships" and he
explained that "representational models are the invisible psychic structures that
organise behaviour and experience in the present, mediating our expectations and

predictions about self-other relationships deriving from the silent past" (2012, p. 178). In Renn's opinion it is these structures, not the memories themselves, nor the events that contributed to their development, that need to be the focus so that implicit memories can be subtly changed and encoded within modified representational models. We could think of this as creating new "maps" because of something occurring relationally or somatically, an experience that leads to what Cramer called "a dynamic disconnection" between past and present (Horne & Lanyado, 2015, p. 115). Matt's experience of his leg kicking is a good example.

Bromberg is another contemporary analyst who emphasises the here-and-now process rather than the content of what is being said (Bromberg, 2011, pp. xxxiii, xxxvi). His particular interest is on the shifting states of mind that organise this content, another way of thinking about the map maker, and on enactments which communicate dissociated aspects of attachment-related trauma. Bromberg described an enactment as "a shared dissociative event … an unconscious communication process that reflects those areas of the patient's self experience where trauma has to one degree or another compromised the capacity for affect regulation in a relational context and thus compromised self-development at the level of symbolic processing by thought and language" (2011, p. 16). He pointed out that in a safe enough therapeutic relationship it can be possible for the painful reliving of early trauma without it being just a blind repetition of the past. The therapist's job is to use the enactment "in a way that the patient's 'not-me' experience can be given representational meaning as a shared phenomenon by enabling a perceptual link to be made in the patient's working memory and the here-and-now self as the agent or experiencer" (p. 22). It is not a once and for all process because enactments take place repeatedly and each time provide the opportunity for a little more to be processed and put into words.

Bromberg's stress on the relationship being safe but not too safe, accords with a neurobiologically informed approach of endeavouring to keep people in their window of tolerance. "The sensitive psychobiologically attuned therapist", as Schore pointed out, "allows the patient to experience dysregulating affects in affectively tolerable doses in the context of a safe environment, so that overwhelming traumatic feelings can be regulated and integrated into the patient's life" (Bromberg, 2011, p. xxxiii). It also accords with attachment theory. As Allen commented, "the content of the story is less crucial than the capacity to create, refine and narrate the story in a secure attachment relationship" (2001, pp. 342–4). In other words, we can provide something developmentally needed to scaffold work on the past and foster the emergence of something new. We can provide a missing experience of safety and connection, of presence and containment. We can act as witnesses and partners in meaning making and in "good-enough" fashion we can act in ways that disconfirm the client's expectation that we will be like the people who failed him and weather whatever shocks, horrors, attacks and enactments that emerge during the journey. If possible, too, we need to be willing to be there for the long haul. In such a relationship the client has the opportunity to gradually let go of fixed beliefs and old insecure attachment patterns.[4]

One aspect of the slow, faltering process of transforming implicit into explicit memory is actually finding words – something that in my experience is a co-created process. The language of shock, terror and pain, so eloquently but mysteriously expressed by the body, defies words. It is a visceral language of heart-breaking, gut-wrenching, mind-blowing sensation; a language with its own idiosyncratic intensity, rhythm and pace – of unendurable, time-expanded moments and of breathtakingly fast occurrences. To symbolise it we have to find metaphors that capture the multi-sensory, out-of-time nature of a traumatic moment. This is again where the relationship is important for our capacity to take something in, digest it and give it back in an empathic, contactful and manageable form helps our clients to feel truly met and find a way to tolerate the unbearable. Often what I reflect back is through sharing images that come to me or that I pick up in what my client is saying. Metaphors are mutative. They help to hold and structure the inchoate language of trauma, the inarticulate speech of the heart and body. We share and build on the emerging metaphors and this helps people to feel deeply met as well as promoting that increased capacity for a language of past, present and future as "mutually interacting modes of time" mentioned earlier.

I have talked about some of the amazing changes that can occur when someone has a new somatic or interpersonal experience. Brief mention should also be made of the power of the imagination. This too can "create the possibility of remembering differently by virtue of establishing new associations with the traumatic memory" (Allen, 2001, p. 330). When people start to visualise something different happening – a different outcome to the old story or visualising somewhere or something that gives them a feeling of comfort and safety, not only does this have an immediate effect on their physiological and affective state, it seems to free something for the future – a loosening of old familiar habits and survival responses, a greater confidence to try something new. Both therapist and client are often surprised and amazed what emerges in such work and to my mind it emphasises the power of novelty, the unexpected and the uncanny to shift us out of familiar ways of thinking and behaving. I suspect that there are links with some of the unexpected things that can emerge towards the end of an EMDR session or using artwork or inviting a client to dialogue with younger parts of self, and that all involve right brain processing. Rachel was one client whose imaginative capacity proved an important resource. Whenever she became hyperaroused, inviting her to imagine sitting by a peaceful stream in a wood and all the sensory details calmed her. She then found it much easier to talk about whatever was distressing her. For another woman imagining the playful things her rebellious inner child wanted to do gave her a feeling of mastery. The rebel creatively turned the tables on the people who hurt her or let her down, or imagined powerful animals helping when she needed to do something she was scared about. If nothing else, laughing about what came to mind always lightened Fiona's mood, and the humour was shared.

To be able to laugh, be playful and imagine are as essential to our being as experiencing states of calm, alert interest, curiosity, determined commitment and excitement. But when dominated by a brain on the lookout for danger our play and exploration systems shut down. We respond to others defensively, hypervigilant for any sign of rejection or attack. We withdraw from active engagement in the world. So, when we notice our traumatised clients becoming curious, developing wider interests, joking or doing something creative, it is a sign that they are beginning to live more fully and securely in the present.

Conclusions

To sum up my conclusions: I have highlighted the need for new experiences. "Exploring the past for its own sake", as Van der Kolk stressed, "has no therapeutic benefits unless it becomes attached to other experiences, such as feeling understood, being safe, feeling physically strong and capable, *and let's add feeling creative and playful to the list,* or being able to empathize with and help fellow suffers" (2007, p. 19). The work of people like Ogden, Levine, Bromberg, Renn and other relational, intersubjective therapists demonstrate some of the amazing changes which can occur when someone has new physical and interpersonal experiences, experiences that in time, if repeated and integrated because the grip of the past takes time to escape, enable new pathways to be made in the brain. I have given examples of body-based interventions to alter the client's physiological state and help her develop new somatic resources and complete arrested defences. I have also talked about the relational processes that support the emergence of something new and loosen fixed beliefs and habitual survival patterns. In some cases, something new is also needed outside the therapy – new relationships or activities, unforeseen happenstances that give a new turn to a client's day and challenge the trauma-related certainties that for so long have constrained his life. Recovery is a complex process, demanding a range of supports, of integrating past and present, grieving and letting go, and discovering oneself – the person who exists now, who has suffered but who can play an active part in shaping a new future.

Perhaps Laura should have the last word on this. At one point she had decided to go and look at the place where she had been abused. Not long afterwards she said, "I feel as if I have got a future for the first time". "I always saw the house in front of me – pulling me back. I could never believe they'd let me go. But it feels as if it is behind me now!" My impression is that this was also a very embodied experience for as she spoke Laura looked over her shoulder, moving her hand behind her as if throwing something away. Then she turned to look at me with a face full of amazement. She had realised at a felt level, not just a cognitive one, that the horrific past really was over. "You are a being in time!" I exclaimed. "The past is over and you can cross the line into a new future." With this realisation came relief, excitement and joy because it opened up so many new possibilities for Laura. Sharing the horror, and in witnessing her body moving in agony I literally felt as if I was with a child being tortured, was an important part of the process. But so too was sharing Laura's joy and emerging hope. We could celebrate together the dawn of a new life.

Notes

1 In other words, having dual awareness or an observing ego.
2 In the language of Family Systems Therapy they have "blended" with a younger, trau-matised part of self (Fisher, 2017, p. 81).
3 Bamber's biographer wrote of the "insolent way" in which it was conveyed to the former POWs that "the authorities – the state, the army, the whole of official Britain – would prefer to forget about them", and of "memories of brutality, of grotesque deaths" which nobody including their families really wanted to hear (Belton, 1988, pp. 11, 16).
4 From an attachment perspective, we know that if a client's earliest experiences were of safety and trust she is more likely to be able to talk about and reflect on traumatic events without becoming overwhelmingly distressed and dysregulated. There will be a coher-ence to her narrative. Moreover, even if someone was insecurely attached as a child, later in life with the support of a person with whom they feel safe, (an "earned" secure attachment), it is possible to develop increasingly elaborate, coherent narratives and the capacity for reflective functioning (Allen, 2001, p. 342).

References

Aleyne, A. 2014. *Intergenerational Trauma*. Confer Online Module.

Allen, J. 2001. *Traumatic Relationships and Serious Mental Disorders*. Chichester: John Wiley.

Belton, N. 1998. *The Good Listener: Helen Bamber, A Life Against Cruelty*. London: Faber & Faber.

Bromberg, P. 2001. *Standing in the Spaces: Essays on Clinical Process, Trauma, and Dissociation*. Hillsdale NJ: Analytic Press.

Bromberg, P. 2011. *The Shadow of the Tsunami and the Growth of the Relational Mind*. New York: Routledge.

Fisher, J. 2017. *Healing the Fragmented Selves of Trauma Survivors*. New York: Routledge.

Horne, A. & Lanyado, M. (Eds.) 2015. *An Independent Mind: Collected Papers of Juliet Hopkins*. London: Routledge.

Kurtz, R. 1990. *Body-Centred Psychotherapy: The Hakomi Method*. Mendocino, CA: LifeRhythm.

Lamb, K. 2017. "Recovery and Reconnection" in J. Boyles (Ed.) *Psychological Therapies for Survivors of Torture* (pp. 56–75). Monmouth: PCCS Books.

Laub, D. 2005. "Traumatic shutdown of narrative and symbolization: A death instinct deri-vative?", *Contemporary Psychoanalysis*, 41(2), 307–26.

Levine, P. 2015. *Trauma and Memory: Brain and Body in a Search for the Living Past*. Berkeley, CA: North Atlantic Books.

McGown, L. 2013. "Reaching into the relational unconscious. Integrating spontaneous mental imagery into clinical practice". *British Journal of Psychotherapy Integration*, 10(2), 21–32.

McKinnon, N. 2017. "The Door to my Garden: Kevin, Me and the Clock" in J. Boyles (Ed.) *Psychological Therapies for Survivors of Torture* (pp. 36–55). Monmouth: PCCS Books.

Ogden, P., Minton, K. and Pain, C. 2006. *Trauma and the Body: A Sensorimotor Approach to Psychotherapy*. London: W. W. Norton & Co.

Renn, P. 2012. *The Silent Past and the Invisible Present*. London: Routledge.

Stern, D. B. 2010. *Partners in Thought: Working with Unformulated Experience, Dissociation and Enactment*. New York: Routledge.

Toibin, C. 2013. *The Testament of Mary*. London: Penguin.

Van der Hart, O., Nijenhuis, E. & Steele, K. 2006. *The Haunted Self: Structural Dissociation of the Personality*. New York: W. W. Norton & Co.

Van der Kolk, B. 2014. *The Body Keeps the Score*. London: Penguin.

Van der Kolk, B., McFarlane, A. & Weisaeth, L. (Eds.) 2007. *Traumatic Stress: The Effects of Overwhelming Experience on Mind, Body and Society*. New York: Guilford Press. (1st edition, 1996. New York: Guilford Press).

Woodcock, J. 2017. "Living with someone else's trauma: extreme events, time, liminality and deep subjectivity". Conference presentation.

Wright, S. 2019. "Alice", *Attachment: New Directions in Psychotherapy and Relational Psychoanalysis*, 13(2).

11

THE IMPACT OF LOSS AND LIFE CRISES ON OUR RELATIONSHIP TO TIME

> Traumatic events including severe illness and deaths also occur in parenthetical time. They are both outside the usual continuity of life – the familiar daily rhythms, and yet, once happened, they deeply influence that continuity like a foreign body in our existence.
>
> *(Rose, 1999, p. 16)*

In this chapter, I will focus on illness and bereavement because they illustrate some of the ways a life crisis impacts our relationship to time and can lead to crises of self and meaning. Although I focus primarily on two forms of life crisis, many of the emerging points are applicable to other disasters – something that devastates our home for instance, like a fire or flood, being involved in an accident, having to flee one's country, learning something about a loved one that completely changes how we see that person. Such events cause ruptures in time.

Rose reminds us that illnesses and deaths can be traumatic, and that can be for both individuals and whole families or communities. I immediately think of the shock of something happening to one's body or mind that feels very frightening, the beginnings of a heart attack, a sudden excruciating pain, the terrifying experiences of psychosis or dissociation. There is also the experience of being rushed into hospital, perhaps in an ambulance, or being restrained, held in a police cell and sectioned. Imagine too, what it must be like waking to find oneself in an unfamiliar place with bright lights, jarring noises and unknown people, or on a psychiatric ward with people doing and saying things that seem "mad", or being in an eating disorder unit having to eat far more than your starved body can tolerate. The interventions used to save your life or stabilise you, although of course necessary, can also be traumatic. Tests can be intrusive. Waiting for a diagnosis and imagining also sorts of "worsts" can be incredibly hard and how the diagnosis is given will play a part in colouring the meaning of these events. How we learn about a death, what we see or know that happened, sometimes too the events leading up to it can be traumatising, and shock and horror can complicate the grieving process. It is understandable that in any of these situations our threat system will be aroused and the survival responses to trauma discussed earlier can kick in. The traumatic aspect of illness and death is not my focus here. But that is the backdrop and for many people earlier stories get hooked in: stories of needing care; of being alone, afraid, dependent; of being in hospital oneself or visiting others; of assaults on one's body. Such experiences leave emotional scars. What meanings do people give to a health crisis or loss? What stories do they tell about it? How can they come to terms with it?

When time becomes strange: time and illness

> All days are nothing, but the same day repeating itself – or rather, since it is always the same day, it is incorrect to speak of repetition, a continuous present, an identity, an everlastingness – such words as these better convey the idea … You are losing the sense of the demarcation of time, that its units are running together disappearing, and what is being revealed to you as the true content of time is merely a dimensionless present in which they bring you broth.
>
> *(Mann, 1999, p. 181)*

All forms of crisis make time strange. They interrupt it for long or short periods; speed it up; suspend it. Mann's description captures this strangeness when ill in bed. On bad days, and for some people dealing with a critical or chronic illness all the time, we can become a self-out-of-time. Clock time no longer has meaning; shared social time feels irrelevant – our rhythms now out of synch with the people around us. For relatives, the need to respond to a sick relative also disturbs their normal daily rhythms. I have spoken to many people pulled into a caring role who speak of their time being devoured as, in addition to trying to work as normal, visits to hospital or the relative's house, running errands for him or her and calls to professionals and other members of the family have to be slotted in. Sometimes everything has to be put on hold in order to dash to hospital. I have heard complaints about there being no time for oneself and neglecting others, of being woken in the early hours by a panic call. I have experienced all these and the strange out-of-time moments sitting in a waiting room or by someone's bed in hospital and of hectic days when I lost touch with what time or day of the week it was.

Pye (2017) also described the strangeness of illness time in a record of his experiences during a brush with cancer. He wrote: "I begin to live in two different sorts of time: ordinary time and cancer time … I get up at 7-ish and make tea for myself and my wife … I write a diary. I read. I walk to Waitrose, buy £5 of food to claim my free newspaper. I come home, read it, become depressed by horrible news. I try to clear my mind. A client arrives. That's the diurnal round, roughly speaking, although not necessarily in that order. Doing these things, in ordinary time, I'm in a comfortingly deluded state." The comforting rhythms of our daily rituals. They help us to stay in a deluded state where the existential challenges of living in time do not exist. And I am struck how in ordinary time our field is wide – Pye's thoughts went to his family, his clients, the world. In illness, external concerns and interests shrink. The preoccupation, especially when immersed in illness, becomes the self and whatever pain one is experiencing. Even if we try hard to focus on the diurnal round, the "foreign body" is there – literally in some cases in the body and meta-phorically in a sharpened awareness of mortality.

For Pye, "cancer time" involved the precision of a treatment schedule. "I would set off from home at the same time each day, for a seven-minute walk to the clinic." There would be two minutes outside looking at a tree that became a kind of companion. Then, inside, there were two minutes to get inside and register his arrival before drinking "the first of six carefully time cups of water at nine exactly". Pye commented that this precision contrasted with his two min-utes with the tree. "If I had a pie-chart of how time felt from arrival, to tree, to the beginning of the treatment regime – the tree would take up far more time than the rest." What a wonderful evocation of the differences between Chronos and Kairos!

Pye's cancer schedule echoes what Charmaz learned from the people she interviewed who suffered from chronic illnesses. They had treatment regimes that took time every day: the precision of timings for medication, for the application of dressings, for appointments with doctors and so on – new daily, weekly and monthly rhythms. Sometimes the regime made it impossible to do things they used to do. Some people tried to squeeze everything in, the "filled present" mentioned in Chapter 2. In other cases, the demands of the schedule intrude on other people's time – the parents who support a sick or disabled child, the wife now carer for a sick, elderly husband. New rhythms, but no longer nurturing ones. Time has become medicalised. The illness "made time disobey its normal habits" (Pye, 2017).

For Pye, treatment interrupted life then, afterwards, resuming his work schedule returned him to ordinary time. Time as an "interruption to life" is one of three ways that Charmaz conceptualised how illness can affect our relationship to time. It can be seen as an inconvenient interruption, an event in parentheses distinct from other events. I am sure we have all experienced illness as interruption, usually short, but sometimes for a defined period of our lives. We assume that whatever we are suffering from will be temporary. We might temporarily put life on hold, taking time off work, perhaps spending a few days in bed. But we are confident that once we have recovered the present and future will be unaltered. Now and then we might experience a longer period of interruption, perhaps beginning with a crisis during which time might speed up or slow down. Charmaz described this as "a searing disruption" (1991, p. 35). We might then go into "waiting time" (p. 30), waiting for results, an operation, to get better when medication takes effect. Quite when these things will be are uncertain. But our sense of self and confidence in returning to "normal" life are not shaken.

Things are different when an illness becomes intrusive. If a condition becomes chronic and severe it progressively intrudes on the day. It is now a permanent part of life rather than a separate event (p. 42). Unpleasant and painful symptoms are always present and can get in the way of ordinary activities, although there are distinctions between good and bad days. As Charmaz discovered, the two can have very different temporal structures. Some people try to ignore or mask their symptoms, determinedly getting on with life. They hang on to their pre-illness Self. Others come to accept the illness, and this means accepting a new identity. Charmaz's third category is immersion in illness. To be immersed in illness means being engulfed in the necessities of whatever treatments are prescribed, trying hard to fit in other things without getting exhausted, and preoccupied with thoughts and feelings about what is going on. It can separate people from conventional time and the rhythms of ordinary life (pp. 75, 82). The boundaries of experience contract as pursuits narrow and shrink. Control over time lessens. It is either fiercely regimented with routines that shape the day or repeatedly hijacked. Many people become socially isolated, like an elderly person who is housebound, no longer in touch with the ongoing flow of life. They turn inwards (1991, p. 99). And like the latter, they can feel "invalid", redundant and useless.

Carol's immersion in ill health was not permanent, but it really shook her and psychologically it took a long time afterwards to fully recover – if indeed recover is the right word, because it knocked something out of her. Her life wasn't the same again. The patterning of Carol's life completely altered when a trapped nerve in her back left her in incessant pain for eight months. She had to go on extended sick leave and doing the simplest household chores took much longer than usual and was at the cost of more pain. Carol hated change. Her daily routine made her feel safe and not working left her with many empty hours – hours in which she felt incredibly lonely, in which she ruminated and memories from the past slipped in unbidden, memories that her work routine usually kept at bay. Familiar beliefs originating in a childhood of fear and abuse took centre stage and her capacity to challenge them, which had been slowly developing during our work, seemed to vanish.

Charmaz focussed on physical health. But many of her findings also apply to people with severe and enduring mental health problems. For instance, the obvious parallel with days being marked by when medication has to be taken, and the week by appointments with health care professionals. But other more personal regimes can devour time. A good example is someone with OCD whose attempts to live according to ordinary time are repeatedly thwarted by the need to go back and check or to repeat a compulsive behaviour multiple times. I also think of someone with anorexia whose day is filled with thoughts about how much she weighs, what she will eat, how many calories she has consumed so far. I remember feeling deeply sad when one young woman said, "I get a bit of satisfaction now from thinking 'today I stuck to my meal plan or I managed to have a shower … '.

That's not living is it?". No, it is not about living a life with personal meaning. It is about surviving. It is about being immersed in ill health.

Illness, identity and relationships

When severe or chronic illness leads to the loss of taken for granted functions – a body that moves freely, having energy, being able to remember things easily and think clearly – how we see ourselves and how others see us inevitably changes. People often cling to their pre-illness Self until they come to a place of accepting that they are never going to do that again, whether this is to work or compete as an athlete or be able to eat whatever they like again. Without those familiar activities and defining roles and with no sense of what might be realistic, for many people with a disability or chronic condition the question "Who am I now?", even if never explicitly spoken, hangs in the air. Alice, the young woman with ME mentioned when discussing young adults with blocked futures, is another example of someone who was immersed in her condition despite trying hard to do as much as she used to when she was well. She struggled to come to terms with many losses – of energy, motivation and confidence – and often described no longer being sure who she was or what she could become. "I used to be so focussed on my career. I'd always wanted to work in a library. I'd got plans to do more training and one day apply for a job as a branch manager. But that's all gone out of the window." Old beliefs about never being good enough resurfaced. Work had been one of the things that helped Alice feel good about herself. But now she evaluated her days in terms of what she had not managed to do or mistakes made and could not appreciate that in the circumstances she was doing remarkably well. Alice is certainly not alone in her story. Nor was Alice alone in finding it hard that other people don't always adjust their expectations.

In Chapter 5 I shared my interest in observing the temporal contours of the therapeutic relationship, how they can clash and be in harmony. But what about the temporal contours of an ill person's relationships with family and friends? When someone is critically ill or has an enduring condition the rest of family is affected and everyone can struggle adjusting to the need for some radically different ways of structuring their time. It is not only the person directly affected, partners, parents and children can also find it hard to come to terms with all the changes. In poor health, the need to slow down, the blurring of time – for instance, lying awake much of the night and needing to sleep during the day – often leads to family members having very different temporal contours. This can be resented on both sides. Alice believed that her boyfriend and girlfriends were getting fed up with her because she rarely had energy at the end of the day to go out and at weekends often slept a lot of the day. Alice's endeavour to stay working full-time depleted her. There were times too, quite understandably, that she envied and felt angry with friends who were having a good time and doing the things she should have been doing as a young adult. Alice also spoke of feeling guilty at always saying "no" and of loneliness. "No one really understands and there's only so many times you can tell people how exhausted you feel or how everything hurts." Whatever the age of people with persistent ill health, comparing themselves with others and with how they used to be, and feeling useless, unneeded and rejected – in a similar way to elderly people – is common. And it can hook in old self-with-other scripts originating in early childhood.

Enduring ill health inevitably brings losses and they need to be faced, mourned and assimilated into our life story. Illness narratives illustrate how part of that assimilation is to identify time markers, significant dates such as the anniversary of when we were first diagnosed, had an operation, learned of a loved one's death, was given the all clear or the times of year when things were at their worse. They form part of our personal calendar and become benchmarks to evaluate present health. For example: "I feel much better than before I had a heart attack, changed my diet" or "worse than I was three years, six months ago". These time markers also become part of family history. "Do you remember the day when Grandma had a fall?", or "of Dad's funeral?", or "when our brother lost his leg?", or "Jill was sectioned?" Time markers, or what Charmaz also called identifying moments, can astonish or demean the ill person. "Like the small shocks of ageing, unsettling reminders of a changing self and a new identity can emerge when one loses his or her health" (1991, p. 208). She cited one elderly woman who nearly fell after using the toilet: "I realized then my days of living independently are numbered" (p. 208). I also know people who often mention what they were doing in the months before illness struck as if using these as markers.

The theme of loss and what those losses mean often emerged in Charmaz's discussions with her interviewees, and because she met with them over a period of up to seven years, she also conveyed how the losses continued. When someone has an enduring physical or mental health condition, they know that it can get progressively worse or that they will have periods of relative remission, but there is always the risk of further bad times, crises and hospitalisations. Coming to terms with all this and finding a way to mourn what is lost is far from easy. Nor is it easy for even the most resilient and positive person to retain hope and stay positive all the time. And some people find that with each downturn it is harder to "bounce back". This was true of Liam whom I saw at intervals over many years. A man disabled by acute anxiety, he had been an inpatient on many occasions since he was 20 years old. The effort of getting through the day, the pain of feeling intensely lonely and the despair about this being endless sometimes took him to a dark, suicidal place. "It gets worse each time and longer to get back to anything like normal. I don't want to keep doing this", Liam told me. "What is my life about?". Former dreams of doing something he had worked towards and that felt meaningful to him had all been thwarted by his anxiety. "What is my life about?" "Who am I now if not …?" These are also questions that emerge in therapy with people struggling with the loss of loved ones. And for them too, their relationship to time can radically change. It is to this group that I now turn.

Traumatic loss and bereavement

> Death creates a fracture in time – a rent in the fabric of existence, it disrupts, causes discontinuity.
>
> *(Rolls, 2010, p. 332)*

> Death is outside life but it alters it: it leaves a hole in the fabric of things which those who are left behind try to repair.
>
> *(Vickers, 2000, p. 3)*

Having discussed how we react to the thought of our own death in Chapter 6, I want to explore how the deaths of others affect our relationship to time, both in the aftermath and the future. What narratives emerge after a traumatic loss or a wrong time death? How does this affect the ongoing self and our structures of meaning? How do we repair the rent in the fabric of our existence? Let me begin with Rolls' moving account of how one woman tried to support her two young children after their father was involved in a fatal accident (2010). It provides a vivid account of how her thoughts shifted back and forwards between different time-zones. It also illustrates a number of the functions of narrative discussed earlier. As she shared her shifting thoughts and feelings after the accident and contemplated making some crucial decisions regarding her children, her "story" was containing. She contained something for the boys in her ongoing reflection, and she used Rolls as a holding other to share her emerging thoughts and decisions with. The woman's story also involved meaning-making. She tried to make sense of her reactions and decisions, and she "did meaning-making" for the children by oscillating between past, present and future. This meaning-making took time over time as she tried to repair the rent in time and maintain continuity of meaning between past, present and the now lost "hoped for" future. Sometimes she grappled with the immediate future, for instance thinking how to manage an important family event later in the same week of the accident. She also tried to work out what she should tell her children about what had happened to help them make sense of events both now and in the future. Sometimes her focus was their future in years to come. For example, how might the boys deal with things later in life if they had not had a chance to say a final goodbye? "I thought hard for them", she said, "and awful as this scene is going to be, if it doesn't help now, maybe later on" (p. 331). She wanted to minimise their biographical disruption by "finding, creating and reconstructing coherence and meaning" (p. 332).

The mother was very conscious of her changed identity – now a single parent – and of the importance of her continuity for the boys across time. "I had this consciousness that I was all they were going to have for ever and ever amen … They had to know that I did everything with them in mind, and I didn't walk over their feelings and just do what I thought was best for them" (p. 331). One way of conceptualising this is that she was actively trying to transform their relationship with the past and this, as I argue later, is part of the healing process of telling the story after traumatic events. But here it had the additional element of transforming how all three of them might relate to it in the future. As Rolls argued, implicit in her narrative was the hope that her current actions would reap future benefit (p. 333).

Grief narratives

When a death makes mothering hard

Rolls' example of the containing, meaning-making function of telescoping different time-zones (distant/recent past, near/far future) into the present process of narrating and reflecting has made me more aware of how and when oscillating in time is evident in the stories my own clients bring. It was evident, for example, when Zoe started to tell me about her much-loved father's death. She shifted between describing interactions with her children during the week, her own childhood, her father's illness and what happened just before and after he died, and these short narratives were interspersed with thoughts and feelings about different generations and worries about the future. There had been little time to process her feelings because, as well as needing to make regular visits to the family home to visit her father and later help her mother deal with all that followed, Zoe had two young children to care for and worked part-time as a solicitor. Her grief began to catch up with her a year later. Not only did she become depressed and start questioning whether her career held meaning anymore, but her unresolved loss had begun to interfere with her relationship with her two-year-old daughter Melanie.

Now, in the present, Zoe engaged in a complex process of reminiscing, contemplating how the loss of the lynchpin of the family had affected relationships between her and her siblings, and thinking forward to her mother's future and beyond that, the future of the family farm. The narrative process was, as in all therapeutic narrating, not linear. One moment she would be telling me how much she missed her father or fondly recalling moments with him as a child, the next she speculated how she might feel when her mother died. She also slipped between telling me about her "difficult" daughter's temper tantrums, to recalling with increasing sadness how she did not have time to enjoy really getting to know her as a baby because her mind was so caught up in everything she had to do. Sometimes, rather than staying with the difficult emotions that were coming up, Zoe leaped ahead to seemingly unconnected events in the future. At such moments, I felt disconnected from her in the same way, I imagined, she had needed to disconnect from baby Melanie, and still did, at times. I named my response, and slowly Zoe began to notice the links between her daughter's "difficult" moments and her own emotional state. In the present, significantly, their relationship started to improve.

Silenced grief

Like trauma, grief can also become frozen, unassimilated into the survivor's life story, and this makes it harder to deal with later losses. Such was the case with

Joseph. His mother died suddenly when he was five. Everything became topsy-turvy for a while: A week when nothing happened as normal. Then two weeks at his grandparents. Then back home to live with his father. No one talked to Joseph about what had happened. His grandparents, rather mistakenly, had tried to cheer him up, acting as if he was with them for a holiday and distracting him if he talked about Mum. His father got angry when Joseph asked questions about her. "She's not coming back," he said. "We've got to move on." And when Joseph cried, he'd say "stop being silly. Girls cry. We don't." Later, as a teenager needing to know more about his mother in an attempt not to lose his now rather shady memories of her, Joseph tried questioning his father again. Again, he was met with impatience. "Stop raking up the past", was the only reply he got.

Joseph's was a silenced story. He never had the chance to make sense of his experiences, nor did he experience the comfort of shared grief. Instead, he was left thinking he was wrong in missing his mother. When, tragically, one of his children died a cot death and not long afterwards a close friend had a fatal accident, Joseph became his own "silencer". He could not join his wife in shared mourning and they grew apart. Losing her – she left him taking their two other children several years later, was the last straw, and after some wake-up calls because of binge drinking, he found his way to counselling. Slowly we made sense of the patchy memories of all that happened around his mother's death and found ways for Joseph to express and stay with a flood of held back emotions. Once again our work was very much an oscillation in time as Joseph darted between scenes as a five-year-old, a teenager, the parent of a deceased infant, and the man who came home one day to find his wife and children gone – what he thought he had come to therapy to address. We could not change his past. But his present improved and he worked to regain contact with his sons and slowly started to form new bonds with them.

The death of illusions

If, as Rolls said, "death creates a fracture in time", the death of somebody who harmed you can freeze time and complicate the grieving process. And when all his life someone has been able to imagine the possibility of a future because he clings to hope, then the death of the person the hopes were pinned on kills the illusion. This was the case with Adam. Imagining the "hoped for" kept Adam alive during some of his darkest moments. One day his first words as he entered my room were: "I've had enough of grief, ten years of it!" In that period Adam had lost several close friends, his partner Ellie, and his maternal grandfather, the one adult he felt able to turn to as a child. All had been preceded by long illnesses and Adam had spent many hours visiting and doing what he could to offer support. It was understandable then that when his father, with whom he had a highly ambivalent relationship, died, this was the last straw. It knocked the stuffing out of him and got in the way of his grief process for Ellie which, 20 months on, he had been finding a way to come to terms with. He reverted to heavy drinking and had one or two minor brushes with the law.

Adam's father was an authoritarian figure, highly critical of his son, who regularly shamed him in public and was quick to seize a belt if he infringed any of his house rules. "Spare the rod and spoil the child" was his motto. Adam was stuck with the fact that there had been no final conversation with his father. He had slipped into a coma a week before he died. I asked, "what would you have liked to have said to him if you had?" "I wanted him to say he was proud of me, that he loved me. Just once." I reflected how this felt so important because it affected his sense of self. If his father had acknowledged what had happened in the past it would have wiped away some of the shame Adam carried like a badge. "Maybe then I could start believing that I wasn't bad and unlovable. That I'm not a bad person now", Adam said. "But he didn't. I was stupid to imagine he might have done. It was a fantasy. The old bastard was still picking holes in me right up to the end." I noted how he had slipped into self-criticism and said, "It was very important to you. To think of the ideal Dad gave you some comfort. It kept you going. The difficult thing is that with the death of your real Dad, the ideal, wished for Dad was killed". This was the grief work Adam needed to do, and my task to support him in this, gently noting when he slipped back into self-criticism or into attempts to justify and excuse his father, for instance, by saying he had a tough life. Along with the death of his hope, for a while at least, the loss of his father and all that meant to him killed Adam's sense of joy in the few pursuits that gave him pleasure. He slipped into a heavy, depressed state. He felt old, as if he had buried something more alive in him along with his father. "Each time someone goes, I lose another bit of me", Adam sadly concluded.

Emotional kinship

My last example comes from the analyst Robert Stolorow. He wrote movingly of his responses to the death of his wife four weeks after being diagnosed with cancer. Eighteen months later at a conference, surrounded by people he had known a long time, Stolorow was acutely aware how strange and alien they all seemed. They were "vitalized, engaged with each other in a lively manner". By contrast he felt "deadened and broken, the shell of the man I had once been. An unbridgeable gulf seemed to open up, separating me forever from my friends and colleagues. They could never even begin to fathom my experience, I thought, we now lived in altogether different worlds" (2007, p. 14). Stolorow's account speaks of the loss of one's former sense of self after a traumatic loss and, importantly, the loss of connection to others. His sense of being-in-the-world was permanently altered. It was what he called a "shattered absolutism", his world as one of the traumatised and that of his colleagues were now "felt to be essentially and ineradicably incommensurable" (p. 15). What he needed was "kinship-in-the-same-darkness", and he found it in time with his colleague George Attwood who had lost his mother at the age of eight (p. 49). Stolorow knew he understood.

Implications for practice

What can we learn from these examples? "How someone dies lives on in the memory of those who survive him", commented Cicely Saunders, the founder of the hospice movement (BBC Radio 4, June 2019). So too does how the survivor was responded to by others. Who told him and where? How was he told? Was he given time to take this in, to express his feelings? Or like with Joseph, was the death not discussed? Was everyone else in the family so overwrought with emotion and all that they had to do, that he was not kept in mind? Did he feel "met"? The examples I have given are of losses occurring at different stages in the life cycle. How does this variable influence their thoughts about the past and the future?

The impact of death when you are young

Some of the hardest deaths to deal with are wrong time events, when a child loses a parent or a parent a child. When a sibling or parent dies while you are still young, there will be multiple losses. There is the loss of the ongoingness of life, both in terms of the daily round, but also the loss of secure trust in the ongoingness of the people closest to you. Pulled far too early into knowing about the first challenge of living in time, many children harbour a fear that if one parent dies the other might too. There is also the need to assume other roles. For instance, some children feel they need to be "wife" or "husband" to a bereaved parent. When a sibling dies there is a double loss – of the brother or sister, and of needed attention during his or her illness and afterwards, because the parents are inevitably caught up in their own feelings and all they must now do. A child can become invisible or need to grow up far too early. Assumptions are made about their capacity to cope. The young person might react by becoming a responsible carer, always trying to behave and not cause problems. Or they might rebel and act out understandable frustration and anger. I can think of clients who took both positions at different times.

As we saw with Joseph, the loss of a parent when young can haunt people years later. Joseph's grief was stuck. It cast a shadow over future losses. In healthy mourning the survivor goes through the pain of grief many times and in many different forms. They accept the reality that the loved one is really gone. But internally there is a continuing and comforting bond. Some people become perennial mourners, like Dickens' Miss Havisham in her unchanging room, frozen in time, now a dark, decaying place. This is the state Freud described as melancholia (Freud, 1915). And when grief is suspended, its shadow can fall over future generations. In their book *Ghosts in the Consulting Room*, Harris and colleagues spoke of "present absences", absences that can emerge in the form of confusing body sensations and unexplained symptoms, actions, relational patterns and, in therapy, in transference/ countertransference dynamics (2016). Such ghostly hauntings are the result of overwhelming feelings that have not been processed and symbolised. They are the "remnants of losses that cannot find resolution" (p. 200).

Such hauntings can be transmitted across generations so that children or grand-children can feel, enact or dream what they do not know. For example, I became curious why a trainee nurse became so distressed talking about a woman whose son died of leukaemia when he was 10. She could not get her out of her mind. She imagined scenes with the dying boy that the woman herself had never described. One day, when she mentioned this again, I asked whether there might be anything in her family history that might echo this. Uncannily, the week before Jo had discovered that her great grandmother had lost two children after long illnesses and that afterwards she had retreated to her room, interacting only sporadically with her remaining children. Jo's grandmother had been born into a world of sickrooms and loss and suffered from depression. Jo's mother was "delicate", meaning "don't upset her and don't talk about difficult things". It was only because Jo found a box of letters belonging to the great grandmother's brother when clearing a cousin's house that she learned what had happened. Another silenced story. But it explained to Jo why she had often experienced periods of deep sadness with no clear cause. Her emotions belonged to another time-zone.

When our relational map is disrupted

Another theme for us to be aware of is the impact of bereavement on identity. It disrupts our relational map. It calls us to question "who am I if not his wife, mother, sister? And who am I now in relation to the surviving members of my family?" Perhaps the eldest now, which can be a daunting thought when the pre-sence of parents no longer buffers us from the reality of our mortality, or alter-natively it might lead to a sense of responsibility, if for instance, a death leaves us as the eldest of a group of siblings. Argano spoke of identity being in disarray. "Sud-denly the self-with-other identity has been supplanted by a self that is without. Initially, and for a long time, we are defined by what we have lost, our social role demoted from wife to widow, our inner selves withered like parched roots … neither what we were nor what we might become we hover uncomfortably, in the disintegrative space of liminality." However, I agree with Argano's emphasis that identity is repeatedly made and remade (2007, p. 35).

Judith Ryan also wrote eloquently about how a sudden traumatic loss can "assault" our identity and force us to slowly alter our configuration of self and self within the family (2007, pp. 61, 64). Her 23-year-old son died whilst mountai-neering. Ryan described the complexity of how she should refer to herself now: "We are still a nuclear family of five, although now we are only four. I am a mother of a son, even though he is not alive. 'How many children do you have?' If I choose to say 'two' to the hapless and unsuspecting questioner, the answer is also 'three'" (p. 64). And Ryan's daughter wrote: "When I received that early morning phone call, my identity, my sense of self, and my notion of who I am were thrown into an upheaval. My family was no longer five, or was it? Was I still the middle child?" (p. 64). As Ryan summed up, "the work of mourning is not just to accept that a loved one is never coming home – but to learn to tolerate the meanings of his death to one's sense of self" (p. 62). And with time and support, it is possible to find ourselves or, newly emerging, a stronger, wiser self.

The need to mourn

Like Pye's awareness of the co-existence of "cancer time" and mundane time, after a death and for some time before, people do live in different temporal worlds. Zoe had to juggle between the suspended time of her father's sickroom, the time urgency of a screaming baby demanding to be fed, the precision of school time for her older son, and the demands of her own work schedule. "I used to scream", she said. "I craved time for me." The mother described by Rolls would still have been making breakfast and running the children to school in the months after her husband's death, whilst simultaneously being preoccupied with thoughts about time gone and yet to come; and Joseph experienced the confusing craziness of seeing his father going through the daily routine as normal when the lynchpin of those familiar routines was gone. There is an absurdity for any of us, when our lives have been halted by a death, to sit in a team meeting debating future business plans or asked to make decisions about a social event in six months' time when internally, time has stopped. Earlier cultures were wise in the time they allowed for mourning and the space and respect they gave to the bereaved. Long gone are the days when it would be normal to see curtains closed in the days after a death and widows wearing black for periods of up to a year afterwards. Such visual elements of a rite of passage symbolise the survivor's changed status and honour their need for separation from ordinary time and its activities for a while.

Jewish tradition still allocates time for the bereaved to remain with their grief and gradually assimilate what the death means to them, rather than needing to engage prematurely in activities and social interactions that, for a while, feel unimportant. Slochower described how the tradition of observing *Shiva* for seven days after the death of a close relative "alters virtually every aspect of social behaviour" (2007, p. 89). The mourner is symbolically separated from the community, the second stage in a rite of passage. He or she wears a ripped garment, does not wash or work and is fed by others rather than needing to entertain those who call. Slochower pointed out the similarities with a therapeutic holding environment. The "community of callers" support this holding by being "reliably present, non-impinging, yet responsive". The mourner can "be alone in the presence of the (m)other", free to experience and express emotions and not need to worry about other people's reactions (p. 90). Customs for 30 days after the death and the anniversary also support grieving and healing.

For many people these days, it is a question of getting back to business as quickly as possible. This is in the context of changing attitudes to death over the centuries and in the ways it is dealt with. The transition to the "Dirty Death" and its medicalisation has deprived us of many former holding structures. It is also part of detraditionalisation, the erosion of former structures of meaning and support that bound communities together in the past. Do we ever mourn *these* losses I wonder? I think not, and that they therefore show their presence in other ways.

Concluding thoughts

Grieving is an ongoing process, and this is true whether the loss is of a person or of capacities and roles because of illness and disability. Grieving does not move neatly from one stage to the next, although to simplify things we often conceptualise it in this way. Nor is it a case of what Freud believed, a stage to go through, in order to break the bonds with a loved one. Losses and the feelings that go with them can still be evoked, often triggered by significant dates and places, for years after the death – like an old injury that can still twinge, although the intensity fades over time. And loss narratives are constantly being revisited, updated and rewoven and assimilated into our life story. In therapy we often see people who, like Alice, Liam, Joseph and Zoe, engage in a recursive grief process. Their story loops back and moves forwards. And of course, we see people who develop all sorts of strategies to avoid the work of mourning.

Grieving is important, said Slochower, "but so too is memorialisation". I mentioned some communal memorials in Chapter 8, but we also need to create individual ones. In Slochower's view rituals "involving symbolic and literal acts ... allow the mourner to contact, re-visit and recreate memory". They counter our "perhaps equally strong need to forget, to sidestep the loss, fear, guilt or rage that death evokes" (2007, p. 84). She gave several examples of acts of memorialisation. Some occur at specific sites, cemeteries or where a death or massacre occurred.[1] Some take the form of cultural and religious ceremonies. For example, on the yearly anniversary the Jewish mourner recites *Kaddish* in a synagogue. What makes it important is that although a private ritual, if the deceased was known locally it connects the individual to the community. A brief memorial ceremony is also held on Yom Kippur and three other major festivals (p. 92).[2] Slochower writes, "there is comfort in the awareness that the pain of our own loss is both separate from, yet connected to, that of others" (p. 96). The Jewish traditions support mourning across the lifecycle and allow for both connection and separateness. They provide the emotional kinship in darkness that Stolorow discovered is so essential to containing and integrating deep emotional pain.

The novelist Sally Vickers observed that in ancient stories when heroes die, "the first thing their comrades do, having made due observances to the gods, is sit and eat" – interestingly, sharing food is what we do after a funeral – "Then they travel on, challenging, with their frail vitality, the large enigma of non-being" (2000, p. 3). There is something in these traditional ways of honouring a death that connect life and growth, frailty and death. To quote another novelist, "one moment we are pottering about our errands as usual and the next we are dying, and our eternally impending ending does not put a stop to our transient beginnings and middles until the instant when it does" (Hamid, 2017, p. 2). Rituals, whatever form they take, "allow the individual to integrate the experience of aloneness and loss within an intersubjective context that reaffirms life in the face of facing loss" (Slochower, 2007, p. 96). We could put this another way, they reaffirm ongoingness.

To sum up: I have noted some similarities between the crises of illness and bereavement. They pull us out of consensual time and the usual continuity of life for long or short periods. When immersed in a life crisis we can experience parallel times as we grapple with the demands of mundane life and respond to events and emotional states that occur at very different paces. And both can cast shadows deep into the future. Moreover, health crises and bereavement are linked in a deeper way. The former often carry a silenced and unmourned story. To illustrate this, I want to return to Carol, the lady with the trapped nerve. For her, the integrations between self and other, past and present, the "potterings" of daily life and encounters with horror and loss, were never possible. Carol's story of years of terrifying childhood abuse had been silenced. And she had learned to silence her emotions. They remained trapped, frozen like her memories in time. After the death of her brother, the person she was closest to, Carol tried to carry on as normal. "I have to", she said. "It's the only way I can cope." I noticed how she kept putting off organising a plaque for his grave and how his room – they had shared a house for years – was left just as it was before he died. When I gently enquired about her plans Carol told me, "I know I've got to do something. But I can't. I'd lose him if I did". Carol had been unable to memorialise John's death. She had not shared her grieving with others. Nor had she been able to share and memorialise the abuse in her childhood in a communal way. Not for Carol was the company of kin-in-the-same-darkness. And so her body became the voice of protest and pain, trapped like the spinal nerve. No longer would it be silenced. It *was* the memorial to all her suffering.

Notes

1 Recent acts of memorialisation in the UK have included events or services at Grenfell Tower and the site of the Manchester bombings. Flowers are often placed at the site of a fatal car accident or in profusion at the site of a terrorist attack.
2 Other faiths also have annual services for commemorating the dead, even though in an increasingly secularised world fewer people take part in them than in the past.

References

Argano, A. 2007. "Transforming Mourning: A New Psychoanalytic Perspective" in B. Willock, L. Bohm & R. Curtis (Eds.) *On Death and Endings: Psychoanalysts' Reflections on Finality, Transformations and New Beginnings* (pp. 21–41). New York: Routledge.

Charmaz, K. 1991. *Good Days and Bad Days: The Self in Chronic Illness and Time*. New Brunswick, NJ: Rutgers University Press.

Dickens, C. 1996[1861]. *Great Expectations*. London: Penguin Classics.

Freud, S. "Mourning and Melancholia", *Standard Edition, Vol. 14*. London: Hogarth Press.

Hamid, M. 2017. *Exit West*. London: Penguin.

Harris, A., Kalb, M. & Klebanoff, S. (Eds.) 2016. *Ghosts in the Consulting Room: Echoes of Trauma in Psychoanalysis*. New York: Routledge.

Mann, T. 1999[1924]. *The Magic Mountain*. London: Vintage.

Pye, J. 2017. "Full Circle: 'We had the experience but missed the meaning'". Conference presentation.

Rolls, L. 2010. "Narrating time: Minimising the disruption and discontinuities of children's experience of death", *Illness, Crisis and Loss*, 184, 323–39.

Rose, S. 1999. "Naming and Claiming: The Integration of Traumatic Experience and the Reconstruction of Self in Survivor's Stories of Sexual Abuse" in K. Lacy Rogers & S. Leydesdorff (Eds.) *Trauma and Life Stories: International Perspectives* (pp. 160–79). London: Routledge.

Ryan, J. 2007. "Affects, Reconfiguration of the Self and Self-states in Mourning the Loss of a Son" in B. Willock, L. Bohm & R. Curtis (Eds.) *On Death and Endings: Psychoanalysts' Reflections on Finality, Transformations and New Beginnings* (pp. 60–67). New York: Routledge.

Slochower, J. 2007. "Beyond the Consulting Room: Ritual, Mourning and Memory", in B. Willock, L. Bohm & R. Curtis (Eds.) *On Death and Endings: Psychoanalysts' Reflections on Finality, Transformations and New Beginnings* (pp. 84–99). New York: Routledge.

Stolorow, R. 2007. *Trauma and Human Existence*. New York: Routledge.

Vickers, S. 2000. *Miss Garnet's Angel*. London: Harper Collins.

12

JOURNEYING IN TIME

Psychotherapy and the change process

In a fraction of time, in a moment, something momentous can occur. For change "what 'really' happened has to be met by something that is 'really' happening and is 'really' different.

(Slavin and Rahmani, in Lord, 2018 p. 61)

Change happens slowly, sometimes disappointingly slowly.

(Eger, 2017, p. 337)

Our views about therapeutic change will inevitably be theoretically biased. My ideas, based on my trainings, reading choices and clinical practice will be different from yours. A vast amount has been written on the subject and I am not claiming to offer any radically new ideas. But what I want to bring to the debate is the place of the temporal dimension in the change process. Writing this book has repeatedly drawn me to certain questions: What is it that occurs during the life of a therapeutic journey, however long it lasts, that makes a difference? Why is carving out a special temporal space for such a journey important? What helps to change people's memories – or rather, their relationship to them? And what do I do that supports this process? I have also thought about therapeutic change as both a revolutionary process and an evolutionary one, something momentous in a fraction of time or at a slowly, evolving pace.

A number of writers have conceptualised the change process as a hermeneutic one of creating a new relationship between past and present, and we could add, with the future as well. Freud was the first, with his concept of *nachtraglichkeit*, to appreciate the backward action of the present on the past. As Harris pointed out, it captures the paradox in temporal experience that we can be in more than one time-zone at once (2009, pp. 1, 12). More recently Steven Mitchell wrote, "pasts, indeed, are not reconstructed; they are constructed in the here and now" (1993,

p. 59). In similar vein, Donnel Stern argued that "the vitalization of the present by the past or the past by the present requires that experiences be linked across time" (2012, p. 53). In this process time needs to "turn back on itself" (p. 56). It is a recursive process, a repeated looping back, that makes it possible to change the meanings of what took place in the past and free us from its constraints. The future can also be altered. In a sense then, the therapeutic encounter with memory involves a doubling and tripling of time as we inhabit two or more time zones at once. Rolls' account of the mother who created meaning by oscillating in time is a good example (Rolls, 2010).

What is needed for the vitalisation of the present?

In my ongoing grappling with the question "what leads to change and transformation in our clients' relationship to past, present and future?", these are the things that strike me: I see it as a process that cannot occur without certain conditions. It could be argued that all the conditions, and they are interlinked, involve something mutative occurring in real time. Sometimes one will be in the foreground, then the process will become dominated by another. The other common feature is that they all involve something new being connected with the past that alters procedural memory. It occurs when earlier states are accessed (i.e. state dependent memory), and in this altered state of consciousness there is an opening, a plasticity, for a new experience to profoundly change our beliefs, alter our self-other patterns, and for sensing and relating to our bodies in a different way. From the perspective of non-linear dynamic systems theory, even small differences are sufficient for movement and "slight shifts in experience can give rise to change and greater complexity and difference within very short time frames" (Harris, 2009, p. 6). Daniel Stern's thesis is that change is based on lived experiences that alter the functional past. As he said, "in and of itself, verbally understanding, explaining or narrating something is not sufficient to bring about change. There must be an actual experience, a subjectively lived happening. An event must be *lived*, with feelings and actions taking place in real time, in the real world, with real people, in a moment of presentness" (Stern, 2004, p. xiii).

DeYoung made a similar point when outlining the key elements of relational psychotherapy: Insights, she argued, have no power to change anything "unless they are performative insights, or insights that are intimately connected to interactive, emotional experience" (2003, p. 4). "Whatever keeps going wrong (the old scripts or self-other-patterns) will turn into a story you can tell together, and then there will be a way to bring a new story into being … things will change when the two of you can do your relationship in a significantly different way. That's a performative therapy." There is a sense of aliveness, immediacy and risky potential in what both these therapists advocated. The old, stale story could be replayed endlessly in the therapeutic relationship, *or* something excitedly new could emerge provided that both partners are willing to risk being authentically with the unknown. To use Ron Kurtz's evocative phrase, it is about finding the "fertile ground at the margin of the moment" (1990, p. 79).

Stern and DeYoung emphasised the importance of a new intersubjective experience, whereas I argued in Chapter 10 that the novel experience can be intersubjective, intrapsychic, somatic or involving the imagination. Intersubjectively, change can occur when a rift or enactment challenges the therapeutic relationship, both partners caught up in old patterns and fixed beliefs belonging to their respective implicit pasts. But as I have illustrated, transformative moments can also occur when someone has a new experience of his or her body, for instance, a feeling of mastery or of embodied safety, the completion of an action that became stuck during a traumatic event, or when he is able to envisage something hitherto unknown through imagination and metaphor. Diana Fosha's work fits my wider application of the idea of a transformative moment. She proposed that "moments of meeting be redefined as all moments that evoke a 'click of recognition' and a resulting state shift". This, she argued, would allow us to consider the important role of transformative moments "not only in relational change, but also in changes in emotion processing, affect regulation, and somatic experience, to name just a few" (2018, p. 268). I like her term "wow moments". I also want to stress that these experiences cannot take place except within the holding matrix of a secure relationship. As Stern argued, central to the transformation of the functional past is the shared evolving present moment, and the word 'shared' merits emphasis. It is our attunement and encouragement that enables the client to venture into what Bromberg called "safe surprises" (Bromberg, 2011, p. 17). It provides a "sanctuary of safety" that evokes the social engagement system and enables the client to enter a different mental and physical state (Siegel & Solomon, 2013, p. 10). To be effective, as DeYoung said, remembering needs to be remembering *with*, to have someone there who acts as a partner in thought and helps us to find meaning in our experiences (2003, p. 113). And it is our marvelling with the client that helps to integrate the change, and our witnessing and remembering what just occurred that ensures it can be drawn on later as new memory and employed to inform the future.

The juxtaposition of something new in the present with something dysregulating, distressing and limiting from the past is central then to therapeutic change, and it occurs within a supportive relational context. The novelty of the "something new" is part of its potency. We habituate to what we know. But stale beliefs, rigid ways of behaving, and fixed expectations about how others will treat us become unhinged when we encounter something not known, seen or experienced before. It surprises us into change. But the new should offer a "safe surprise" rather than shock us, because when shocked we cannot assimilate what has happened. In what follows I am going to discuss seven conditions which support this transformative revitalisation of past and present. I shall then explore the differences between revolutionary and evolutionary change.

Seven conditions supporting transformation

Memorial activity and making connections

The first condition involves what I talked about in Chapter 8, the re-collecting and possessing of our life-story, an integrative process of memorial activity. Cozolino argued that "change in psychotherapy is all about memory: the exploration of past memory, the impact of the past on the present, and the ability to modify what is stored in memory to affect changes in thoughts, feelings, and behaviors" (2016, p. 68). For change then, we could say that we need to have a "dialogue with time", a self-reflective engagement with the reality of time. (Giddens, 1991, pp. 72, 77). In Chapter 1, I described memory as something capricious. It is not fixed, not, as Loewald pointed out a *fait accompli* "leaving traces on a wax tablet brain". Instead he viewed memory as action, or rather, as a linking activity. Through the "memorial activity" of the mind we can link disparate bits of experience into a nexus "which has meaning and gives meaning to each element by subjective virtue of the reciprocal relationship created between them". We make our history and thereby shape our identity by virtue of this memorial activity "in which past-present-future are created as mutually interacting modes of time" (1972, p. 409).

There is something important in this which goes to the heart of how psychotherapy supports change. Change is about making connections – "Only connect" – and in connecting we find meaning. I am reminded here of Haynes' observation that "meaningful becoming depends on two principal actions: the act of creation (which is inevitably twinned with destruction), and memory", and change entails not just connecting and integrating, but separating and differentiating (Siegel, 2010). Haynes continued: "Unlike the processes that are required for the recording of history, precise or accurate memory, in this context, is less desirable than an ability to make links that allow us to weave the particularity of one life to the pattern of all lives" (2007, p. 212). The communal narratives mentioned in Chapter 8 illustrate this weaving of self and others. Different therapies emphasise the importance of connection and integration in different domains. Some prioritise the connection between self and others; some between different parts of self; others between thoughts, feelings and emotions; whilst body therapists focus on the connection of body and self. There is also the connection between unconscious and conscious. Where we stand on this goes back to my point about theoretical bias.

If change is about making connections and in this integrative process finding meaning (and I am thinking both of meaning as insight and meaning as purpose), contrast this with situations when the creative activity of memory is suspended – for instance, when trauma breaks the reciprocal relationship between past, present and future so that what is experienced is a meaningless now. Trauma freezes the past and deprives it of the plasticity needed to connect with the present (Stern, 2012, p. 56). People become embedded in their experience. They blend with younger parts of self, for the memories held by those parts have not been updated, and they find it hard to hold multiple perspectives.

The presence of an engaged witness and co-narrator

The second condition is the presence of an external witness, a co-narrator, a companion on the journey. It is someone who is not only available to listen, but who can share the process at an emotional level. It is a witness who is moved with you but can contain his or her feelings. It is someone who communicates under-standing, who gets it, and that is at a level much deeper than any cognitive understanding.[1] Our engaged participation is important in the emergence of the something new. Mair spoke of the need for therapists to adopt the role of an intermediary, a role in which we engage in forms of communication that "refresh and bring a person to life, open them to new possibilities". If we listen with the whole of ourselves and suspend the need for literal accuracy, he argued, we can help give voice "to what is being said in the living space of both the speaker and the receiver" (2013, pp. 44, 45). There is an imaginative opening up of alternative perspectives. From a different standpoint Mitchell wrote about the analyst adding imagination: "a facility with reorganising and reframing, a capacity to envision different futures, different endings" that supports a shift in narratives that are ste-reotyped and closed (1993, p. 76). We need to be willing to bear imagining what our client's earlier experiences might have been like, to step into the shoes of the frightened, lonely, confused and disconfirmed child,[2] *and* to be able to dream dreams about the person he could become. In such imagining we are doing what an ordinary parent does – holding the prospective adult in mind, and then encouraging and supporting the child to achieve his own dreams. In the use of our imagination we are oscillating in time, holding our client's present self, his past selves and his potential self in mind when he is unable to do this for himself. Some of our more intuitive, experimental interventions will often be to access a child-state or to invite a client to imagine or embody how they might deal with some-thing in the future. To return to Mitchell's words, it supports them to envision different futures and endings, and to see themselves as they were, or others as they were back in the past in different lights.

Even if we introduce something more technical, for instance, to suggest trying out a certain movement, or offering a visualisation or creative exercise using objects, its transformative potential at that particular point comes from resonance, not just theory. Cox and Theilgaard spoke of the therapist's experience of "a sense of fit and coherence linked to an imperative urge to respond to a patient in a particular way", and this often occurs because of "associative echoes" that are evoked in us (1987, p. 36). Without this emotional 'fine tuning' the intervention will feel clunky and removed from the present experience, and although it might be effective at some level, perhaps offering a fresh insight, it does not have the quality of a deeply transformative moment.

When we really engage at an emotional level, we support the reconstruction of the past and also the construction of a more coherent and perhaps compas-sionate sense of self. And we do this by intuitively turning to a form of com-munication that is qualitatively different from ordinary conversation. It is the language of caregivers and babies, a language of immediacy, attunement and communion/togetherness. The attuned mother manages to step inside her baby's experience and reflects back her empathic understanding through the tone and pace of her voice, her facial expressions and her gestures. These repeated moments in micro-time of what is called protoconversation shape our emergent self (Meares, 2012, pp. 20–23). A therapist who captured simply and beautifully the quality of this right-brain, non-linear language of connection was Ron Kurtz. Kurtz explained that "offering a short, simple comment on the client's present experience" shows that we are following what is going on for him (1990, p. 77). The connection is also made by communicating that this is the client's time. We listen, watch and wait until something indicates that he is ready for us to say something. These "contact statements" help capture what otherwise is likely to get quickly lost as thoughts, feelings and sensations go rushing on (p. 76). We might contact what we see: "Lots of feelings, huh?" "Something happens when you think of that"; or what the client is talking about: "You were really scared, huh?" "So confusing for a little girl" (pp. 78–82). Kurtz argued that when the client feels listened to and understood he relaxes and goes deeper. It moves the process along.

Feeling understood settles us. It can have a dramatic effect on our physiology. It quietens anxiety and reduces shame. And over time it is essential in the formation of our identity. Two early writers appreciated this. Erikson, for instance, defined identity as an "accrued confidence that inner sameness and continuity are matched by the sameness and continuity of one's meaning for others" (1965, p. 253). There is a good-enough fit between how we experience ourselves and how, from their responses to us, other people appear to experience us. The fit confirms us. Sander described this as a process of recognition, and cited Winnicott's account of his observations playing the Squiggle Game with children (1995, p. 589). As they embellish each other's squiggles they come to a moment of shared awareness in which "the child becomes aware that another is aware of what the child is aware of within" (1990, p. 228). I cannot think of a better way to describe the look on a client's face when we make a contact statement that is just right – a moment of connection that is way more than communicating an understanding of facts. Maybe this is an or *the* essential feature of the "something more than …" that the Boston Change Group discuss. Winnicott called it a "sacred moment". It is a moment of meeting, an event in a tiny moment of present time which can profoundly alter the experiencing of and learning from the past[3].

Winnicott described playing the Squiggle Game with a 16-year-old girl and a point when she drew something and said, "It's all cramped up, it's not free and spreading". Winnicott replied, "It's you, isn't it?" He was contacting instinctively what was implicit in her words and she agreed. "Yes. You see I'm a bit shy." Winnicott responded by acknowledging that she did not know him or why she had come or what they were going to do and the girl, clearly feeling understood, said, "the squiggle is not spontaneous. I'm all the time trying to make an impression because I'm not sure of myself. I've been like it for ages". Winnicott, again getting her, said, "It's sad isn't it?" to show that he had heard and had feelings because of the implications of what she was telling him (1990, pp. 122–3).

Another example comes from my work with a woman called Kim who suffered from acute loneliness. On this occasion, she had started by saying that she could not imagine ever not feeling lonely. She described how during the week the pain in her chest felt unbearable, "like spikes being pushed into it". Kim had tried to focus on stroking her cat, her pets usually bringing some comfort. But that had reminded her of a dog she had been particularly fond of, and the pain felt even worse. Kim welled up as she spoke. "You really miss him", I said. "I keep thinking, maybe I didn't make the right decision about having him put down", she said, suddenly biting her nails. "Such worries", I contacted, "they gnaw away at you." I sensed she felt understood as she looked away, then said, "I can hear him … his bark when he was excited playing ball". She paused. "It was the right thing to do." "Yes, part of you knows that", I commented, "that now he can be free to play somewhere else". Kim smiled.

There are various situations when a good-enough fit between how we are experiencing ourselves and how others respond to us is lacking with consequences for the formation of a coherent sense of self. They include very early experiences with a depressed mother who was unable to "give the baby back himself", or with incoherent and inconsistent parents. They also include situations when abusive adults deliberately tried to confuse the child in order to keep her scared and subservient. And lastly, there is the trauma of disconfirmation when our reality is repeatedly discounted or disconfirmed (Bromberg, 2001, p. 57). The example of Rose in Chapters 5 and 8 is a case in point.

An internal witness

We also need to be able to witness ourselves, or to put it another way to occupy two or more self-states at the same time. This is Donnel Stern's argument. He explained that the linkage across time occurs when we are able to "occupy self-states in both the past and the present" each bearing witness to one another. This is the internal work of accessing and dialoguing with different selves, those hurt and traumatised selves that have been split off, silenced and repudiated as "not me". In such dialoguing we will come up against internal conflicts, for instance all too often it is accompanied by harsh self-criticism, a voice full of "shoulds" and "oughts", or that scorns and wants to get rid of other parts of self. As the external witness we need to welcome all the conflicting parts of self into the dialogue and invite curiosity and compassion about their individual beliefs and strategies.[4] By encountering and learning to tolerate them, it becomes possible to hold multiple perspectives. This leads to freedom rather than the constraints of rigid single-mindedness (Stern, 2010, pp. 102–3). It also leads to a much more benign form of internal witnessing without which change is far less likely to occur. Our capacity for internal witnessing has its roots in symbolic play (Meares, 2012, p. 24). It is possible because as children we experienced an attuned other who gave our experience back to us in manageable form. And, as discussed earlier, it is a process that can get derailed by overwhelming events that sever the connections between different parts of self.

An "affective bridge"

Change also entails creating "affective bridges" between feelings and knowledge and past and present (Stern, 2012, pp. 55, 60; Modell, 2009). Talking about past events is only a small part of memorial activity. Processing memories entails accessing and being with the emotions, sensations, impulses, thoughts and beliefs that go with the details of whatever happened. Here I return to Siegel's point that "making sense goes way beyond having a logical understanding of past events – a coherent story involves all our senses, head to toe" (2010, p. 178). The use of metaphors supports the creation of affective bridges. But what do we mean by metaphors? And why are they transformative?

Thinking in metaphors is a right-brain process, "the currency of the emotional mind" (Stern, 2012, p. 55). It is synchronic and belongs to the realm of Kairos, the kind of time that is non-linear and can turn back on itself. Metaphors re-present experience. They "stand for" and have an "as if" quality. To explain this Stern described how when a present experience reminds us of something from the past things feel they belong together. There is a "feeling-connection", an affective bridge, between two episodes, and that is because our brain "maps" certain experiences onto others such as an emotional state onto a sensory detail or bodily experience (Stern, 2012, p. 54; 2010, p. 132). For instance, we might associate feeling safe with the smell of baking cakes or feeling anxious with the sound of raised voices because these sensory-affective states are reminders, albeit not consciously recognised, of situations in the past. Metaphors provide links between emotional memory and current perceptions and act as "pattern detectors" (Stern, 2010, p. 135; Modell, 2009, p. 8). This, I suggest, is an important aspect of memorial activity.

Mair used the term 'vehicle' for metaphors (2013, p. 33). We use metaphors to "give form, shape, and expression" to our experiences. In this way, we create associative links between otherwise separate experiences, something Stern believed is crucial to psychic growth (2010, p. 136), and find ways to explore and relate our inner and outer worlds. This brings me back to the importance of connection and integration. Creating links is an essential part of sense making, and as we discover meaning in our experiences it opens the door to new ways of being with ourselves and others. Mair evocatively captured how metaphor can enrich experience when he said, "through metaphors, new possibilities of meaning, of living, can be entered and explored, new costumes, new plays, new parts, new access to the scripts we did not know we were being spoken by" (2013, p. 18).

We can appreciate how crucial the process of creating links and organising emotional memory is when we think of trauma survivors who find it impossible to do this or to make sense of what happened to them. As Modell pointed out, "in health, metaphor retains its complexity, generating a multiplicity of meanings". However, "in interpreting the memory of trauma, metaphor loses its play of similarity and difference and becomes frozen, involuntary and invariant, and recognizes only similarities" (2009, p. 8). In Modell's view, in the wake of trauma the past becomes timeless in the sense that is exists beyond the experience of time. In consequence, the traumatic events stay fixed "as a concrete record that cannot be contextualized in the present" thus draining meaning from both past and present (Stern, 2010, p. 135). This adds weight to my emphasis on the need for something new to be connected with the past.

Because of its "as if-ness", the use of metaphor helps us to oscillate in time. When we play with images, we find it easier to look at events, whether in the past or imagined in the future, from a distance. We can scrutinise the image from a number of angles, each revealing new perspectives and meanings. It is having a dialogue with our experience that opens up new possibilities for living. The "as if" quality of metaphors resembles the language of play, and through play, using objects to stand for something external, a child often discovers highly creative ways to alter his felt experiencing of a situation. I recall hearing Van der Kolk's lovely example of a little boy whose picture of the Twin Towers had trampolines at the bottom to catch people as they jumped. In this way he transformed something of the horrors he had seen. Mair took the playful aspect of the therapeutic process seriously. "It seems so necessary to help people to detach a little from the grim insistence of the cultural imperatives they live amongst, which they have had to take as real, the way things are, the enduring reality they know, and encourage them to pretend, *to act as if* … at last a way of make-believe can allow someone to say how it really feels, however foolish it would seem at home to be so fanciful" (2013, p. 73).

Just as the capacity to play initially depends on an engaged witness, so when someone is struggling to find something that will make sense of her life, to have another person with whom to play with metaphors is important. Perhaps like the falling tree that only makes a sound if someone is there to hear it, it leads to feeling heard at a deeper level, to a sense of togetherness. In the moment, we grasp and share a felt response to the enormity and pain of the experience being discussed. When, for instance, Rose said it felt as if her mother's repeated accusations – "You're too …"; "You always …" – were killing her, I sensed the profound impact these words had and reflected it was like a barrage of arrows attacking her. They annihilated her sense of self and, in consequence, she found it hard to know and speak her truth. I could tell that Rose felt understood when I amplified her word "killing" and sensed that she also understood herself a little more deeply.

Let me end this section by returning to Kim, the woman who suffered from acute loneliness. It is an example that illustrates how metaphors can open up new possibilities and be containing. Kim both longed for and was terribly scared of intimacy. She had been seeing a man on and off for several years and often spoke of her distress at being unable to really let in his care. The pattern was echoed in our relationship and became the focus in the third year of work. On one occasion, Kim had been talking about the previous session when she had asked to hold my hand. She had been preoccupied with the need to "get it right" and to feel something and this made it impossible to be fully present to the experience. I asked

Kim how it would be to hold my hand now and simply notice what colours came to mind. She did not actually take it, but immediately said it would be a rainbow and spontaneously started to play in her imagination. It was as if my invitation freed her access to linking, cognitively in terms of reflection and metaphoric processing and intersubjectively because it challenged her pattern of freezing at the thought of contact with another person. The first image that came to her was of a younger part of self playing and occasionally darting up to touch my hand and running off again. But curiously there was not just one hand but a number, all of different colours. This was followed by an image of my hand in a block. When Kim wanted, she could come and look at it, seeing it from different angles, but not needing to do anything with it.

My sense is that the transformative element in these images was that in this imaginative realm our contact was under Kim's control. Moreover, I believe that she was beginning to internalise me as a good object even if, at that point, she could only make use of me cautiously. It opened up the new possibility that in her relationship with others she might be able to ask for contact when she needed it and to say no or enough when she did not. In other words, it was about managing the tension between aloneness-togetherness. In her family, Kim had taken the role of a caretaker and mediator between her parents from a young age, and was called on by them whenever their relationship was strained. Her own emotional needs went unnoticed or dismissed. Later, Kim's first adult relationships, entered into to escape loneliness, were with men who were either coercive or very needy. The intensity and temporal contours of contact were never hers to regulate.

The absence of agendas

Agendas, whether our own or those of the client, or other people eager to see them change, can get in the way. We can be too speedy, too eager, try too hard when we have something in mind that we think should happen. It prevents us hovering at the fertile margin of the moment. What is more important is to be able to wait, allowing the client space to find herself and her truth. In time-suspended moments both client and therapist can enter a more liminal space, a place of reverie. It enables us both to digest what has been coming up, to notice how something is resonating at a somatic-affective level, simply to breathe and centre ourselves again. It is the listening, watching and waiting that Kurtz advocated. And in these few minutes "in parentheses" it is interesting how often our client discovers a new thought.

I know my tendency when excited by a new idea – what Winnicott rather splendidly called a "brain child" – to eagerly share it with my client. I need to remember his wise advice to hold back on premature interpretations. As Kurtz said, "every client is an experience that wants to happen not a problem to be solved." (1989, p. 146). Getting out of our own way and cultivating what Gestalt therapists call "creative indifference" is important. We can also get hooked in by the seeming urgency of our clients to change something about themselves or their world. This need to fix something and do it quickly is an aspect of the world today and reflects the difficulty we have waiting and tolerating discomfort or not knowing.

This brings me back to the temporal contours of the therapeutic relationship and the contrast between speed, urgency and intensity, whoever it belongs to, and being able to pause and wait patiently. Both polarities were very evident in my relationship with Abigail. I had ended one session frustrated with myself. We had journeyed through something intense, risking more connection and getting in touch with a fragile, younger self. Abigail was unusually calm. Then I spoiled it, mis-attuned and too fast, tried to suggest something she could take away. I became the mother who impinged when Abigail, as a baby, needed to withdraw her gaze and rest. My sense is that their rhythms frequently clashed. And the musicality of our dance kept shifting from in to out of synch. The learning from this helped me next time. I allowed Abigail more time for pauses to digest what had gone before and find her reality and at the end, after some minutes of quietness, each of us in our own thoughts, she smiled. "It feels so good not to be rushed. To be by myself, but knowing you hadn't gone."

A chance to mourn

"Return and repetition are always elements of change" said Harris, (2009, p. 4), and grieving is an essential feature in that return. As DeYoung pointed out, "grieving brings past and present together into coherent meanings, dense and rich with feeling" and "from the crucible of mourning relational losses, a once-fragmented self emerges as a self of integrity" (2003, p. 115). Judith Herman observed how grieving is at once the most needed and the most dreaded task of recovery after trauma. People fear that once they start to grieve, they will never stop. They resist it with fantasies of revenge, compensation and forgiveness, and their resistance is perhaps the most common reason for stagnation. The unmourned keeps trauma active. As said earlier, it stays split off as a present absence, a gap, a ghostly haunting (Herman, 1992, pp. 188–9; Harris, Kalb & Klebanoff, 2016).

In the analytic tradition, much as been written about the transformation of melancholia into mourning. In the halted time of melancholia there is a romance and an omnipotence that banishes need and loss for it "carries the imaginary power to change outcomes" (Harris, Kalb & Klebanoff, 2016, pp. 192, 197).[5] But the reality of death and, after trauma, the loss of how things were before and of the things one needed but were never forthcoming, has to be faced. Unless we can mourn and face our pain, an ongoing and repetitive process, we will not be able to internalise what we valued in the past, or fully enjoy what is available to us now (Salzberger-Wittenberg, 2016, p. 3). "Only through mourning everything she has lost", wrote Herman, "can the patient discover her indestructible inner life" (p. 188). Once again, the presence of an engaged witness supports this process. It allows emotional pain to be transformed into grief (DeYoung, 2003, p. 155).

What I have said here and in Chapter 11 is about grieving in the face of the first existential challenge of living in time, the loss of loved ones and other personal losses. But what about our grief in the face of the second challenge – that of contemplating our insignificance in the context of deep time as individuals and a species and, increasingly figural, the potential annihilation of the familiar natural world? And what about the need to mourn the consequences of the third challenge, the loss of supportive structures and traditions linking individuals and communities in our globalised, decontextualised world? How might our feelings about all this be "languaged" by the body or in action when they cannot be symbolised and shared? As Bednarek pointed out, when we think about bereavement, we mostly focus on the loss of people. "Rarely does a personal loss include the catastrophic loss of attachment to nature itself, the loss of living in a functioning community, the loss of meaningful rituals or the loss of connection to place – even though these are losses so deep that they change who we believe we are" (2018, p. 11). Yet our "deep but silent grief" for connections already lost or anticipated as being lost is emerging more and more, if we listen out for it. Bednarek has commented on our grief-phobic culture in which grief, anxiety and despair about these pressing existential challenges gets pathologised as excessive and unfounded (2019, p. 37). But what if our emotional responses are healthy reminders of things we have lost, not personal shortcomings? (2018, p. 14). And what if, to adapt the words from Herman used earlier, we could say that "from the crucible of mourning existential losses, a once-fragmented social world" could emerge as something more connected and whole? If, as with other griefs, these understandable emotional responses are repeatedly silenced how then will our bodies speak? How are they speaking now? Mourning needs to be respected and given space and time.

Integration

Whatever it is that leads to transformation, the new experience needs to be integrated otherwise it will not stick. It is all too easy for both of us to rush ahead with a new thought or issue. But we need to spend time allowing a new sense of the body or fresh insight to land and take root. Integration entails differentiation and linkage – noticing separate details of an experience and bringing together, combining or weaving parts into a whole (Siegel, 2010). It entails being with and honouring the range of emotions that suddenly burst forth – excitement, amazement, relief, calm – and often frozen grief, because this new experience throws into relief all that was not, the time lost, the opportunities that could not be fulfilled. There is a bittersweetness to change. We can support our clients' deepening awareness of the "something new" by encouraging them to stay with and savour the experience, to allow the emotions to sequence, then to discuss ways of integrating the change. To enjoy a new feeling, body sensation or belief in the safe, transitional space of the therapy room is one thing. But it will not have meaning unless there are ways of applying it to how our clients live their lives and relates to themselves and others in the future. Diana Fosha presents a cogent argument for deepening into positive emotions when they emerge and metaprocessing what it is like having these experiences, including being heard, with the therapist. Fosha's term for what she does is "turbo-charging". In her approach, processing the transformation is essential. In response to each moment of meeting the therapist asks, "what's that like?" "And what's that like?" As she says, it is a "recursive process in which each round's reflection on the experience of change-for-the-better yields a new experience, which then in turn becomes the focus of the next round of experiential exploration and reflection." Such metaprocessing, Fosha argued, "involves a dialectic bouncing back and forth between right-brain-mediated, somatically based experience and left brain-mediated experience-near reflection, promoting a prefrontal cortex-based integration" (2018, pp. 273–4).

In the following example, you can see how I tried to deepen the transformation. In this particular session George began describing some recent family events that had evoked powerful self-with-other patterns. He felt frustrated that he kept giving in to their requests. The theme of something being forced into him emerged and we explored this creatively using imagery and the body. When George said he felt like he had swallowed something big that got stuck in his stomach I asked what colour and shape it was. We played with the emerging imagery and then with imagining a protective boundary around him. He visualised a prickly, thorny hedge and shouting no if anyone approached. "What does that feel like?", I asked. "Good! Like I'm learning to the language of no", he replied. "Notice that feeling", I urged (so that the small new experience could be integrated). George told me that inside the hedge it felt safe enough to be himself. Again, I asked, "What's that feel like?" But now George was more tentative. It reminded him how of his two-year-old acts if she has done something wrong and is expecting to be told off. I immediately thought of a child believing he is naughty if he exerts his will and says no, and intuitively said: "If there's any part of you who is worried about disagreeing with people, can I tell that child "it's not naughty to say 'I don't want that'". This had an immediate body response – a somatic "moment of meeting". George said he suddenly felt solid and grounded. "And it's not just things I don't want", he added, "It's about being who I am". "Yes", I said, "that's so important" – and "it's not naughty to be yourself." This had an even bigger impact. I could see George taking it in, a look of amazement and excitement on his face. He told me that the tension in his body had vanished. Instead he felt very calm and centred. He'd never felt quite like this before. "It's really big", I said, and invited George to take his time to let this really sink in, that being himself wasn't bad. I also suggested that he repeat to himself those words so that his younger selves did not forget. We agreed not to do any more that session. This was absolutely enough.

I chose this excerpt because it illustrates how something new can emerge when a client is in an altered state of consciousness, a heightened state of self-awareness, in which it is possible to step out of the known. We can help people access such states by asking questions involving mindful self-awareness, inviting them to play with metaphors and imagery, or asking them to imagine themselves as the child they used to be. The example also illustrates that sometimes the new experience entails saying something to a "child" part of self that radically challenges what he had been told or believed back in the past. We might make such statements to clients when they are in ordinary consciousness, but they don't stick. The power of a transformative message is that in the altered state of consciousness past and present are directly linked. The same applies with new somatic experiences.

Evolution or revolution?

The final theme I want to explore is whether the change process is of necessity a slow one, and the creation of a secure relationship takes time, or whether the deepest transformations occur in "the fertile place at the margin of the moment". In other words, is change evolutionary or revolutionary? Hilary Mantel commented that an objection to analytic psychotherapy is that it is simply slow. "Though the important creative leaps may be made within a matter of seconds, analysis is slow in the way that writing a novel is slow; it is an open-ended commitment to watching a narrative unfold, and you can't force the pace without selling yourself short. We need to wonder if our addiction to quick fixes makes us gullible". She continued: "The most frustrating question a writer is asked is 'how long did your book take?' The only reasonable answer is 'my lifetime'. No matter what the subject, the book is the sum of your lived experience and the product of the character that experience has helped form. Similarly, in a psychotherapeutic engagement we bring the whole of our lives and more" (Haynes, 2007, p. 5). There is much I could say about the importance of not forcing the pace, of having time for things to slowly unfold, of the value of a relationship that endures over time and has both its own history – to which we can keep referring back – and gives the client a needed experience of someone who can hold her history in mind. Having said that, I also know that some amazing changes can occur in "moments of meeting" when something new and surprising emerges in the present that alters the client's (and ours too?) relationship with his or her past.

Mitchell pointed out that evolution emphasises continuity and smooth, continuous growth and development with change taking place gradually and incrementally. Meanwhile, revolution emphasises difference, novelty and discontinuity. It challenges and discards things (1993, p. 84). Stern used the terms progressive and dynamic change when discussing how the functional past can be changed – and by functional past he meant "the past that is activated and now influencing present behaviour". The dynamic, more dramatic route occurs during "now moments" and "moments of meeting" when the functional past is rewritten and the old record is erased in the course of one experience (2004, p. 222). In the shared, evolving, present moment, something in real time alters how client and therapist relate to each other, and how the client sees herself and her world. Another way of putting this is that it alters old internal working models and changes our relationship to our memories. First there is a now moment. "There is novelty and an 'upset', as well as a mounting emotional charge. The situation emerges unexpectedly and something must be done". "In such moments the participants are pulled fully, even violently, into the present moment that is now staring them in the face. ... Presentness fills the time and space. There is only now" (pp. 166, 167). The second stage is when an authentic response resolves the crisis created by the now moment – a moment of fittedness, of meeting (p. 168). These are the occurrences that a client will often remind us about years later, an event we have probably forgotten, but hugely important for them. In the language of non-linear dynamic systems theory, the happening involves an emergent property and represents an irreversible shift into a new state. The intersubjective field has been expanded with fresh possibilities for being together (p. 169). Stern explained that the potency of such experiences compared with empathically listening to the narrative of an event, rests on the experience being shared as it unfolds. He used the evocative term a "shared feeling voyage". "There is no remove in time. It is direct, not transmitted and reformulated by words" (p. 173). Mair's ideas about speaking from within an experience relates to something very similar.

Such "wow moments" stand out for their clarity and novelty, in the same way that a just-right metaphor does. That is why we remember them. We habituate to what we know, but the brain lights up to novelty and this makes neural change possible. This is a key aspect of neuroplasticity. However, the novel moments do not come out of nothing. Therapist and client could not reach moments that feel radically different if they were not part of a much longer process of getting to know each other's idiom and building trust. It is our steady patience and understanding over time that makes the difference and the hard work of repeatedly trying to understand each other better and to fashion a shared language. It also rests on the hard work our clients do between sessions as well as on the processing we do afterwards.

This is the progressive, evolutionary route to change. It is slow, repetitive and incremental and arises in the moving along process of therapeutic conversations. It is the result of courageous patient work in which old fears, shame and grief shrink a little each time part of a story is revisited. It involves taking in and integrating new information bit by bit. It also involves a recursive process of trying something new, darting back to the old way which feels safe because of its familiarity even if it brings problems, then bravely stepping forward again. And the therapist needs to offer a steady, reliable presence through all of this, willing to be there for the long haul through moments of stuckness when "progress" seems miles away, to get caught up in intense momentary dramas, and still hold the longer evolving history in mind. The intersubjective aspect of the process is what is most salient for Stern. In the moving along process, which occurs on a micro-time scale, he pointed out that therapist and client co-create ways-of-being-with-one another. "They are implicitly learning ways of regulating their intersubjective field". These subtle, new intersubjective present moment experiences create a novel "present remembering context" when details from the past are reassembled to create a new functional past (2004, p. 222). As Stern emphasised, the new experience does not repair the past by filling a deficit. What happened has to be acknowledged and grieved. But it creates a new experience that can be carried forward and built on in the future (p. 179). When the client starts to experience something new in relationship with the therapist then she will gradually experience "many small, interconnected differences in how she relates and feels in other contexts" (DeYoung, 2003, p. 7). The change becomes generalisable. This, argued DeYoung, is an example of the type of change that occurs in complex, systemic, non-linear ways in a relational therapy. It is very different from a linear sequence of "working on symptoms, producing a catharsis or insight, and then having symptom relief" (p. 7).

As an example of progressive change, one of Stephanie's enduring trauma-related certainties was that I would either tell her abruptly that I did not want to see her anymore, or that I would become seriously ill. It was a rejection/abandonment script that surfaced on numerous occasions. But over time Stephanie gained some distance from the fears. She was able to say, "the adult me knows that you have never done this, but it's the teenager. She finds it hard to trust anyone". And when her life was more stressful than usual or if there had been a small rift between us, Stephanie would keep checking if I was OK. There was a dissonance between what she knew explicitly and the implicit memories that coloured her responses. This, as Stern explained, is because the content of language and narrative is an abstracted experience, once-removed from the temporal flow of direct experience. It can only rewrite the explicit past, not the implicit experienced past (2004, p. 221). And that is why the relational, affective, imaginary and somatic dimensions of our work are so important.

Conclusions

To sum things up, for mutative action the therapeutic process needs to be embedded within a secure, attuned, containing relationship. It necessitates some doubling or tripling of time and processes that give words to past events, make sense of and alter their meanings. The writers who speak about the uncanny process of recursiveness and the looping back of time, are all in tune with more right-brain, analogical processes – something creative, relational, and liminal that involves stepping out of the ordinary, known and categorised. To step out demands dropping into a different sort of language, the language of feeling, imagination and metaphor – and this is a language of connection. It also demands accessing feelings about what has happened and in particular, working through grief. Lastly, something needs to take place that integrates the changes.

When we can hold different time zones in mind simultaneously– one foot in the present and one in the past or future – and reflect on our experiences now and then, including the experience of something new occurring right now, a space is opened up for something new to emerge. Harris put it this way: Structural change – and here I would include a new experience of our body, such as feeling strong and empowered, or the completion of truncated actions; greater dialogue between and acceptance of different parts of self; the ability to express and hold difficult emotions or a loosening of fixed, limiting beliefs – "alters our experience of temporalities, of timelines, or in reverse, a change in the experience of being in time (whether past, present, near future, or horizon): alters identity, object history, and internal worlds" (2009, p. 13).

Notes

1 The "witness", at least if we ascribe to the relational turn, also needs to be able to engage in his own memorial activity, to catch and reflect on emerging personal memories and how they relate to what is going on in the therapeutic relationship.
2 In response to something a client is telling me or how they are reacting, images often come to me of a child or a baby. These images speak to me about how things might have been or about missing experiences. They help me to understand at a deeper level the fears, concerns and longings of my client in the present, and to get an intuitive sense of what might be being said implicitly or what might be needed for something to change. This is the territory of implicit relational knowing.
3 Pye thinks of moments of meeting as happenings "when past and present can configure a different future" (2017).
4 The work of Janina Fisher exemplifies this approach (2017).
5 When might we, as therapists, be stuck in a more omnipotent place of trying to engender change in a "rescuing" way, because we cannot bear to hear the story or to see someone in such distress? And when is our client stuck in omnipotent denial?

References

Bednarek, S. 2018. "How wide is the field? Gestalt therapy, capitalism and the natural world", *British Gestalt Journal*, 27(2): 8–17.
Bednarek, S. 2019. "Is there a therapy for climate-change anxiety?", *Therapy Today*, June, 36–9.
Bromberg, P. 2001. *Standing in the Spaces: Essays on Clinical Process, Trauma, and Dissociation.* Hillsdale, NJ: Analytic Press.
Cox, M. & Theilgaard, A. 1987. *Mutative Metaphors in Psychotherapy.* London: Tavistock Publications.
DeYoung, P. 2003. *Relational Psychotherapy: A Primer.* New York: Brunner-Routledge.
Eger, E. 2017. *The Choice.* London: Penguin.
Erikson, E. 1965. *Childhood and Society.* Harmondsworth: Penguin Books. (1st edition, 1950. New York: W. W. Norton & Co.).
Fosha, D. 2018. "Something More than 'Something More than Interpretation'" in D. Lord (Ed.) *Moments of Meeting in Psychoanalysis: Interaction and Change in the Therapeutic Encounter* (pp. 267–292). London: Routledge.
Giddens, A. 1991. *Modernity and Self-identity: Self and Society in the Late Modern Age.* Cambridge: Polity Press.
Harris, A. 2009. "You must remember this", *Psychoanalytic Dialogues*, 19(1), 2–21.
Harris, A., Kalb, M. & Klebanoff, S. (Eds.) 2016. *Ghosts in the Consulting Room: Echoes of Trauma in Psychoanalysis.* New York: Routledge.
Haynes, J. 2007. *Who Is It That Can Tell Me Who I Am? The Journal of a Psychotherapist.* Bristol: Cromwell Press.
Herman, J. 1992. *Trauma and Recovery: The Aftermath of Violence.* London: Pandora.
Kurtz, R. 1990. *Body-Centred Psychotherapy: The Hakomi Method.* Mendocino, CA: LifeRhythm.

Loewald, H. 1972. "The experience of time", *The Psychoanalytic Study of the Child*, 27, 401–10.

Mair, M. 2013. *Between Psychology and Psychotherapy: A Poetics of Experience*. London: Routledge. (1st edition, 1989. London: Routledge).

Meares, R. 2012. *A Dissociation Model of Borderline Personality Disorder*. New York: W. W. Norton & Co.

Mitchell, S. 1993. *Hope and Dread in Psychoanalysis*. New York: Basic Books.

Modell, A. 2009. "Metaphor – the bridge between feelings and knowledge", *Psychoanalytic Inquiry*, 29(1), 6–11.

Pye, J. 2017. "Full Circle: 'We had the experience but missed the meaning'". Conference presentation.

Rolls, L. 2010. "Narrating time: Minimising the disruption and discontinuities of children's experience of death", *Illness, Crisis and Loss*, 184, 323–39.

Salzberger-Wittenberg, I. 2013. *Experiencing Beginnings and Endings*. London: Karnac.

Sander, L. 1995. "Identity and the experience of specificity in a process of recognition". *Psychoanalytic Dialogues*, 5(4), 579–93.

Siegel, D. 2010. *Mindsight*. London: Oneworld Publications.

Siegel, D. and Solomon, M. (Eds.) 2013. *Healing Moments in Psychotherapy*. New York: W. W. Norton & Co.

Slavin, J. and Rahmani, M. 2018. "Moments of Truth in Psychoanalytic Treatment" in D. Lord (Ed.) *Moments of Meeting in Psychoanalysis: Interaction and Change in the Therapeutic Encounter* (pp. 45–64). London: Routledge.

Stern, D. B. 2010. *Partners in Thought: Working with Unformulated Experience, Dissociation and Enactment*. New York: Routledge.

Stern, D. B. 2012. "Witnessing across time: Accessing the present from the past and the past from the present", *Psychoanalytic Quarterly*, 811, 53–81.

Stern, D. N. 2004. *The Present Moment in Psychotherapy and Everyday Life*. New York: W. W. Norton & Co.

Winnicott, D. 1990. *Playing and Reality*. London: Routledge. (1st edition, 1971. London: Tavistock Publications).

EPILOGUE

Towards an appreciation of time

And we begin to see that we are time. We are this space, this clearing opened by the traces of memory inside the connections between our neurons. We are memory. We are nostalgia. We are longing for a future that will not come. The clearing that is opened up in this way, by memory and anticipation, is time: a source of anguish sometimes, but in the end a tremendous gift.

(Rovelli, 2018, p. 175)

Whether it be a reputed physicist like Rovelli; a philosopher; a therapist, curious how individual history seems to repeat itself; a medieval cleric or an Arabic scholar writing a treatise on the recursive nature of history, humankind has always been puzzled by the mysterious nature of time and struggled with its challenges. In this book, I have touched on the "big" mysteries and challenges: our place in the cosmological drama as individuals with a finite lifespan, although we do not know exactly when it will end, and as a species facing the thought of our annihilation. I have also talked about individual people and their relationship to time – after loss and trauma, in the face of chronic illness, or dealing with everyday time pressures familiar to us all. The process has heightened my appreciation of the time I have and, using words from a poem cited below, "sharpened my nerve ends" to all that is beautiful, amazing and ordinary in my world. It has also led to a deeper awareness of when and why I become anxiously preoccupied with time and sometimes wish the clock had never been invented. However, and this was unexpected, I have come to appreciate how clock time can organise our days in comforting ways. Without it how would we structure the everyday rhythms that anchor us or coordinate with others? A recent brief conversation led to another realisation, that what I value about time's structure is not so much numeric clock time, but social time. When I said to someone, "Oh! You're the lady I see in the park every morning", she surprised me by saying: "Yes, I know if I'm early or late depending on where we pass each other". How fascinating, I thought, that I had become her 'clock'. And yes, I do that too. I 'measure' time on my walks by when I see the first sign of the sun creeping over the hill or where the dustcart is on a Thursday morning or a certain car passes me.

We have idiosyncratic time-markers, intersubjective timepieces, hardly the most accurate guides, but no less so than things our ancestors trusted like the cockerel's call or shadows cast by a hill. Another appreciation is the richness of such time-pieces, for they are about our connectedness to others and the natural world. Isn't it interesting how instinctively and emotionally we still lean towards Aristotle's view of time rather than Newtonian absolute time? We measure passing time by what changes – by things that occur in cycles, a familiar rhythmical time. This surely is the instinctive language of our bodies, a harmonisation of our body clocks and those of the natural world, without which we are sorely depleted.

I have learned a great deal from conversations with others about time and our temporal existence, from radio programmes and from reading, and as I end, I turn to other people's words and some inspiring quotations that help me when I struggle with the existential challenges of living in time. I want to share them and to leave you with some questions to ponder. If your time became short, what would be most important to you? How would you want to live your final months and days? Such questions are raised in the words of a poem called *Monday week at 3pm*. The anonymous writer invites us to set aside a time to die such as 3 p.m. on Monday and to concentrate fully on living until then. "*How the nerve ends would sharpen*", he argued, "*as each wasted second annoyed, a little more than the one before. How the eyes would sparkle when set before outrageous beauty, then change to panic at the wanting more*". What would we choose to do? "*Would we try and please others or seek a more private comfort, under a favourite hat?*" Yes, indeed. Would old scripts still drive us or, being acutely aware of our imminent end, would we at last, risk abandoning them? And when "*the appointed time came*", would "*we be content by then, by Monday week at 3pm?*"

My other question, which was probably there subliminally when I began writing this book but has become increasingly refined, is: Instead of endlessly trying to deny, defy, expand and slow time down, what if we accept its passage and look for the values of living in time? What might they be? I recall the quotation from Molnos regarding therapy, that "what makes a difference is not the absolute length of time, but what we do with it" (1994, p. 52). The same is true about life, and an aspect of Buddhist practice is to keep meditating on death so that we are prepared for it and learn to truly live the life we have. Can we, in the wise words of Nkosi Johnson "do all that you can, with what you've been given, in the place where you are, in the time that you have".[1]

A writer who speaks powerfully about our attitude to death is Marcus Zusak. In his novel *The Book Thief*, the narrator, Death, asks "what colour will everything be at that moment when I come for you? What will the sky be saying?" A more challenging question would be, "do we live our lives? Do we notice the present moment in all its richness or sleepwalk through it?" (2005, p. 14). There is a cruel irony that evolution has privileged man with a brain sensitive and sophisticated enough to remember, predict and "make an ordered sequence out of a helter-skelter chaos of disconnected moments", but leaves us unable to live fully in the present. As Watts argued, "the power of memories and expectations is such that for human beings the past and the future are not *as* real, but *more* real than the present" (1992, p. 31). If we are so preoccupied with resentment or guilt about something in the past how can we notice what is different right now? And what use is it to be able to plan what to eat next week if we cannot enjoy meals when they come? The present does not really exist.

In the view of "Death", "people observe the colours of the day only at its beginning and end". "To me", he said, "it's quite clear that a day merges through a multitude of shades and intonations with each moment" (Zuzak, 2005 pp. 2, 14). If we read 'life' for 'day' I think this is correct. Some people get stuck focussing on pain and loss and as a consequence become embittered and hopeless. But there are others who manage to find gifts in the "shades and intonations" of the moment and in their connections to others as their world shrinks. Within a few days of being told he had less than six months to live, Sacks described how "I have been able to see my life as if from a great altitude, as a sort of landscape, and with a deepening sense of the connection of all its parts" (2015c, p. 18). And he expressed gratitude for having loved and been loved, for having been given much and having given in return and the fact that "above all, I have been a sentient being, a thinking animal, on this beautiful planet, and that in itself has been an enormous privilege and adventure" (p. 20).

Shabad pointed out that transience heightens appreciation (2001, p. 9). "It sets up an urgency about how best to use and treasure each moment", and he presented us with the interesting challenge, to imagine what a deathless life would entail. Would we bother to get up in the morning if an infinite series of mornings stretched ahead? Would greetings and partings matter if we knew someone would be around forever? Shabad stressed, it is "the absence of life that complements life's presence" and that without death our perspective on time would change so profoundly that our sense of our own identity and the quality of human relationships would be radically altered (pp. 9–10). So much human activity, observed Watts, is designed to "make permanent those experiences and joys which are only lovable because they are changing" (1992, p. 30) – the ongoing rhythm and flow of music, the flickering flames of a fire, the sky as the sun sets. None of these could be appreciated were it not for their embeddedness in a flowing process of change and death, presence and absence.

Research from academics like Carstensen and Charmaz back up these points. I recall Carstensen's point that as our horizons contract and when we see the future ahead of us as finite and uncertain, and this is independent of our age, our focus shifts to the here and now, to everyday pleasures and the people closest to us (Gawande, 2015, pp. 94–9). One woman with breast cancer reflected, "If you face death, life becomes more valuable. I had never really been here, in the present, before. I always looked ahead or worried about the past. Now, I feel like I'm really here. I'm sorry I had to learn the hard way". Another woman with a disabling condition said, "Isn't it a shame that it takes illness for someone to realize what's important in life" (Charmaz, 1991, p. 247). The words of these women are echoed by Paul Kalanithi and Oliver Sacks when both were diagnosed with terminal cancer. Kalanithi spoke of the dilemma in not knowing how many months or years he had left. "Tell me three months, I'd spend time with my family. Tell me one year, I'd write a book. Give me ten years, I'd get back to treating diseases" (2017, pp. 160–62). In similar vein, Sacks said he felt "a sudden clear focus and perspective. There was no time for anything inessential. I must focus on myself, my work, and my friends. I shall no longer look at *NewsHour* every night. I shall no longer pay attention to politics or arguments about global warming. This is not indifference – I still deeply care about the Middle East, about global warming, about growing inequality, but these things are no longer my business; they belong to the future" (2015c, p. 19).

Facing the finitude of time, owning regrets and grieving losses is the route to transcendence. But do we need to wait until our last months before we do this? It is interesting that when something brings us face to face with life's finitude, for a while, we appreciate all that we have and all that is around us with more depth and intensity than usual, and we make resolutions about how we want to live. However, as Charmaz pointed out, "transcendence is not a static state of being" (1991, p. 258). Our immersion in the intense present tends to be a fragile arrangement and "like the glow of compassion during religious holidays or the commitment to New Year's resolutions, daily routines dull and supersede the intense present. The wonder of having a reprieve lessens" (p. 249). Returning to the familiar, mundane rhythms of life and our usual preoccupations and ways of being after a period of crisis or prolonged ill health, can dilute the intense appreciation of what we have and we forget the resolutions made when facing mortality.

This shift from intensity, aliveness, and excitement is what I have often encountered after what felt like an amazing moment of transformation in a therapy session. In that euphoric moment so much seemed possible for both client and therapist. Maybe this was it, what we'd been looking for all the time. Then something happened to puncture the bubble and that charged moment was forgotten as we returned to life's ordinary dramas. I am also familiar with a snakes and ladders process. Someone begins to make significant changes in her life. But this new territory feels scary. We don't have any maps for it, and it is tempting to return to the old country even if we know it is not good for us. We know its rules and how to position ourselves, and that is comforting. So, as people contemplate and engage with change there are many changes of direction – towards the new country, which is both appealing and frightening, then back to the familiar known. Both life and therapy call us to keep revisiting old issues and questioning who we are and why we are here. I believe that each of us then must take his or her own journey towards an appreciation of time and an acceptance "of one's own and only lifecycle as something that had to be" (Erikson, 1965, p. 260).

Near the end of his life Einstein wrote: "the distinction between past, present and future is only a stubborn illusion" (Rovelli, 2018, p. 100). But it was not in a scientific paper. Nor written as a physicist. This was Einstein the man, writing to the sister of a lifelong friend who had just died. And his statement was preceded by the words: "Now he has departed from this strange world a little ahead of me. That means nothing …". His words, Rovelli commented, were "prompted by the experience of life itself. Fragile, brief, full of illusions" (p. 101). They also speak of connections, attachment bonds which transcend time, the connectedness Sacks and Kalanithi experienced and which we appreciate all the more because of transience. We inevitably oscillate between appreciation, intensity, new resolutions and back-lashes as the daily round or crises and complications pull us out of celebrating the present into repeating or rehearsing the past or focussing on the future. We move back and forwards in time. We cycle between loss and transcendence, transcendence and loss. Endings and beginnings, births and deaths. This is humankind's dance in time!

Note

1 Nkosi was born with Aids. He became a spokesperson for children with Aids and died when he was 12. This is his gift to the world.

References

Charmaz, K. 1991. *Good Days and Bad Days: The Self in Chronic Illness and Time*. New Brunswick, NJ: Rutgers University Press.

Erikson, E. 1965. *Childhood and Society*. Harmondsworth: Penguin Books. (1st edition, 1950. New York: W. W. Norton & Co.).

Gawande, A. 2015. *Being Mortal: Illness, Medicine and What Matters in the End*. London: Profile Books.

Kalanithi, P. 2017. *When Breath Becomes Air*. London: Vintage.

Molnos, A. 1995. *A Question of Time: Essentials of Brief Dynamic Psychotherapy*. London: Karnac.

Rovelli, C. 2018. *The Order of Time*. London: Allen Lane.

Sacks, O. 2015c. *Gratitude*. London: Picador.

Shabad, P. 2001. *Despair and the Return of Hope: Echoes of Mourning in Psychotherapy*. Lanham, MD: Jason Aronson.

Watts, A. 1992. *The Wisdom of Insecurity: A Message for an Age of Anxiety*. London: Rider. (1st edition, 1951, Pantheon Books).

Zusak, M. 2005. *The Book Thief*. London: Transworld Publishers.

INDEX